'GELIGNITE'
JACK MURRAY

'GELIGNITE' JACK MURRAY

AN AUSSIE LARRIKIN LEGEND
PHIL MURRAY

For my father, the Aussie larrikin legend 'Gelignite' Jack

and for you ...
all the people whose lives he touched and left you with a smile.

FOREWORD

What an honour to be asked to write the Foreword for this book.

I well remember the REDEX Trial of 1954. I was ten years of age, in the days before television. We would either listen to the Trial on radio or watch the Cinesound reports at the Wynyard Newsreel Theatre. These were normally compered by Jack Davey, the famous quiz show host we would often listen to on the radio at night.

On the starting day of the 1954 REDEX Trial, I walked up to Lindfield on the Pacific Highway north of Sydney. The crowds there were ten deep at night as the cars screamed through at enormous speed. Quite reckless—but there were few safety rules in those days!

'Gelignite' Jack Murray became the most famous driver that year, not only from the notoriety he gained by throwing sticks of gelignite out the window (he was an absolute maverick), but because he won without giving up a single point. How was that even possible? Remember, the roads were almost all dirt in those days, and 'Gelignite' had plenty of the Aussie larrikin 'attitude' of thumbing his nose at bureaucracy.

Thanks to that race, 'Gelignite' Jack instantly became a hero of mine. I often wondered if I could replicate some of the things he did. Of course, as you read this book, you'll understand that this was just not possible.

Years later, after being hopeless at school, I managed to start a small car radio servicing business with just $610. I called it Dick Smith Electronics, and with little to spend on advertising, I had to find other ways to gain publicity. Inspired by Jack's larrikin spirit, I towed a fake iceberg into Sydney Harbour on April

FOREWORD

Fools' Day. Later I jumped a double-decker bus over seventeen motor bikes. (Evel Knievel had done the reverse.)

Then in 1977 I came up with the idea of chartering Qantas 747s to fly to the South Pole for the day. I was delighted when Jack and his partner, Dorothy Rosewell, booked a flight. I remember saying: "Gelignite' Jack, you're a hero of mine. Thanks for coming.'

From that point on we became good friends. By July 1979, Dick Smith Electronics was making a fortune and looking for sponsorship opportunities to generate extra publicity for our shops around Australia. Jack and his son John asked if I would sponsor them in the Repco Reliability Trial. I said: 'For sure—I would love to.' And that's what we did. Having 'Gelignite' Jack, the ultimate larrikin, endorse Dick Smith Electronics, with our fun spirit of business, was one of the reasons we did so well.

Of course I always wanted to drive in a REDEX Trial, but by the time I got my licence and could afford it, the trials had ended. No problem. I came up with a different idea and called it the Bourke to Burketown Bash—a trial using twenty-year-old cars to raise money for the Variety Club of Australia.

The first Bash set off in June 1985, in the spirit of the original REDEX Trials. In fact, REDEX sponsored my car. What a pity that Jack had died two years earlier! But it was fantastic to have Dorothy and John come along, bringing the humour and fun that reminded us all of 'Gelignite' Jack.

Over time, Jack has become synonymous with having a go, being a renegade, an eccentric character who was also greatly admired.

I recommend this wonderfully written book to anyone. Conceived, researched and written by his son Phil, it takes a fresh look at those REDEX Trials, as well as Jack's early years, including the 1930s, World War II and his decades of winning in motor car performance sports.

I learned many fascinating things about 'Gelignite' that I didn't know—such as how he taught Wernher von Braun, father of the moon landing, to waterski on the Hawkesbury River. This is just one of many wonderful anecdotes.

Jack had an extraordinary life, from high jinks as a young boy through to his incredible success running his own business. He was passionate about making a good living and looking after his family.

This is one of the best books I've read in years. I hope you enjoy it.

Dick Smith AC

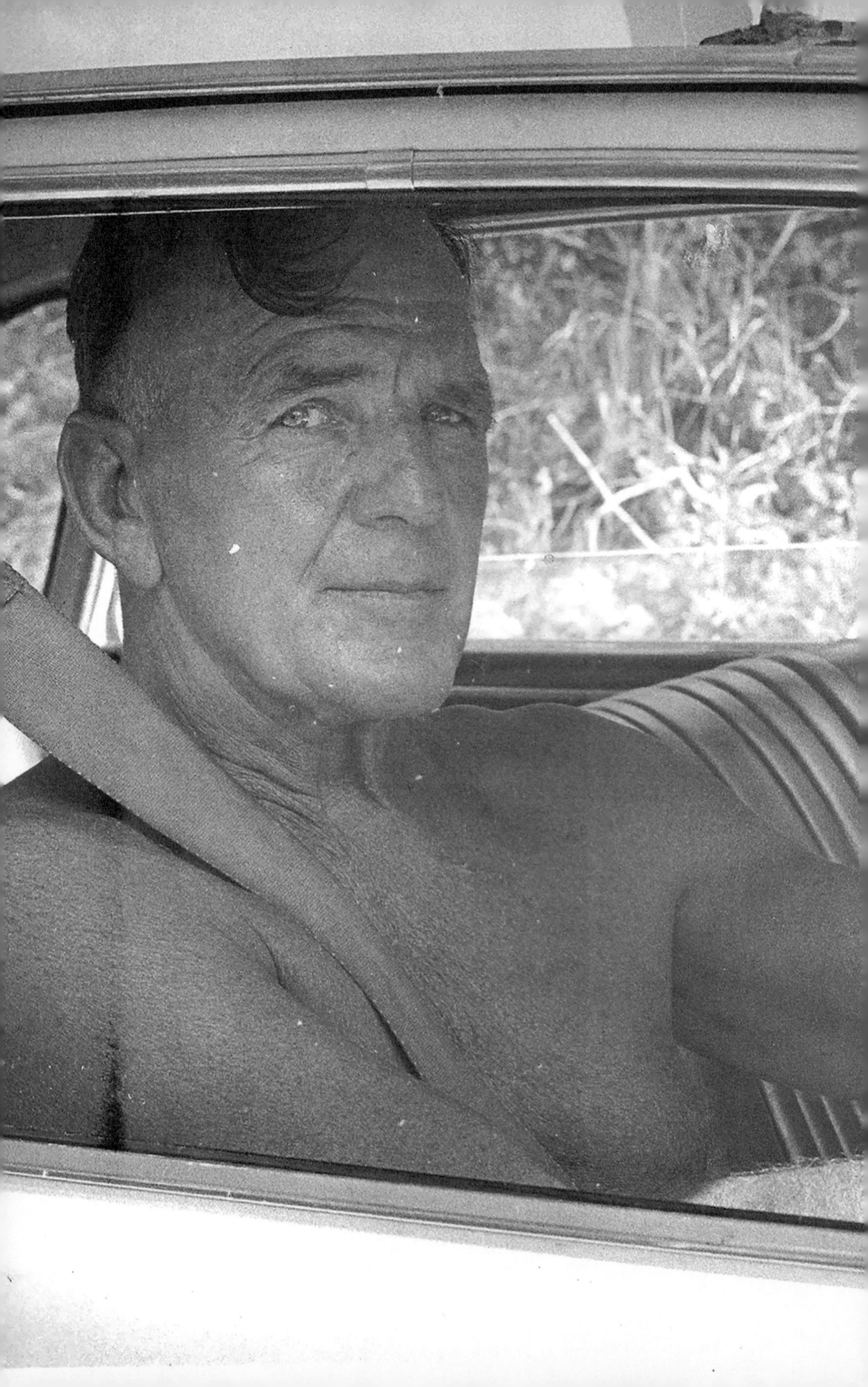

PREFACE

Mention the name 'Gelignite' Jack Murray and any Australian from the Baby Boomer era or older will simply smile. Everyone from that era seems to have a Jack story: 'I remember lining up ten deep in the main street and seeing Jack Murray come through our town' or 'I was in Townsville the time he let off the jelly' or 'I met Jack out Birdsville way'.

'Gelignite' Jack Murray was best known as the rally driver who in 1954 won the REDEX Round Australia Reliability Trial without the loss of a single point. But Jack's sporting interests and achievements were eclectic and far ranging. In his own words, at different times throughout his life he was 'engaged in various sports with various successes': cycling; VFL schoolboy football; stock car racing; hill climbing motor races; circuit car racing; car endurance events; Australian and NSW Grand Prix racing; international and Australian rally driving; wrestling; boxing; crocodile, kangaroo and buffalo hunting; ocean boat racing and waterskiing—to name most, but not all. Oh yes—Jack even raced a bathtub once, plug in.

'Gelignite' Jack Murray, in addition to being a larrikin legend, was also my father. My older brother John and I grew up in a time when Jack's adventures and escapades made national headlines. Jack died in 1983. Encounters with those who met him, knew him and loved him now grow fewer and fewer as the years pass and the reliability trials of the 1950s drift into Australian history and folklore.

It is over 30 years since Jack left us. Now, more than three decades later, what can a biographer set out to achieve? And what can we add to the 'Gelignite'

PREFACE

Jack Murray story that has not already been said? A great deal, I would suggest.

For those with an historical interest in sports or Australiana in general, there is material already available on Jack Murray's life. The television show *This Is Your Life* featured Jack as the honoured guest in 1978. Two years earlier, Neil Bennetts interviewed and recorded Jack for the National Library of Australia. Jack has an entry in Toby Creswell's and Samantha Trenworth's *1001 Australians You Should Know*, and with the 21st century upon us, today Jack even has an online presence.

Many newspaper and magazine articles have been written about my father. They vary in quality—unfortunately, most are poorly researched, often mixing hyperbole and myth with fact.

Evan Green, journalist and author, has written extensively about the many adventures, trips and shenanigans the good friends shared over 30 years. All this material is publicly available and can be sourced in hard copy, online or via application to organisations such as the National Film and Sound Archive.

A sportsman's biography should encompass far more than just a chronological listing of the events they competed in and the trophies they won. The anecdotes of friends and fellow competitors give colour and substance to the public figure. And it is only the memories, recollections and thoughts of family and those closest to Jack that can complete the whole picture.

There is much more yet to be told. Jack's personal and non-public life, showing the man behind the derring-do, has never been fully explored, written about and woven into the fabric of the whole. Given the conservatism and attitudes of the 1950s and 60s, this silence is understandable. But with the passage of time much water has passed under the proverbial bridge. Those who perhaps may have been embarrassed or uncomfortable with candour, openness and discussion of such matters—especially my father and mother—have now left us. To tell Jack's story, to write a biography and not commit to a complete and comprehensive story would not only be disingenuous, but would do a disservice to those of us who loved him and were loved by him. I disagree with the French philosopher Voltaire: I believe we owe *both* respect and the truth to those who are gone—and also to those of us who remain.

My father and mother married in 1942 and remained married until Jack's death. However, in the late 1950s my father met another lady and they fell in love. Their relationship blossomed, grew and also endured until Jack's passing. It was a love that spanned 25 years. As Jack lay dying in St Vincent's hospital

PREFACE

in Sydney, the two women who shared Jack's life, my mother Ena Murray and Dorothy Rosewell, stood on either side of the bed. The man they both loved lay between them, dividing but at the same time uniting them in their shared grief and imminent loss. This is a part of Jack's story, but an integral part none the less. It deserves telling and being incorporated into a biography.

Duality is a theme that runs through Jack's life. 'Gelignite' Jack really did burn the candle—or the gelignite—at both ends. As we will see, in many ways Jack lived two parallel lives and I recall that for some reason that never was fully explained to me when I was growing up, he even seemed to have two birthdates. My father crammed the experiences, travel, sports and sheer zest for life of at least two men into his 76 years.

Double the speed. Double the adventure. And double the fun.

It was Mark Twain who wrote, 'Truth is stranger than fiction' and then added, 'but it is because fiction is obliged to stick to possibilities. Truth isn't.' This became Jack Murray's favourite saying. But Twain's expression was Australianised and paraphrased by Jack: 'I say, truth would leave fiction for dead. But you tell people and they don't believe you—so I never bother telling them.'

The 'Gelignite' Jack Murray story proves both Mark Twain and Jack to be right.

The starter's flag has dropped and it's time to open the throttle and rally through 'Gelignite' Jack's incredible life of adventure, sport and, above all, fun. It's a hell of a ride, beginning at the moment Jack himself described as the 'most exciting thing I've done': winning the 1954 REDEX Trial.

modern
MOTOR
MARATHON
TEST
REDEX TRIAL
10th.
ANNIVERSARY
SHELL X-100

CONTENTS

	Foreword	6
	Preface	9
Chapter 1	The REDEX Trials	15
Chapter 2	Behind the Wheel	55
Chapter 3	The War	71
Chapter 4	Cutting Mad Capers	85
Chapter 5	A Decade of Wins	99
Chapter 6	The Garage	143
Chapter 7	The Swinging 60s	159
Chapter 8	The Long Drives	183
Chapter 9	Adventurer, Hunter, Diver and Fireman	195
Chapter 10	Family	217
Chapter 11	Growing up with 'Gelignite'	243
Chapter 12	Dorothy	257
Chapter 13	Wrestling and Waterskiing	279
Chapter 14	This Is Your Life	311
	Epilogue	333
	Acknowledgements	349
	About the Author	353
	Sources	355

REDEX TRIAL

Listed below are the 263 entries received for this year's round-Australia 9,600 mile Redex Trial:—

1—Marshalls Motors (G. Marshall), N.S.W. (Standard 8)
2—N.Z. Team (K. Berge) (Peugeot)
3—Pound Motors, Vic. (Renault)
4—Akers, R.; Fallon, R. K., Qld. (Citroen Lt. 15)
5—Farmer, N., Qld. (Rover)
6—Setter, G. P., Qld. (Zephyr)
7—Adamson, C. R., Sydney (Holden)
8—Doherty, D. E., Vic. (Zephyr)
9—Carrington, J. B., N.S.W. (t.b.n.)
10—Marshalls Motors (E. J. Lefoe), N.S.W. (Vanguard)
11—Burrows, L., N.S.W. (t.b.n.)
12—Liebert, R., Vic. (Holden)
13—Buchanan, W. K., N.S.W. (A40)
14—Warwick, M. H., Vic. (Custom)
15—Dawson, R., N.S.W. (Mercury)
16—Forward, I. A., N.S.W. (Peugeot)
17—Campbell, G., N.S.W. (Ford V8)
18—Mitchell, A., Qld. (Holden)
19—Reno Autosales, Vic. (t.b.n.)
20—Cape, F. C., N.S.W. (Holden)
21—Dunkley, G., W.A. (Jaguar Mk. VII)
22—Roberts, J. E., Qld. (Vanguard)
23—Holland, A., N.S.W. (Holden)
24—Conway, Mrs. M., N.S.W. (A40)
25—Standard Motor Co. (D. Whiteford), Vic. (Vanguard)
26—Boundy, P., Vic. (Armstrong-Sidd.)
27—Rayward, H., N.S.W. (Peugeot)
28—Mayne, W. S., N.S.W. (Customline)
29—Patterson, G. W., Vic. (Peugeot)
30—Nelson, E. A., N.S.W. (t.b.n.)
31—Rootes Ltd. (T. Sulman), Vic. (Super Snipe)
32—Fulton, C.A., N.S.W. (A70)
33—Farrell, T. H., N.S.W. (Customline)
34—McFadden, J., N.S.W. (M.G. TF)
35—Burton, V. R., Qld. (Oxford)
36—Christy's Motor Auctions, N.S.W. (Chevrolet)
37—Evans, D., Qld. (Zephyr)
38—Cox, R., S.A. (Vanguard)
39—Maloney, C. G., Broken Hill, N.S.W. (Holden)
40—Rothwell, R. F., N.S.W. (Holden)
41—Page, R., N.S.W. (Peugeot)
42—Duffner, H. G., N.S.W. (Velox)
43—Coorey, A., N.S.W. (Ford)
44—Melrose, A., W.A. (t.b.n.)
45—Commonwealth Motors Pty. Ltd., Vic. (Citroen Lt. 15)
46—Antill, D. H., N.S.W. (M'cedes Benz)
47—McCaffety, J. F., Qld. (Holden)
48—Miller, S. M., N.S.W. (Customline)
49—Quinn, J. W., N.S.W. (Customline)
50—Bell, P., N.S.W. (Renault)
51—Herbert, C. F., N.S.W. (Standard)
52—Walker, R. B., N.S.W. (Vanguard)
53—Hecker, S. W., Qld. (Holden)
54—Regent Motors Pty. Ltd., Vic. (Volkswagen)
55—Automotive Tech. Service, N.S.W. (Rover 75)
56—Ahern, E. G., N.S.W. (Holden)
57—Rootes Ltd. (W. Nunn), N.S.W. (Super Snipe)
58—Kendall, R., Qld. (Rover 75)
59—Murray, R., N.S.W. (Holden)
60—Hicks, C., N.S.W. (Customline)
61—Kook, H., N.S.W. (Vanguard)
62—Robinson, W. J., N.S.W. (Peugeot)
63—Kreig, C., S.A. (Holden)
64—Gibbs, S., England (Zephyr)
65—Luiting, G., N.S.W. (Peugeot)
66—Anderson, J. G., Qld. (A70)
67—Goodwin, J., N.S.W. (Holden)
68—Hay, J., Vic. (Super Snipe)
69—Brit. Aust. Motors, Qld. (Armstrong-Siddeley)
70—Wilson, R. E., Vic. (Volkswagen)
71—Palmer, G., N.S.W. (Hillman Minx)
72—Happ, B., W.A. (Holden)
73—Yard, H. L., S.A. (Plymouth)
74—Perkins, J., Qld. (Holden)
75—Davey, J., N.S.W. (Customline)
76—Johnson, R., Vic. (Vanguard)
77—Pomroy, P., Vic. (Citroen)
78—Kleinig, F., N.S.W. (Peugeot)
79—McArdle, C. N., S.A. (Vanguard)
80—Gudgeon, R. E., A.C.T. (Hudson Super Wasp)
81—Reddie, M., Vic. (Velox)
82—Hall, Mrs. L. E., N.S.W. (A40)
83—Green, G. W., N.S.W. (Peugeot)
84—Egan, J. E., N.S.W. (Holden)
85—Smith, C. G., N.S.W. (Peugeot)
86—Sears, R., N.S.W. (Peugeot)
87—Macguire, F. R., N.S.W. (Nash)
88—Emry, G. M., Vic. (Peugeot)
89—Pryer, R., Tas. (M.G.)
90—Ferris, J. H., Vic. (Peugeot)
91—Wattle Corrie Motors, Vic. (Holden)
92—Place, N., Vic. (Plymouth)
93—Flinders Towing Service, N.S.W. (t.b.n.)
94—MacDonald, D., Qld. (Consul)
95—Gibson, E. A., Qld. (Chevrolet)
96—Gibson, A., N.S.W. (M'cedes Benz)
97—Witter, A. J., N.S.W. (Hudson)
98—Leigh, V. H., N.S.W. (Austin)
99—McHardy, J., Vic. (Peugeot)
100—Lenaghan's Belmont Taxis, N.S.W.
101—Rootes Ltd. (A. Peck), Vic. (Super Snipe)
102—Hayes, W. H., S.A. (Peugeot)
103—Cresswell, C. V., N.S.W. (Plymouth)
104—Leslie, H., N.S.W. (A40)
105—Thorpe, Miss S. E., N.S.W. (t.b.n.)
106—MacMillan, I., W.A. (Peugeot 203)
107—Seidel, R. D., S.A. (Morris Minor)
108—Kilpatrick, J., N.S.W. (Holden)
109—Welinski, A., N.S.W. (Holden)
110—Horner, G., Vic. (Customline)
111—Binney Holt, N.S.W. (Peugeot)
112—Thiel, A., S.A. (t.b.n.)
113—Thomas, R., N.S.W. (Zephyr)
114—Carpenter, S., N.S.W. (Zephyr)
115—Culver, Bill, N.Z. (Jaguar)
116—McLachlin, D. A., N.S.W. (Zephyr)
117—Kook, J. B., N.S.W. (Rover)
118—Standard Motor Co., Vic. (Standard 8)
119—Consolidated Press Ltd., N.S.W. (A70)
120—Phelps, I. J., N.S.W. (Hillman Minx)
121—Birmingham, G. A., W.A. (De Soto)
122—Cameron, A., Qld. (Mercury)
123—Henfry and Thomas, W.A. (Vanguard)
124—McGrath, W. T., A.C.T. (Oldsmobile)
125—Williams, R. J., Vic. (Holden)
126—Miller, K., N.S.W. (Holden)
127—Kipling, A. L., N.S.W. (t.b.n.)
128—Harrison, D. R., Qld. (Peugeot)
129—Benson, P. E., N.S.W. (Holden)
130—Dekyvere, V., N.S.W. (Citroen)
131—Parfitt, K. L., Vic. (Singer 9)
132—Osmond, J., N.S.W. (Holden)
133—Ride-Easi Shock Absorber Spst., N.S.W. (Consul)
134—Clarke, R. H., W.A. (Holden)
135—Claridge Motors, S.A. (Holden)
136—Westren, L., N.S.W. (Peugeot)
137—Morgan, W., N.S.W. (Vanguard)
138—Mick Simmons Ltd., N.S.W. (Zephyr)
139—Laister, R., Qld. (t.b.n.)
140—Manly Pacific Garage, N.S.W. (Peugeot)
141—Robinson, Mac., N.S.W. (Citroen)
142—Dunstan, L., Vic. (Holden)
143—Watt, A., N.S.W. (t.b.n.)
144—Selke, M. G., N.S.W. (V8)
145—Courtney and Patterson, Vic. (Zephyr)
146—Austin 7 Club of Aust., S.A. (A70)
147—Varcoe, M. W., S.A. (Rover)
148—Parker Bros. Auto Co., Vic. (Holden)
149—Roberts, E., N.S.W. (Morris)
150—Pedley, J. E., Tas. (A70)
151—Lanock Motors, N.S.W. (Volkswagen)
152—West's Motors, N.S.W. (Velox)
153—Smith, C., S.A. (Holden)
154—Onto, G. S., Vic. (Lagonda)
155—Irish, A., N.S.W. (Peugeot)
156—Walton and Gardner, W.A. (Holden)
157—Pearsall, H. A., N.S.W. (Fiat 1100)
158—Standard Motors (L. Oxenford), N.S.W. (Standard 8)
159—Arentz, M. L., N.S.W. (Customline)
160—Purnell Motors Pty. Ltd., N.S.W. (Holden)
161—Porter, F. W.A., N.S.W. (Buick)
162—Preston Motors (L. Davison), Vic. (Holden)
163—Perkins, E. B., Vic. (Rover 90)
164—Colmer, A. J., S.A. (A40)
165—Advanx Motor Service, Gosford, N.S.W. (Peugeot)
166—Manning Motor Co., N.S.W. (Vanguard)
167—Williams, G., N.S.W. (Javelin)
168—Barnett, D. G., N.S.W. (Custom)
169—Shepherd, F. J., Vic. (Holden)
170—Williams, P. and R., Pty. Ltd., N.S.W. (M.G.)
171—Tottey, D. W., Vic. (t.b.n.)
172—Standard Motors (A. Pilkington), Vic. (Vanguard)
173—Welsh, J., N.S.W. (Super Snipe)
174—Parker, D., N.S.W. (Peugeot)
175—Hall, S., N.S.W. (A40)
176—Anderson, A. A., Qld. (Holden)
177—Perrignon, G. J., N.S.W. (C'line)
178—Eastwell, A. P., (A40)
179—Century Storage Battery Co., N.S.W. (Austin)
180—Norman, E., N.S.W. (t.b.n.)
181—Rootes (G. Gilbert), Vic. (S/Snipe)
182—Farrow, J. N., N.S.W. (Mercury)
183—Gorfain, A., N.S.W. (Velox)
184—Connors, J. R., N.S.W. (Zephyr)
185—Dever, N., Qld. (Holden)
186—Hirst, I. D., N.S.W. (Vanguard)
187—Century Storage Battery Co., N.S.W. (Holden)
188—Shepherd and Scown, S.A. (Peug)
189—Lumb, J., N.S.W. (Rover 75)
190—Shean, N. (driver, D. McKay), N.S.W. (Austin A70)
191—Weal, H. R., N.S.W. (Ford)
192—Carmody, K., N.S.W. (Volkswag)
193—Woollahra Driving School, N.S.W. (Holden)
194—Lawrence, M. D., Vic. (Zephyr)
195—Mair, W. D., Qld. (Renault)
196—Luxton, W. N., Vic. (M'cedes Be)
197—Preston Motors Pty. Ltd. (R. N...), Vic. (Holden)
198—Hurley, W., Vic. (Holden)
199—Crouch, J. F., N.S.W. (Oxford)
200—Rootes (Miss H. Frezell), Vic. (Super Snipe)
201—Lee, H., Qld. (Vauxhall)
202—Worland, N., N.S.W. (Dodge)
203—Vincent's Transport, N.S.W. (Javelin)
204—Morschel, P., N.S.W. (Custom)
205—Hines, H. A., N.S.W. (Holden)
206—Wilkinson, B., Vic. (Austin)
207—Wood, H. J., N.S.W. (Peugeot)
208—Parr, M., N.S.W. (Vanguard)
209—Aird, R. J., Vic. (Holden)
210—Doidge, C. R., N.S.W. (Citroen)
211—Mathieson, R., Vic. (A40)
212—Howie, P. C., Vic. (Citroen)
213—Rootes (R. Lane), Vic. (S/Snip)
214—Coppock, J., N.T. (Holden)
215—Tipping's Garage, N.S.W. (Vangu...)
216—Edgar, C. A., Qld. (A40)
217—McMahon, F., S.A. (Consul)
218—Gregory, John, & Co., Vic. (Morris Minor)
219—Orrman's Service Station, Vic. (Peugeot)
220—Crockford, W. H., N.S.W. (Ford)
221—Raven, D., S.A. (Holden)
222—Hughes, E., N.S.W. (Holden)
223—Ira L. & A.C. Berk Pty. Ltd., N.S.W. (Renault)
224—Robinson, A., N.S.W. (Vanguard)
225—Henty, Dr., N.S.W. (Sunbeam Alpi...)
226—Lee's Newsagency, N.S.W. (Huds...)
227—Rootes (N. Buchanan), Vic. (Super Snipe)
228—Spanner, A., S.A. (Chevrolet)
229—Cooke, G., N.S.W. (Peugeot)
230—Sexton, D., N.S.W. (Peugeot)
231—Parade Motors, S.A. (Plymouth)
232—Falon, C., N.S.W. (A70)
233—Christie's Motors, Vic. (Chevrole...)
234—Templer, R. F., N.S.W. (Rover)
235—Harrison, K., N.S.W. (Vanguard)
236—Nielsen, Mrs. E., N.S.W. (Zephyr)
237—Budd, H., N.S.W. (Holden)
238—Ryan, L. R., Vic. (Holden)
239—McCrohon, K., N.S.W. (Vanguar...)
240—B. & M. Electrical Co., N.S.W. (Peugeot)
241—Savell Bros., N.S.W. (Holden)
242—Coffey, Alan, Motors, Vic. (Zeph...)
243—Kittle Bros., N.T. (Holden)
244—Plummer, J. L., N.S.W. (Fiat 11...)
245—Standfield, A. W., N.S.W. (Vanguard)
246—O'Shea, A., N.S.W. (Citroen 6)
247—Humphreys, L., N.S.W. (Holden)
248—Johnson, F. J., S.A. (Holden)
249—Davies, H., N.S.W. (Holden)
250—Tubman, K. V., N.S.W. (Peugeot)
251—Wyly, O. J., S.A. (Jaguar XK-1...)
252—Klingner, N., Qld. (Vanguard)
253—Standard Motor Co. (H. Firth), Vic. (Vanguard)
254—Carboni, A., Vic. (Ford)
255—Smyth, A. H., Vic. (Customline)
256—Murray, J., N.S.W. (V8)
257—Belling, J. T., S.A. (Zephyr)
258—Bicket, J. A., N.S.W. (Peugeot)
259—Townsend, J., N.S.W. (M/Min...)
260—Preston Motors (S. Jones), Vic. (Holden)
261—Phillips Bros., Qld. (Holden)
262—Johnson, Fred, N.S.W. (Holden)
263—Newstead, V., N.S.W. (V8)

AUSTRALIAN MOTOR SPORTS, July, 1954

CHAPTER ONE
THE REDEX TRIALS

I'd have to say winning the REDEX was the most exciting thing I've done—mostly because I didn't think I could do it. I had my fair share of luck, but then again, I've always had a lot of arse.

So said 'Gelignite' Jack interviewed by *Modern Motor* in August 1981.

The 1954 REDEX

It was a cold, fine Sydney night on 20 July 1954. A speeding police car was the first vehicle the straining spectators saw as they lined the Princes Highway leading into Sydney and towards the Moore Park Showground where a crowd of over 20,000 eagerly waited. In close pursuit of the police came a dust-covered, booming Ford V8 that in the previous eighteen days had covered 9600 miles (15,450 km) over the roughest roads the Australian continent had to offer. The driver, clad in black pants, black t-shirt and flight jacket sat beside his white-overalled navigator. Bonded by a shared love of motorsport and adventure, both men wore their customary flying boots—and broad grins. The four burly officers sardined into the lead vehicle had earlier offered a quiet word of advice to the two Murrays as they reached the southern outskirts of Sydney and now followed closely behind.

As Jack told the story in Neil Bennetts' interview recorded in 1976 for the

Left: The 1954 REDEX Round Australia Reliability Trial list of competitors.

CHAPTER ONE

Above: From left to right: 'Gelignite' Jack Murray, John V. Murray ('Snowy' aged ten, Jack's older son) and navigator Bill Murray (No Relation) atop the Grey Ghost, a 1948 Canadian Ford V8 which had already done 75,000 miles when Jack bought it for £700 early in 1954.

National Library of Australia:

> Across the Nullarbor and practically back to Sydney, it was eventful but not like it had been: lots of bitumen, and got escorted everywhere, more or less nursed back into Sydney, and the police met us up at Moss Vale and said, 'If you let one stick of jelly off, you'll be locked up. You follow us from here to Sydney Showground,' and we followed the police, four of them—I think it was a Ford too—and they went faster than we'd ever been. We were flat out keeping up with them. We got there about half an hour too early and we crossed into the Showground. We had a lot of luck, and that was it—and then we became more or less famous.

As the speeding Fords reached Moore Park and Driver Ave just on 9.25pm, the police car peeled away to let the Grey Ghost enter the Showground in solitary splendour. History was about to be made and 'Gelignite' Jack Murray would become a household name and enter the Australian lexicon of sportsmen, characters and larrikins.

As Jack laconically described events that night: '... then we became more or less famous.' Indeed they did.

> I guess the three happiest people in Australia were my wife, Ena, my ten-year-old son, John, and myself when my car, the Grey Ghost, slid into the Showground on Tuesday night with an unblemished record to win the REDEX Round Australia Trial 1954.

The 1954 REDEX Trial had been the longest event of its kind in the world. From an entry list of 263 came a starters' list of 246 cars representing 30 different makes. Just on half would make the successful circumnavigation of the continent, but only one team would complete the journey with no points lost, an unblemished record for Jack and Bill Murray and the tried, tested and from then on equally famous Grey Ghost. A legend had been born.

Today, for an Australian generation that has grown up with 4WDs, SUVs and dual carriage freeways—or at least surfaced roads linking all the capital cities—the importance and impact of the post-war REDEX trials are difficult to appreciate and understand. Public interest was enormous at that time. Today grey nomads in their motor homes or towing caravans travel around Australia as a normal rite of passage following retirement. In the 1950s, this concept was unthinkable.

Imagine the era. As the REDEX field of 1954 journeyed round Australia, the Petrov spy affair raged in Canberra, Bob Menzies was Prime Minister and Australia's major exports were wool and wheat. A few months earlier on 3 February 1954, Queen Elizabeth II and her consort Prince Philip had set foot on Australian soil for the first time. As a result of this royal visit, 'the REDEX baby' as I was nicknamed at the time by the press was destined to be royally christened. I am Philip Eric Murray, Eric being Jack's middle name.

The same day cars set off for the 1954 REDEX trial, food rationing ended in Britain. It had only been a few years earlier, at the turn of the decade, that petrol rationing had ended in Australia. Television would not arrive till 1956. For news, the public relied on radio, newspaper reports and gathering in their thousands to witness for themselves events such as what was acclaimed in 1954

CHAPTER ONE

as 'undoubtedly the greatest event in motoring history'.

There were three major REDEX trials held in successive years: 1953, 1954 and 1955. It is a little known fact that there was also a series of much shorter REDEX 1000 trials held in the months preceding the long distance REDEX events. In both 1953 and 1954, Jack had class wins in these events—a portent of things to come.

REDEX was a motor vehicle oil additive and Reg Shepheard, an Englishman who came to Australia, owned the selling agent rights. Car clubs and motoring magazines had proffered the idea of a round Australia car trial since before the war, but it was Shepheard's offer of sponsorship and his endeavours to promote and advertise REDEX that enabled the trials to become a reality.

These events were not races as such, nor were they 'rallies'. Rallies are timed to the second, not minute, and are more often conducted on closed roads, rather than open public roads. The winner of a rally is the fastest car from A to B. The REDEX events were termed 'reliability trials'. Very strict rules ensured that vehicles available to the general public were used, with few modifications, and replacement of parts was strictly limited. Along the way, competitors were required to meet and comply with set times established between control points. Being more than five minutes early or late on their scheduled time of arrival at fixed controls attracted a one-point penalty for each minute discrepancy. A margin of three minutes late or early per hour was allowed for secret controls to allow for possible speedometer error, and discrepancies between officials' and competitors' watches. It was a nervous navigator's worst nightmare.

The competitors who completed the trials with the lowest number of accumulated penalty points were declared the winners. Elimination sections, used to separate and test both competitors and cars, were a feature of the REDEX trials. Seemingly unrealistic and unobtainable times were often set between control points on these difficult sections. While frowned upon by police, necessity demanded competitors often travelled very fast to make up time. Balanced against time was the need to both conserve and preserve battered vehicles and weary crews over long distances on roads that at times were described as 'the worst in the world'. It was a delicate motoring and juggling act.

On 3 July 1954, 246 vehicles gathered in the Sydney Showground and patiently waited to be lined up and individually flagged away from Driver Ave. At the Palladium Theatre in Sydney on 7 June, radio and stage stars had drawn names and numbers to decide the starting order.

Teams of competitors, two or three per vehicle, anxiously awaited their scheduled departure time. The official starter was Donald Peers, an English crooner whose popular song at the time, 'Yes, I've told them all about you', foreshadowed the stories and events the press would relate to an eager public over the next eighteen days.

Commencing at midday, cars departed at two-minute intervals. Gordon Marshall, a motor trader at Windsor, was the first away, in Car No 1, a grey Standard Eight. It took over eight hours for the full field to depart under the Start banner. Since the Grey Ghost was Car No 256, it was well after dark before Jack and Bill Murray finally set off on their round Australia odyssey.

Below: Jack, wearing a gorilla mask, lined up inside Sydney Showground waiting to be flagged away from Driver Ave. Jack's son John, with a school friend, stands nearest to the passenger door. Jack's personalised plates, JM 456, adorn the Grey Ghost.

CHAPTER ONE

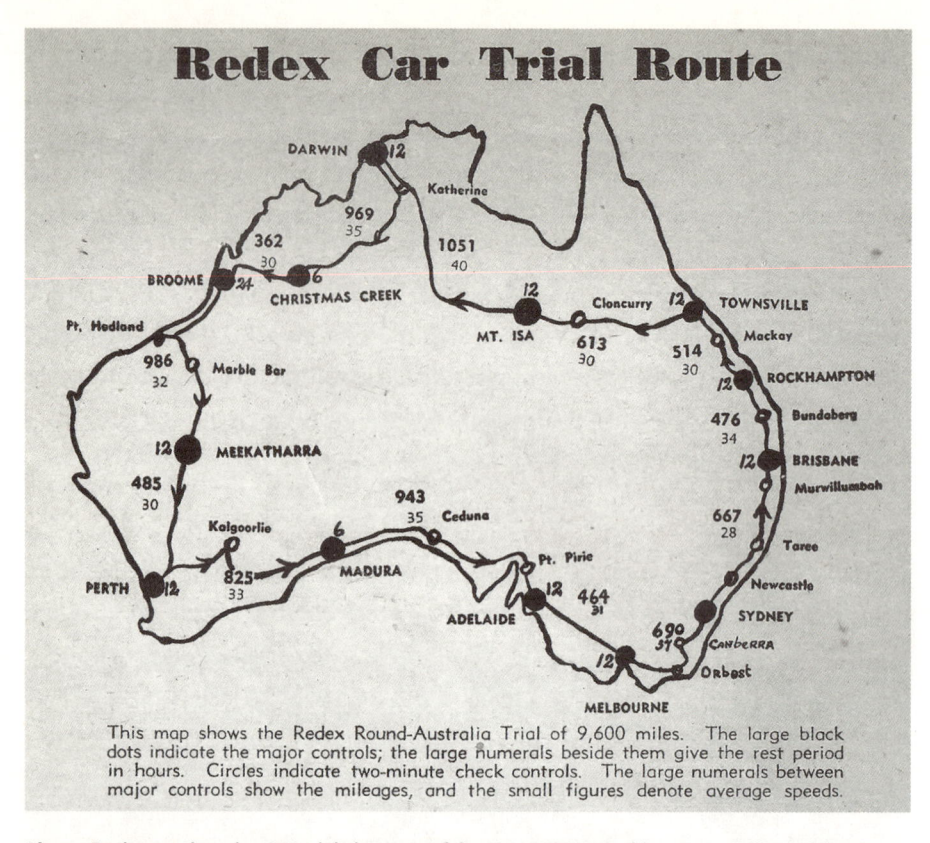

Redex Car Trial Route

This map shows the Redex Round-Australia Trial of 9,600 miles. The large black dots indicate the major controls; the large numerals beside them give the rest period in hours. Circles indicate two-minute check controls. The large numerals between major controls show the mileages, and the small figures denote average speeds.

Above: Far longer than the 1953 trial, the route of the 1954 REDEX would see competitors visit every state and capital city in mainland Australia, driving anti-clockwise.

The REDEX Trials for many of the drivers and navigators were as much about adventure, fun and a chance to see Australia as they were about serious motorsport. The list of 1954 REDEX competitors reads as a 'who's who' of Australian motorsport at that time. Competitors ranged from complete novices such as 22-year-old Bruce Wilkinson from Melbourne, one of the youngest, through to experienced trial and motorsport drivers such as Peter Antill, Jack Brabham, Tom Sulman, Laurie Whitehead (who became the 1955 REDEX winner), Ken Tubman (the 1953 REDEX winner), Reg Nutt, Bill McLachlan, 'Duck' Anderson, Doug Whiteford, Bill Murray (No Relation) and Jack Murray.

Jack's brother and business partner in their Curlewis St, Bondi Garage, Ray Murray, accompanied by Robert 'Ricky' Smallwood, Australian waterski champion in 1953-1954, and State bowls and chess champion in 1952-53, also competed in Car No 59, a grey Holden. Smallwood, a neighbour, built my first billy cart and encouraged me to play chess.

Commentators and the press humorously grouped the competitors into categories: the amateurs, the eccentrics, the professionals. 'Gelignite' Jack earned his very own special category: the professional eccentric.

Press and commentators saw Jack as a larger-than-life character who dominated the event, leading from start to finish and creating a reputation as a man with a touch of Nuvolari (a famous Italian racing driver of the time), Ned Kelly and Guy Fawkes. It was said there were plenty of colourful characters, but no one else combined skill with the colour. Certainly no one else tried exploding gelignite. In a pack of colourful cards, he was the joker.

'The omens were good': Sydney-Newcastle-Brisbane-Rockhampton-Townsville

The first four stages of the event, running north along Australia's east coast, were relatively uneventful. Even my mother Ena felt comfortable with the initial trial journey north:

> I felt the omens were good. The trial started on the twelfth anniversary of our wedding and for as far as Townsville, Jack went on the exact route we followed when we drove to Cairns for our honeymoon. I felt he just couldn't fail with a start like that. (*The Courier Mail*, Brisbane, 24 July 1954)

Despite my mother's confidence, the trial involved far more than just driving up the bitumen covered Pacific Highway as we would picture it today. Eight miles out of Wauchope, a 400-yard-long bog (360 metre) trapped most competitors. Rain between Taree and Brisbane had turned unsealed sections of road into a quagmire. Secret controls near the Bulahdelah climb and also outside Gympie in Queensland had been introduced to prevent speeding, unknown to competitors. Police regulations would be strictly enforced and drivers were booked for speeding and any other misdemeanours.

There was much controversy about the secret controls and many complaints. A four-kilometre discrepancy between the Shell Map and the Vacuum (Mobil) maps used in the trial caused more confusion. Competitors had been told they could use either. Drivers and navigators as one protested that 'the trial will be a flop with secret controls'. Some locals, who turned signposts around, either as a lark or sabotage, did not help matters. Eventually officials relented, points were restored and secret controls removed from the Rockhampton to Townsville section.

In order to placate and appease both the police and the press—who had complained the previous year about dangerous driving—the Australian Sporting Car Club had over-reacted by setting excessively low speed averages. They ran the risk of removing all fun from the trial.

STAGE	DISTANCE	AVERAGE SPEED	TIME ALLOWED	ROAD TYPE	CLEANSHEETERS (NO PENALTY PTS)
Sydney to Newcastle	111 miles (179 km)	22 mph (35 km/h)	5hrs	Bitumen	240
Newcastle to Brisbane (12 hrs rest)	556 miles (895 km)	30 mph (48 km/h)	18hrs 30mins	Bitumen Gravel	203
Brisbane to Rockhampton (12 hrs rest)	476 miles (766 km)	33 mph (53 km/h)	14hrs 30mins	Bitumen Gravel	169
Rockhampton to Townsville (12 hrs rest)	514 miles (827 km)	30 mph (48 km/h)	17hrs	Bitumen Gravel	114

Jack's good mate and fellow competitor, Bill McLachlan, driving a Zephyr was also a competitor in the 1954 REDEX. Two years earlier, Jack and 'Wild Bill' MacLac had journeyed from Sydney to Darwin via outback Queensland in McLachlan's Ford, a vehicle similar to the Grey Ghost. Heavy rains had made many roads impassable.

But it was the driving experience gained in these conditions, the knowledge developed about the clearance levels required, weight distribution in vehicles and protection of vulnerable car parts that lay the groundwork for Jack and Bill Murray's success two years later.

It was at Townsville in 1954 that Jack earned his moniker 'Gelignite'.

'I bet it's those blokes, the two Murrays'

As Jack tells the story:

Above: 1952: Perhaps not Jack's best angle as he digs out Bill McLachlan's Ford V8.

I'll tell you the name of the place this was: it was Townsville. Do you know where the big rock is in Townsville? The great big rock? OK. Well, for the acoustics you've got to have the jelly somewhere in a valley because it really travels round. So we were parked in the showground. There would be about 8000 people, everybody that lived in Cairns and everywhere were all down at Townsville, and it was a beautiful summer's night, nine o'clock the first car was out. So we found it was always good when you were letting the jelly off to go and find a policeman, put it on a long fuse, put it where you wanted it and then go and find a policeman, know where he is and go and talk to him, so when it goes off, it's not you, it's somebody else. How the hell could you let it off?

So we got there, we find this policeman, OK, and there was an outhouse, so we got three sticks of jelly and just threw it up against the tin and went up the street to the policeman. Next thing up went the jelly, and you could hear everybody saying, 'Christ, what was that?' and they turned round, and here's an old guy with his braces hanging down—do you know those policeman's braces, they've got 'Policeman' or 'Fireman' on them—and he came out, looked up at the sky, and just turned round and walked back inside again.

CHAPTER ONE

> That was one of the best jokes we ever played with the jelly. The copper said, 'Christ, what was that?' I said, 'I wouldn't know.' He said, 'I bet it's those blokes, the two Murrays.' I said, 'It's not us—I'm Murray,' and the bloke said, 'You're not, are you?' I said, 'Yeah.' He said, 'Oh well, you're out of it.' I said, 'Yes, of course we are.' So away we went. I'll never forget that one.

In a 1979 interview, standing beside his son John Murray, during the Repco Rally, Jack stated: 'I've never blown up a toilet with anyone in it in my life—never, so help me God.' Hmmm—as Jack was a non-believer, I feel that last qualification is more poetic flourish than solemn oath. Detonated *next* to an outhouse probably technically qualifies as *not actually* blowing up the ablution block itself.

For those who might wonder why three boxes of gelignite would be standard provisions for the Grey Ghost during a REDEX trial, Jack had an explanation which he gave to Neil Bennetts:

> Where does the name 'Gelignite' come in?' When we were doing a test in the Ford, we said, 'Right, on this Mt Isa section, if somebody breaks down, how are we going to get past?' I said, 'OK, let's use this jelly.' Bill knew how to use it and showed me, and I said, 'Right, let's go 20 miles by the speedo and assume there's a car right on the road, busted.' So I went out 20 miles along this road. As I said previously, it was so narrow you couldn't get past anybody. Where we picked the 20 mile, right spot on, we said, 'Stop. Rightoh, get out of the car.' And you couldn't have got past anybody. So he said 'Rightoh,' so I got the axe out of the car and cut a shrub down, put a marker there: OK, we want to be back on the road up that section, just up there that much, and we've got to clear this. It took us about twenty minutes. We lit the fuses and we got back and we blew a couple of trees out, blew some rocks away, cleaned it up a bit and it took us twenty minutes and we got back on the road again. We cleared a section about as long as this office, 30 or 40 feet or something, cleared it, drove the car off the road in low gear, because it was really rough, and he said, 'We'll take the jelly.' So we took the jelly. In the

end they used to demand it. We never did ever use it in the trial to get us out of strife.

Ka ... boom: gelignite

What exactly is gelignite? And how is it used? Jack used to maintain that jelly was 'just like big bungers: the explosion went up and was not dangerous.' Well ... not *too* dangerous.

Gelignite is also known as blasting gelatin or simply 'jelly'. It is an explosive material in which nitroglycerine has been soaked in wood pulp to make it safe and stable. Unlike dynamite, gelignite does not suffer from the dangerous problem of sweating, the leaking of unstable nitroglycerine from the solid matrix. Its composition makes it easy to mould and safe to handle without protection—as long as it is not near anything capable of detonating it.

Gelignite was invented in 1875 by the Swedish chemist Alfred Nobel, who had also invented dynamite and left a Will that led to the creation of the Nobel Prizes.

Dynamite is more dangerous than gelignite. Over time, regardless of the sorbent used, sticks of dynamite will weep or sweat nitroglycerin, which can then pool at the bottom of the box or storage area. The maximum shelf life of nitroglycerin-based dynamite is recommended as one year from the date of manufacture, under good storage conditions. For years, Jack used to have ageing sticks of gelignite scattered about his workplace in various locations. Gelignite, guns and bullets were as common as spanners, tyres and oil in his garage.

Gelignite needs a detonator to go *boom*. Consequently, it can be stored safely. As well as the normal safety procedures for exploding it, Jack would invariably incorporate his own unique final step: walking quickly and nonchalantly away from the impending blast site and finding a policeman with whom to have a casual chat.

So could detonating gelignite for amusement as Jack did be described as a safe pastime? Gelignite is associated with the IRA, British paramilitary groups and 'Gelignite' Jack Murray. Two of the three would be classed as terrorists and one is just plain terrifying. I'll let the reader be the judge.

Townsville to Mt Isa

In 1953 it had been on the Calamity Trail from Cloncurry to Mt Isa that Jack had rolled the Plymouth and ended his dream of winning the 1953

CHAPTER ONE

REDEX. Those lessons learnt, in 1954 the very same section of road would be instrumental in his winning the trial.

'The roads were murder'

One of the main things on a car was the clearance. How far can you get off the ground? You'd even go to oversized tyres, just to get another quarter of an inch or so. Put the springs up and the muffler, everything that was hanging down. You looked at it, you lay under the car, and you'd say 'That, there.' The fuel lines under the chassis, you'd split rubber tubing down and slip it over the pipes. You wouldn't miss anything that was hanging down, because they'd be knocked off the car. You'd practically rebuild the car. You had to do this all the time. When you'd pull in to get a service, you'd hop underneath it, get a spanner and start checking things—because the roads would undo anything at all. The roads were murder. The road from Cloncurry to Mt Isa was 80 miles. That was where we actually won the trial. You see, it all goes on loss of points. Every minute you're late, that is another point.

By the time competitors had reached Mt Isa, only three cleansheeters remained from the original 246 starters: Car No 159, NSW, Martin Arentz (Ford Customline), Car No 25, Victoria, Doug Whiteford (Vanguard Spacemaster) and Car No 256, NSW, Jack Murray (Ford V8).

It had indeed been a 'horror stretch'. A secret control 28 miles out of Cloncurry on the way to Mt Isa had been manned by officials from the Australian Sporting Car Club (ASCC). Lex Davison was caught. He drove a few kilometres to a township and rang his teammate Stan Jones about the secret control. Stan misread his map and also got caught—but not before he had warned the two Murrays. Jack and Bill showed the patience of Job, creeping along the road at the set pace and letting others fly by only to be penalised at the control.

So why did Stan Jones pass on the warning about the control to Jack and Bill, fellow competitors? There was certainly camaraderie among the team members and a feeling of 'them versus us' when it came to the officials. But Stan's benevolence may have had more to do with the 'special paint' used in the REDEX to mark car parts and the returning of a favour.

Chris McLachlan, 'Wild Bill' McLachlan's son had the tale related to him a number of times over the years. As soon as his father's car was marked with the so-called special paint, Bill took a sample back to the laboratory in his paint shop and promptly reproduced a small amount, some for Jack and some for Bill. Partway through the trial, another competitor (Stan Jones?) lost a part in the sand. Jack had the part and offered it. Stan replied, 'That's no good—it doesn't have the special paint.' Jack promptly produced his very own special paint and put a dab on it. With a wink and a smile, Jack then said, 'You owe me.' Indeed he did—and when he learnt about the secret control repaid the help and shared the information with the Murrays. The irony is that while neither Jack nor Bill needed to use the paint themselves, the competitor who did benefit instead lost points through a misread map. Truth is stranger than fiction.

Once past the secret control it was a very different story. Jack and Bill did what they did best: drove flat out to make up time, overtaking 23 cars on the hell road into Mt Isa. Jack always maintained that this was one of the worst stretches of road he ever drove. Only one and a half cars wide, the Murrays risked all on this stretch, climbing on to rocky shoulders to get by. The only damage was broken shock absorber lever arms.

The secret control cost competitors many points, while road conditions meant 30 teams withdrew between Townsville and Mt Isa. Locals commented that the cars looked much more battered by the trial than in 1953.

STAGE	DISTANCE	AVERAGE SPEED	TIME ALLOWED	ROAD TYPE	CLEANSHEETERS
Townsville to Mt Isa (12 hrs rest)	613 miles (987 km)	30 mph (48 km/h)	19 hrs	Dirt	3

Mt Isa to Darwin

The remaining 214 vehicles in the trial set off for Darwin. The army-maintained Barkly and Stuart bitumen highways allowed the ASCC to set an average speed at the speed limit of the road—40 mph (64 km/h). But many cars had taken a battering reaching Mt Isa and needed to use valuable road time for repairs. Cleansheeter Martin Arentz had mechanical trouble and dropped points, leaving only Murray and Whiteford as cleansheeters. There were no secret controls.

STAGE	DISTANCE	AVERAGE SPEED	TIME ALLOWED	ROAD TYPE	CLEANSHEETERS
Mt Isa to Darwin (12 hrs rest)	1051 miles (1692 km)	40 mph (64 km/h)	26 hrs	Bitumen	2

Darwin to Christmas Creek to Broome: 'A lot of arse'

On Saturday 10 July, a week after leaving Sydney, the remaining competitors set out on the long, gruelling leg from Darwin via Christmas Creek to Broome. Many locals knew, and drivers later agreed, that this section offered road conditions that were at times worse than the infamous Calamity Trail from Townsville to Mt Isa.

Christmas Creek in 1954 was a dot on the map amidst desert, dust, sand and stones. Plagued with flies and comforted only by cold rations, the crews waiting out the six-hour rest stop surely thought that if the world ever needed an enema, Christmas Creek was without doubt the place to insert the hose.

A further 26 cars withdrew there, leaving 180 to push on towards Broome.

South of Katherine, near Wave Hill, the dust was so fine and thick that at one time 47 cars found themselves bogged. An enterprising farmer with a handy tractor was extracting £1 from teams during daylight hours and £2 at night before extracting vehicles from the dust bowl. It was on the Darwin to Broome section that one of the two cleansheeters, Doug Whiteford, later to become a three-time winner of the Australian Grand Prix, crashed into the back of a slowing car which had been obscured by the dust. Whiteford's Vanguard Spacemaster had been smashed at the front and the radiator holed; over four hours were lost repairing the damage. Risking all and driving at over 60 mph (96 km/h) on narrow, dusty tracks to make up time, Whiteford's Car No 25 arrived in Broome with 70 points lost.

It was during the Darwin to Broome section that luck was with the boys in the Grey Ghost. As Jack once famously said:

I had my fair share of luck—but then again, I've always had a lot of arse.

However, for *Truth* newspaper Jack was far gentler in his description of events:

A plug of gelignite outside the Hotel Roebuck to celebrate

We ploughed through to Broome and it was on this stretch that the gods gave us a smile. Thirty miles out we stopped, dead out of gas. I said to Bill: 'Just how many points do you reckon we're going to "do" getting gas?' He grabbed a can and started walking, but had not gone 100 yards when he topped a rise and saw a Holden on the side of the road with its crew wearing a sort of despairing air. They had broken down and had no chance of moving without a tow.

I am a businessman, so I made a deal.

'We'll swap you a tow for your petrol,' I said.

There was no argument so we syphoned their gas into the Grey Ghost, hooked on our towrope and towed them to Broome.

At the Broome control we were told we were alone in the lead.

We celebrated by letting off a plug of gelignite outside the Hotel Roebuck in Broome.

They had taken one hell of a gamble. That section from Christmas Creek to Broome had included a 28-mile (45 km) detour into Derby for fuel. That meant 28 miles into the town and 28 miles back to rejoin the main road to Broome. Gambling that there would be no secret Derby control, the two Murrays had only put in enough fuel in their judgement for the straight drive from Christmas Creek through to Broome. This risky decision was despite the official program initially listing Derby as a checkpoint. As Jack told the *Truth*, agonisingly close to Broome the fuel ran out, the Grey Ghost coasted to a stop and a dust cloud drifted by. Silence. Sure enough, the fuel had run out—but Jack's 'arse' had not. Clem Smith and his broken-down Holden with plenty of fuel were just over the hill, and were the Murrays' salvation.

At Broome, which marked roughly the halfway point in both time and distance, Jack and Bill Murray and Car No 256 stood alone with no points lost. They were leading the 1954 REDEX Round Australia Reliability Trial. While some exhausted competitors tried to sleep, Jack amused himself by donning his gorilla mask and letting off sticks of gelignite, much to the delight of locals. Jack asked if other competitors who might still be awake had any 'spare flies for his flywheel'. Well—there's no fun sleeping, is there?

Victorian Bill Patterson was placed second in his Peugeot, with 8 points lost and Queenslander A.A. 'Duck' Anderson in a Holden was third, with 14 points lost. But many miles of driving, poor roads and challenges lay ahead on the journey home.

STAGE	DISTANCE	AVERAGE SPEED	TIME ALLOWED	ROAD TYPE	CLEANSHEETERS
Darwin to Broome (6 hrs Christmas Creek) (22 hrs Broome)	1331 miles (2143 km)	33 mph (53 km/h)	43 hrs	Gravel Dirt	1

Broome to Meekatharra to Perth

Only 167 competitors remained as cars left Broome and headed south towards Port Hedland and then inland to Meekatharra. Sand drifts made the going tough and rock-hard humped road edges ripped the sumps out of cars. It was in this section that Jack Brabham's trial ended when he hit a huge creek boulder. Rugged ranges and creek crossings claimed more competitors. South Australian A. Spanner's Chevrolet (Car No 228) rolled several times. But the Murrays arrived in a cloud of dust at Meekatharra with 80 minutes to spare.

Now that they were leading the trial, most competitors in Jack's position would have focused purely on the task at hand, keeping a low profile and easing the Grey Ghost home. 'Gelignite' Jack Murray has been described many ways over the years, but 'like most competitors' was never one of them. As we have seen, he never took life too seriously.

Above: Left: Jack often found himself talking to police. Right: Jack enjoys a sedate cup of tea at Meekatharra. Perhaps a fuse is burning somewhere nearby.

THE REDEX TRIALS

'Police book REDEX trial leader Jack Murray for exploding gelignite'

It was at Meekatharra that Jack had yet another run-in with the law concerning some unexplained explosions that had disturbed the local peace. Accusations were even made that he was throwing gelignite at competitors who would not move over to allow the faster Grey Ghost to pass.

So did Jack throw gelignite to encourage slower traffic to move aside? He was once quoted as saying:

> I've got too much respect for gelignite to toss it from a moving car.
> But then we used to make a few stops, and that's a different story ...

The rest period had been doubled at Meekatharra to twelve hours and Jack, never being one for excessive rest, used the spare time to great advantage.

In writing this book, one thing I have learnt is not to rely on the accuracy of newspapers and magazines. Facts never seemed to get in the way of good copy. Having said that, the *Daily Telegraph* of 15 July 1954 reported the following:

> MEEKATHARRA, Wed.—Police tonight booked REDEX trial leader Jack Murray for exploding gelignite in the street of Meekatharra.
> Murray was driving out of the one-street town on the way to Perth.
> He threw a stick of gelignite out of his car.
> It exploded with a terrific bang, which startled all the residents.
> Constable Reg Carr stopped Murray and took him and his co-driver, Bill Murray, to the police station.
> He detained them for five minutes, took the number of their car, and allowed them to leave.
> As he entered the car Jack Murray said: 'This is a curl the mo job.' [a traditional Aussie term meaning excellent or really good]. Tonight Constable Carr refused to say what action police would take against Murray.

On 13 July 1954, the *Daily Telegraph* reported the following:

> BROOME, Mon. —Leading REDEX drivers Jack and Bill Murray have blasted their way to the front—with gelignite.

CHAPTER ONE

>Other trial drivers explained the Murrays' tactics today.
>
>They said that in the early stages the Murrays found that some drivers were reluctant to give way to let them pass.
>
>So the pair bought two cases of gelignite in Queensland.
>
>Since then many a trial driver hearing an explosion behind him has pulled up thinking he has had a blowout.
>
>Before he has had time to get out and investigate a 1948 Ford V8 has sailed past ...

Well, this certainly makes great copy! I doubt, however, if many (or any) trial drivers would mistake an explosion for a tyre blowout.

Did Jack throw gelignite from a moving Grey Ghost? We are going to have to wait over twenty years for Bill Murray to answer that one during the filming of TV's *This Is Your Life*.

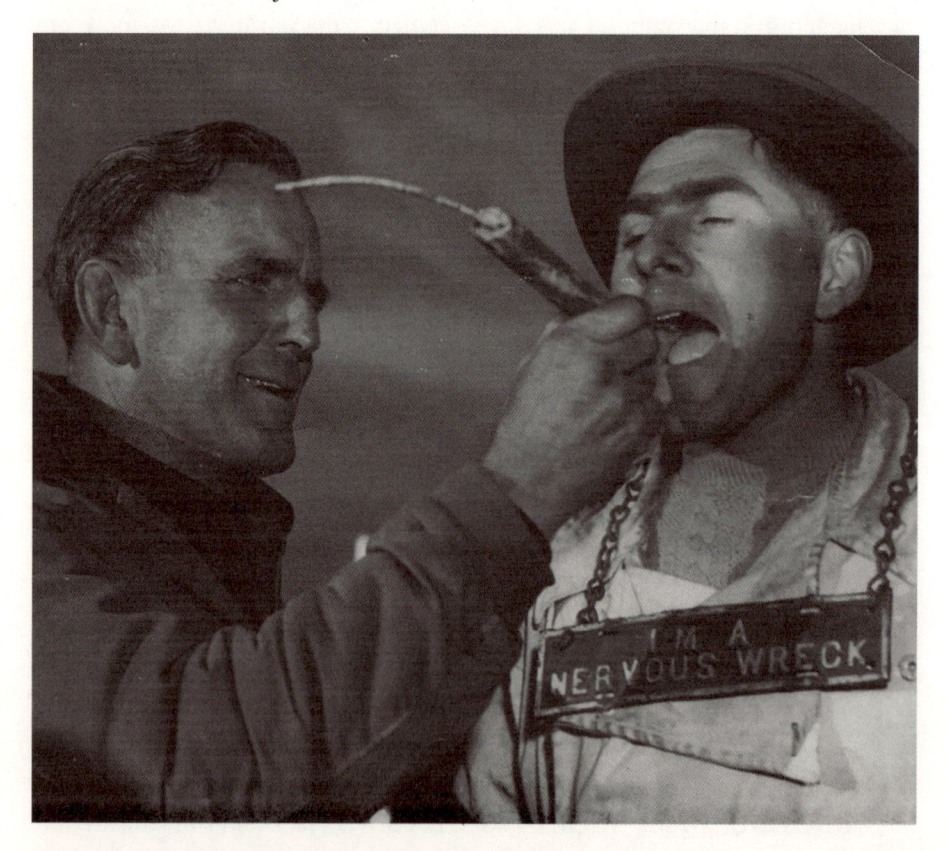

Above: Jack Murray with Keith Wilson, Peugeot Car No 140, grazier from Gilgandra.

STAGE	DISTANCE	AVERAGE SPEED	TIME ALLOWED	ROAD TYPE	CLEANSHEETERS
Broome to Perth	1471 miles (2368 km)	30 mph (48 km/h)	45 hrs	Dirt Bitumen	1

By the time competitors reached Perth, the 1954 REDEX Trial had really captured the public imagination. The massive crowds that had gathered to wish the drivers well surged in waves as cars passed, making it tough for competitors to reach control points on time. 'Gelignite' Jack and Bill Murray were now hot news. Reg Shepheard must have been thrilled at Jack's antics. For weeks the trial's progressive results and the name REDEX were emblazoned on newspaper front pages across the country. The publicity generated more than met the costs of sponsorship.

Perth to Madura to Adelaide

A reduced field of 144 cars left Perth on a day of torrential rain. The road to Kalgoorlie was mostly bitumen, followed by an eastern route out over the Nullabor towards Madura and a much-needed six-hour rest. The Nullabor section proved to be dry, dusty and pot-holed and all cars took a beating. The road beyond Madura lay mostly underwater due to the rains—but ironically it was fire, not water, that brought about the demise of Car No 246, a Citroen driven by Arthur O'Shea from NSW.

'Get out!'

At Koonalda, just east of the Western Australian and South Australian border, the Citroen burst into flames while travelling at 50 mph (80 km/h). Skidding to a halt, the driver yelled 'Get out!' just before flames engulfed the car, the back tyres blew and the reserve fuel tank exploded.

STAGE	DISTANCE	AVERAGE SPEED	TIME ALLOWED	ROAD TYPE	CLEANSHEETERS
Perth to Adelaide (reduced to 11hrs rest)	1768 miles (2846 km)	34 mph (55 km/h)	49 hrs	Dirt Bitumen	1

CHAPTER ONE

Above: The burnt-out wreck of Car No 246. Photo courtesy Hal Moloney.

Adelaide to Melbourne 'I only had to sneeze and I could lose points'

Despite the usual confusion, this time about starting times for leaving Adelaide, most competitors moved quickly along the bitumen roads from Adelaide to Melbourne to get to workshops for much-needed maintenance before they checked in.

As the field raced into Melbourne, police escorted the Murrays and Car No 256 into the control point—possibly more concerned about errant sticks of gelignite than anything else. The second placegetters sat only eight minutes behind the Grey Ghost. 'I only had to sneeze and I could lose points,' said Jack.

While there were no secret controls between Adelaide and Melbourne, when the cars arrived scrutineers went through them with the proverbial fine toothcomb, and some teams lost points for replacing shattered components.

STAGE	DISTANCE	AVERAGE SPEED	TIME ALLOWED	ROAD TYPE	CLEANSHEETERS
Adelaide to Melbourne (reduced to 6 hrs rest)	575 miles (926 km)	31 mph (50 km/h)	18 hrs	Bitumen	1

34

Melbourne to Canberra to Sydney:
A snowman and snowballs

Of the 246 cars that had started in Sydney all those days and miles ago, just over half, 127, left Melbourne. Teams had finally been given the secret route cards that showed the way home via the Snowy Mountains, but drivers were fearful not only of the icy conditions that lay ahead, but of warnings about secret controls.

One of the toughest sections of the trial still lay ahead. Mt Talbingo, just north of the Victorian border in the Snowy Mountains, was a steep and slushy descent. As Bill Murray commented:

> The very steep mountain road near Talbingo rivalled for toughness the Mt Isa section. The car's brakes failed on the mountains and we drove down at 40-50 miles an hour in second gear. Quite often we had close calls in keeping our points-free record. On the Talbingo section we had only minutes to spare.

While there was no snow on the actual road, the Australian Alps afforded Jack and Bill the opportunity to have some typical Murray fun. The boys stopped on the roadside, built a snowman and then amused themselves by throwing snowballs at startled passing competitors. The aptly named Superintendent Snowden from NSW Police had warned, 'I drove over the Snowy Mountains road a few days ago. To travel faster than 25 mph would be unsafe.' Jack and Bill averaged 55 mph (88 km/h)—with a 'snowman stop'.

No doubt there was tension, anticipation and excitement in the air as the finish line drew closer—but never enough for 'Gelignite' Jack when the opportunity for a bit more fun presented itself.

After the Australian Alps and Canberra, the field set off on the final leg to Sydney. Newsreel footage of the time shows lines of cars snaking down Macquarie Pass at break-neck speeds, headed for the coast. From early in the afternoon, people had begun to line the streets to get a clear view of the cars and by nightfall the Princes Highway, from Dapto to Bulli Pass, was lined with cars full of people to give tired drivers a cheer. As one man commented, 'Only the Queen received a greater welcome.' Of the original 246 starters, only 120 cars arrived back in Sydney after eighteen days and 9600 miles of car-wrecking roads, disputes, secret controls, dust, more disputes, misleading maps,

CHAPTER ONE

weariness, even more disputes—and, of course, gelignite.

As non-smokers and teetotallers, both Jack and Bill celebrated the win not with the traditional magnum of champagne, but rather with homemade cake. It had been baked by Mrs N. Hawke, wife of Alec Hawke, a fellow Curlewis St, Bondi garage owner. It was decorated with the words 'Gorilla Jack' and featured a model car. The boys tucked in with gusto.

In both the 1953 and 1954 REDEX trials, Jack and Bill Murray were termed a 'two up' team. Some crews opted to have three members. While this extra teammate shared the workload, the downside was the added weight. In a very practical sense, 'Gelignite' Jack Murray, Bill Murray and the Grey Ghost bonded as a team of three, each playing their part and reliant on the others for success.

At this point, Bill Murray's story and that of the Grey Ghost deserve telling.

Bill's motorsport career was both unusual and exceptional, involving major victories in each of the three different areas of motorsport: an Australian Grand Prix (1947), a major trial (1954 REDEX) and a Class win in the Armstrong 500 (1960).

Above: To the victors go the spoils: let them eat cake. Jack and Bill tuck in. Photo courtesy Hal Moloney.

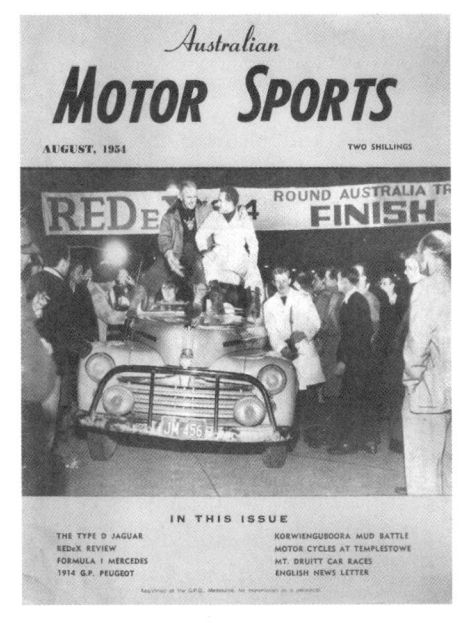

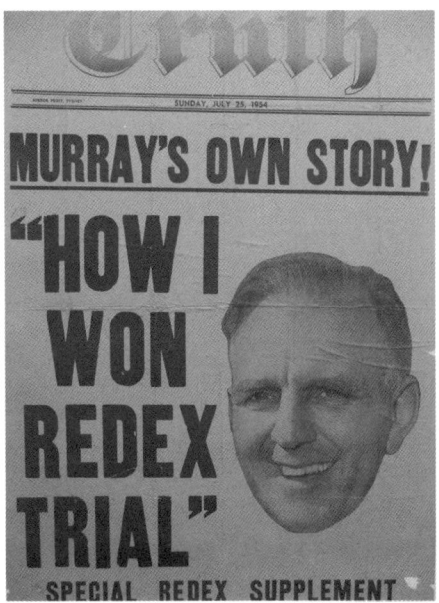

Above and Below: 'Gelignite' Jack Murray and Bill Murray (No Relation), winners without loss of points of the 1954 REDEX Round Australia Reliability Trial.

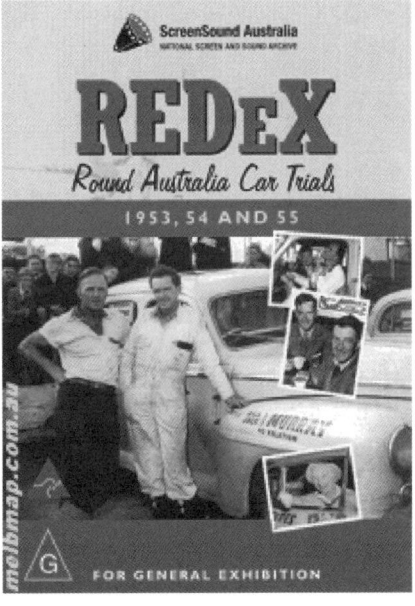

CHAPTER ONE

Bill Murray was a bulldozer driver experienced in using gelignite. Perhaps it is best left to Jack to tell the story of his good mate:

> Well, Bill Murray was an explosives expert and he used to build dams and this sort of thing around Bourke and Wilcannia ... and all those places. So we said we'll take it in case there are trees across the road and we'll blow it out—OK. The tree comes up; we timed ourselves. It took us quarter of an hour to blow the tree out of the road and go around the side in first or second gear—but we never had to use it for that.
>
> And so we started playing jokes with it and so I got the name 'Geli' Jack. It shouldn't've been mine—it should have been Bill Murray's. And they all used to write in the paper Jack Murray and Bill Murray and they then would put in brackets (No Relation)—and they still do it. (ABC Radio interview with Mike Jeffries, 1979)

Bill won the 1947 Australian Grand Prix driving an MG TC at Mount Panorama, Bathurst. In 1952, Bill Murray made his first (and last) reappearance at Bathurst since 1947, placing an impressive third, one ahead of 'Gelignite' Jack Murray, in the seventeenth Australian Grand Prix. Bill drove an Alfa Alvis and Jack his Allard J2 (Cadillac V8). The Murrays' good friend Bill McLachlan placed thirteenth that year in the Grand Prix.

In the *Truth* newspaper a few days after the 1954 REDEX win, Jack paid due credit to the 'other Murray':

> At the outset I want to say that my co-driver and navigator, Bill Murray, who is not my brother or any relation, played as big a part as anything else in our victory.

Bill Murray's name has entered Australian motorsport history. Every October, it's become traditional, even for non-motorsport devotees to sit down and watch at least part of the 'great race' on Mount Panorama at Bathurst. As cars attempt to wash off the almost 300 km/h speeds at the end of Conrod Straight before entering Pit Straight, they must negotiate the infamous Murray's Corner. This treacherous left-hander was not named after 'Gelignite' Jack Murray and nor was it named after Bill Murray in honour of his 1947 Grand Prix win.

On Monday 7 October 1946, as competitors battled for position in the NSW Grand Prix of 100 miles, Bill Murray braked heavily for what was then termed Pit Corner at the end of Conrod Straight—but his Terraplane crashed into the sandbags.

In the darkness of the evening, as the competitors left the circuit, Alf Najar used a piece of charcoal from a campfire to scratch Murray's Corner on the Pit Corner timber fence. That's the real story of how an iconic Bathurst location got its name. I notice that as the years pass the latest sponsors' names are more frequently attached to sections of the course. But to the traditionalists, it will always remain Murray's Corner.

'Good winners, and deservedly so'

In his 1976 interview with Neil Bennetts, 'Gelignite' Jack explained the characteristics and detailed preparation of the famous Grey Ghost that helped give him and Bill the winning edge:

> **MURRAY**: The real trial was the year after—it was 1954. Having been around in Bill's [McLachlan] car earlier, in the Ford, I was still keen on a Ford. It was a V8 and it had a lot of punch in it and it had the right springing, transverse springing: the front spring and the back spring transversed, and up very high. There's a lot of clearance under a Ford, and they had a very strong chassis on 'em.
>
> **BENNETTS**: This was 1954?
>
> **MURRAY**: That would be '54. The one we had was a Canadian one, built in Canada and exported here. They didn't bring a lot of them. Why we picked that, they had [special] shock absorbers.

In these trials, I've seen the shock absorber at night, on a rough road, glowing under the mudguard. Now, that sounds crazy. Burning the paint off them, going like that all the time, they generate heat. You know when you blow a bike tyre up—ever felt the heat in the pump? Well, the shock absorber is just going like that all the time on a rough road, and it will burn the enamel off the shock absorber, I've

CHAPTER ONE

Above: Bill Murray in white overalls, 'Gelignite' Jack Murray and the famous Ford V8 Grey Ghost.

seen them glow of a night time. You never tell anybody this; they think you're telling lies—but that's a fact. Many times I've seen it.

Well, these had a type of shock called a Houdaille. It's a hydraulic shock and it's a circular arrangement. It's different altogether to a tubular shock: it's circular and has an arm out the side and goes down on to the axle. It has a different type of action. All the action is in this circular housing; it's like a water pump to look at. They are French designed, beautiful shocks. We never ever touched it from the word go. On an ordinary Ford, you're doing six or seven shocks in, you keep doing them all the time. There's no shock absorber would last you round Australia; they hadn't made any good enough yet. That's why we picked this particular Ford with the Houdaille French designed shocks on, the Canadian Ford. The body was better than ours, the ones they make here and had little bits and pieces on them—but the shocks were the main thing.

In a rally car, if it's a rough road, your shocks—well, even now they're building shocks in Germany filled with gas and they get so hot that they explode. I've seen one explode under the bonnet and blow a hole 12 inches in diameter and blow the horn. It was bolted on to it, and blew the whole lot out of the car. The guys got out to fix the wire on the horn—this was in the London-Sydney Marathon—and there was no horn there. It blew a hole underneath the mudguard and took the horn and all out and there were two wires down. But you never tell people this. As I say, truth is stranger than fiction—any day.

Anyway, you can't make up the stories like the true things that happen, especially on motor cars. So we looked for one of these Fords; we had twelve months' notice. When they talked about having this trial after the short one, they said, 'Let's go for the big one, right round.' So there was a chap in the North Bondi Surf Club. Here's another story: you're not going to believe this. Only yesterday I was round at a Holden dealer's place here, and I was leaning over the counter talking about something and a guy bumped me and said, 'How are you? You don't remember me, do you?' I said, 'No. I know your face, but it's a long while ago.' He said, 'Have you ever heard of the Grey Ghost?' That was what they called the old Ford, it used to be black before I got it and they painted it grey. This was the guy that owned it and sold it to me. Yesterday, this only happened yesterday down here at the Holden dealer's. I recognised him then. He said, 'I've never seen you since the day you bought that car—the old Grey Ghost you called it.' I said, 'That's right.' He said, 'Isn't it amazing, to meet you here?' It was a Holden dealer, Vern Potts, down in Rose Bay, and he said 'Haven't you seen him since?' I said, 'I've never seen him until today.' And he just shook his head and walked away. He'd say that was a lot of bull or whatever you like to call it but that's what happened yesterday.

Anyhow, he had this beautiful Ford. It was immaculate. We got it into The Garage and took the engine out, and I took it to bits and I gave it to Eric Webster, a friend of mine working at de Havilland in the propeller section, and he had it all magnafluxed, all the crankshaft, the con rods, pistons and diffs, had all the engine done, we fitted rings to it and imported bearings. Everything was imported from the States. We done the motor, then I took the wheels off, had the brakes done, Ferodo supplied the lining. Then we had a radio fitted to it supplied by—what's the Australian radio, can't think of it now, they supplied the radio [a Ferris short-wave car radio]. We got plenty of support from the motor trade. We took every bit of it to pieces—everything. Then we went to work on the lights; we got good lights, beautiful lights. The door handles, we took all those off. We took everything off. Then everything was 'locktited' [a thread locking adhesive], bitumen inside the doors and then I used the car for rallies for about five months, till you could just drive it and when you came home just put it away and there was nothing wrong with it.

When the trial started, it was as good as you could ever buy or get a motor car in the condition. Everything was protected, the sump and bits and pieces we'd put on underneath, you know. You'd find it out in the trial and come back and alter it. It paid off. We didn't have to do anything to it.

BENNETTS: And Jack, who christened the Ford V8 the Grey Ghost?

MURRAY: Well, the name—they give you a name, and the guy that gave us the name was a famous cricketer, Ginty Lush [John Grantley Lush, aka 'Ginty' 1913-1985]. Have you ever heard of him? Well, he gave us the name, the old Grey Ghost, and it just stuck to it. That's what they used to call it, the Grey Ghost, and it just stuck. It never left me, the name.

There you have it: 'Gelignite' Jack Murray, Bill Murray (No Relation) and the Grey Ghost—the team that won the 1954 REDEX trial with no points lost.

Protests

All three of the REDEX Trials were mired in controversy. Controversy would reign before, during and after each of the REDEX Trials. Disputes and protests were lodged over a plethora of issues: the use of secret controls; speed limits being set too high or too low; route maps being unclear or even wrong; signposts that had allegedly been moved; the general non-co-operation of police; varying interpretation of the rules and regulations; inclusion of unplanned special stages; and arguments over repairs and modifications allowed to cars plus points being lost during post-race inspection for cracks and damage to vehicles. All these and more caused much angst for all concerned, both competitors and officials. Victorian driver Lex Davison complained that the trial was not a test of driving skill, cars or stamina, but rather 'a test to see how long your ulcer could hold out till the next secret control'.

Spare a thought for Terry Byrne, an Australian Sporting Car Club official, who in 1954 bore the brunt of complaints from the competitors. As the ASCC travelling scrutineer, poor Terry was given the unenviable task of single-handedly checking the 169 cars that had made it to Broome. At around 140, Terry actually collapsed with what was described as 'nervous tension' and was taken home to bed. When Jack and Bill Murray crossed the finish line on 20 July 1954, Car No 256 was only declared the *provisional* winner.

A protest was lodged by well-known fellow competitor and successful rally driver, Peter Antill, against Car No 256. Antill claimed the Murrays did not finish the trial in a standard vehicle, since they had disconnected their shock absorber arms and roll bar. The protest failed, since Norm Pleasance, Trial Director, said there were no regulations in the rules forbidding this. Scrutineer Terry Byrne was given the job of scrutineering the Grey Ghost, no doubt worsening his bout of nervous tension. After two hours of thorough examination, he found that the Murrays had replaced no part in the car. He must have breathed a sigh of relief as he passed Car No 256 without loss of points.

The final placings in the 1954 REDEX Round Australia Reliability trial were as follows:

WINNER	'Gelignite' Jack Murray Bill Murray (No Relation) (NSW)	Car No 256 The Grey Ghost	Ford V8	No points lost
SECOND PLACE	Gerald 'Bill' Patterson (Vic)	Car No 29	Peugeot	8 points lost
THIRD PLACE	A. 'Duck' Anderson (Qld)	Car No 176	Holden	14 points lost

The 1953 REDEX:
'We turned it over'

The first REDEX Trial had not ended well for Jack and Bill Murray. Jack managed to turn over his 1952 Plymouth Chrysler, No 119, on the infamous 84-mile section between Cloncurry and Mt Isa christened the Calamity Trail. The Plymouth actually rolled twice and was a write-off. This was also the section of road that organisers would use to decide the winner, in the event of a draw at the end of the trial. No doubt all competitors, and Jack in particular, would have been speeding and pushing hard—too hard—during this section. As Jack recounted to Bennetts:

CHAPTER ONE

The 1953 REDEX, in the Plymouth. We turned it over. We flipped it over in an up-jump, came out of one of these, came out of the last one and there was a bull standing in the middle of it. I swung to avoid the bull and when we came out, the road turned hard left, hit the bank which was about 18 inches, and just flipped the Plymouth over on its side.

The windows flew out, Bill flew out and the windscreen flew out and hit him on the head and gave him concussion. And half a dozen cartons of jelly just burst open. Of course, you've got to detonate it to let it off; it's quite safe. The sticks were all lying around and Bill was lying on the road. I picked him up, put him against a tree—it was about half past nine in the morning, a beautiful summer's day—and I said, 'This would be a beautiful place for a sunbake.'

By eleven o'clock we moved him into the shade of the tree; it was about 120 in the water bag. (laughs) I'll never forget it. The cars would pull up and say, 'Are you all right?' and I'd say yes, and they'd say, 'What are you doing there?' I said, 'I'm thinking of opening up a shop.' 'You're what?' 'Thinking of opening up a shop.' They said, 'Do you want a lift?' and I said, 'Oh no, we've got a truck coming out.' The truck came out and got hold of the car and drove us into Cloncurry.

There was a friend of ours out from there about 30 miles, Walter Hacon. He had a couple of properties there. I rang him up and he came and picked us up in his car and we went and stayed there for four days. Bill couldn't go shooting; he couldn't let a gun off, because he had concussion and if a gun would go off, he'd nearly faint. Anyhow, he recovered all right, he was all right, and we came back to Sydney. That was the end of that trial.

'Got a ring spanner?'

In addition to Jack's one-liner about 'opening up a shop', it was another of his quips to passing competitors as the boys sat beside the wrecked Plymouth in the 1953 REDEX that gave rise to one of the most frequently told anecdotes about Jack. It became Evan Green's favourite story about his larrikin mate. Evan even opened his book *Journeys with Gelignite Jack* (first published in1966 by Rigby) with the story:

As another concerned competitor slowed to a stop next to the overturned wrecked Plymouth in '53, the ever-present dust cloud drifted on by. A voice yelled out:

'What happened? You all right?'

'Got a ring spanner?' Jack called back. 'Nine-sixteenths SAE?'

Thinking ... followed by the puzzled query: 'A ring spanner. What the hell do you want that for?'

'I thought I'd do the brakes while the wheels were up like this.'

Top and Above: 1953: the wrecked Plymouth. Brakes adjusted? Photos courtesy of Graeme and Ann Cosier and supplied by Hal Moloney.

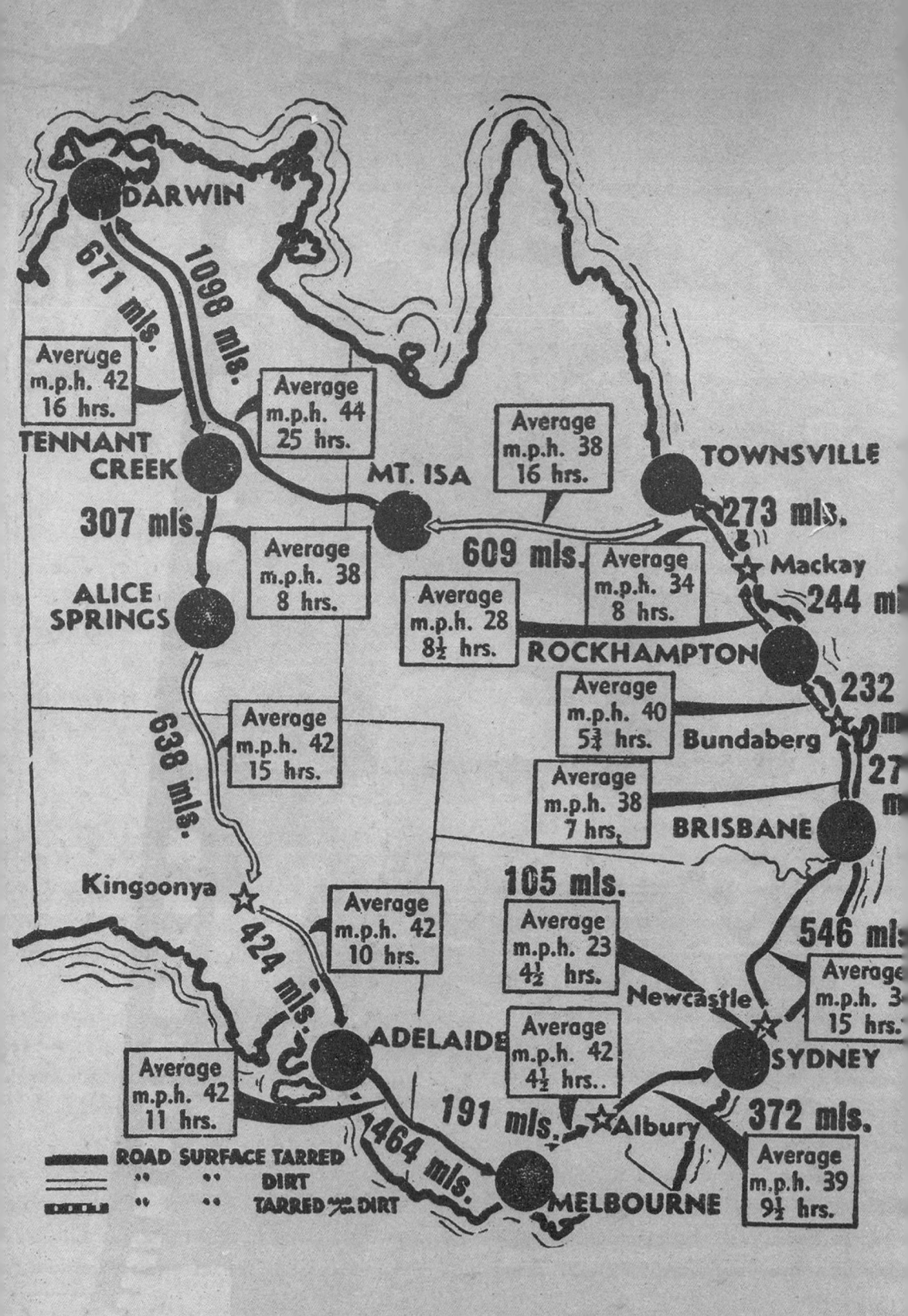

The route of the 1953 REDEX Trial.

Silence ... then everyone started to laugh, even the poor 'No Relation' Bill: bleeding, concussed and nursing a very sore head.

It was Jack's signature cheekiness and that typically Australian attitude when faced with adversity that endeared him to so many people. As his life story unfolds we will see that there would be other, far more serious adversities Jack would face later in life. Yet the man who asked for a ring spanner back in 1953 was essentially the same as the one who was to meet those challenges almost 30 years later.

A shrug, a smile, a joke—and get on with it. That was 'Gelignite' Jack Murray.

The route of the 6500-mile 1953 REDEX, eventually won by Ken Tubman and John Marshall in a Peugeot 203, did not actually go 'round Australia' but cut a path through the centre of the continent.

As we have seen, the following year Jack went on to win. In the *Australian Dictionary of Biography*, Volume 18 (Melbourne University Press 2012), Andrew Moore's account reads:

> Given that he enjoyed but one principal sporting success, the outpouring of stories about 'Gelignite Jack' is surprising. The larger-than-life Murray encouraged and propagated hyperbole.

Jack's supposed overnight success in winning the 1954 REDEX Trial had in fact been a lifetime in the making. As we shall see, the win was both preceded by, and followed by, numerous successes in various fields including motorsport, waterskiing and wrestling. And then, of course, there was the gelignite.

Luck played a part in Jack's 1954 REDEX win—but luck without skill, preparation and determination never won a reliability trial.

The 1955 REDEX:
' ... more or less a shemozzle'

With the success and publicity generated by both the 1953 and 1954 trials, a third REDEX trial in the middle of 1955 seemed inevitable. But it would prove to be the last.

The route of the 1955 REDEX was similar to 1954, but at 10,500 miles (16,900 km) was slightly longer.

CHAPTER ONE

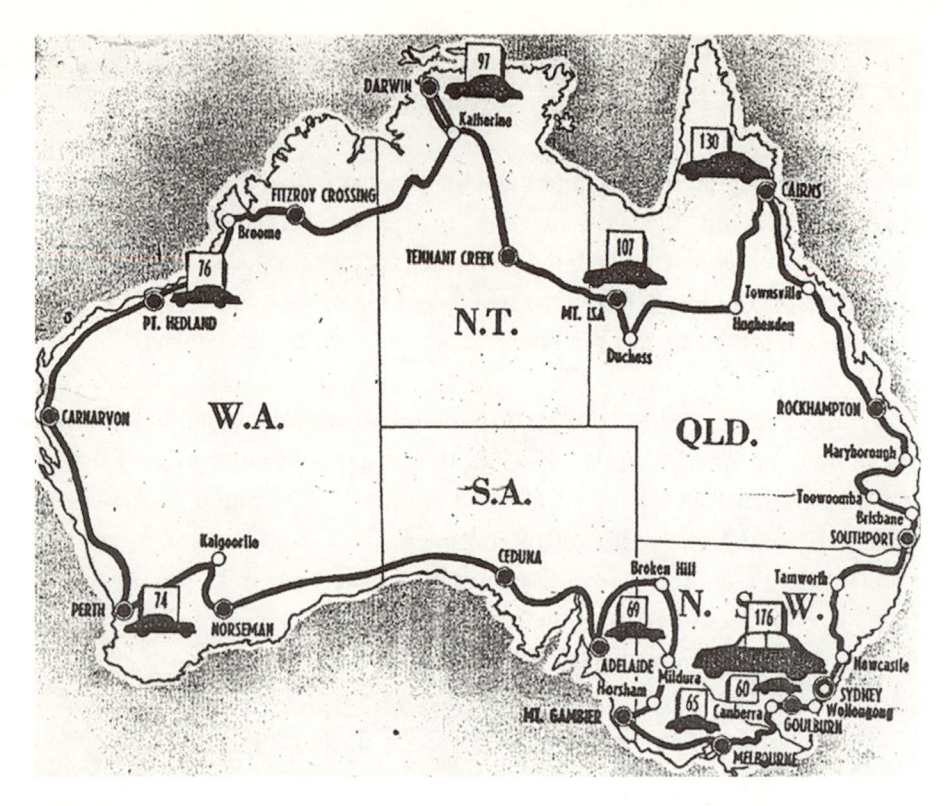

Above: The 1955 REDEX route included excursions to Tamworth (NSW), Carnarvon (WA) and Broken Hill (NSW).

From a field of 167 vehicles, only 63 officially finished, 21 days later.

As the trial neared completion an originally unplanned diversion at Werong (near Wee Jasper and 12 km south of Yass), used to determine the winner, meant that some cars and their drivers were bogged for ten hours or more. Jack, with his brother Ray as navigator, was running third at that stage, with the loss of only 36 points. The Murrays were so disgusted that, although they finished, they refused to submit the Grey Ghost for scrutiny and were disqualified, forfeiting fourth place. Car No 129 (B. Rogers in a Holden) and Car No 36 (N. Klinger in a Standard Vanguard), also protested the officials' decision to run the field through a mud bog by refusing to submit their cars for scrutiny.

Throughout the trial, particularly towards the end and even post-trial, controversy and arguments reigned. Newspaper headlines were full of emotion as they proclaimed *REDEX Boilover* and *Hopeless Mixup*. At the end of the trial

30,000 people who paid to see the finish in Parramatta Park hardly glimpsed a trial car.

Melbourne journalist Laurie Whitehead, driving a Volkswagen, was declared provisional winner with the loss of 21 points. During scrutineering, he was penalised 500 points for alleged damage to his car. Subsequently this decision was reversed. Although the trial ended in September, the farce and disputes continued and the placings were not officially awarded until December 1955. The final results were:

WINNER	Regent Motors/Laurie Whitehead/Bob Foreman	Car No 90	Volkswagen	21 points lost
SECOND PLACE	Eddy and Lance Perkins	Car No 2	Volkswagen	27 points lost
THIRD PLACE	Regent Motors/Mal Brooks/Frank Tate	Car No 60	Standard Vanguard	45 points lost

Jack related his version of the events of the 1955 REDEX to Neil Bennetts:

> Well, the '55 one, that was ill-organised, and all sorts of things happened in that. The finish of that was, it was an easy trial and they put us into a paddock up at Goulburn [*sic*: it was near Wee Jasper] about a five- or six-mile run, and this paddock had no bottom and it had been raining, and if you stopped to do something you couldn't get traction again. They had more than 50 per cent of the cars parked there all night and in the morning they were all down to the running boards. (They had running boards then; they don't have them now.) You had to be towed out. Of course, it was the finish of the trial; there were only about half a dozen cars finished. We got back to Sydney and didn't clock in, and the Victorians drove back to Victoria. They said they'd never go in another trial. Of course, this was something that was extra, put on in the last 24 hours. It should never have happened. They had a winner, they had a first and a second, whatever they wanted—so it wasn't something where they had a lot of cars dead-heating; they were all well spread out. But the chap—I won't mention his name but he

CHAPTER ONE

was the instigator of it and he's never forgiven himself since; he's still alive— but that trial ended up in more or less a shemozzle, and they didn't hold a trial the next year. I think it was three or four years before they could get anybody to go in one, and it lost a lot of its colour, you know. People said it was more or less a swindle, you know. They wanted the Volkswagen to win it—that was the story, actually. (laughs) But that's another story.

Trials, rallies and controversies seem inextricably linked—the 1955 REDEX even more so than usual. Unsubstantiated gossip at the time suggested that perhaps Jack did not finish the trial and submit the Grey Ghost for scrutineering because parts had been replaced and the car would not have passed. Other similarly disgusted competitors shared Jack's view and also chose to protest by not submitting their cars for scrutiny.

In their book *From REDEX to Repco* (Gregory's, 1979), Bill Tuckey and Thomas Floyd referred to the Wee Jasper bog catastrophe as 'a monumental organising blunder that is still talked about in motorsport circles'. The facts speak for themselves and no amount of revisionist re-writing of history can change them. What do you call half a field of trial cars buried in mud overnight? I'd suggest that Jack got it right: a shemozzle.

Jack's views of sport, adventure and competition give an insight into the motivations that drove my father. He told Neil Bennetts:

> I suppose you wonder why I do these trips. Well, they have been offered to me by various people. I like motoring. I like to win—but I don't care if I lose. What do they say—they've got an expression for it—'Modest in victory, gracious in defeat.' That's it. I like the sport, I always liked sport, competing with somebody whether it is physical or with cars, it's mechanical, more or less. When I say I like to win, if I'm competing with somebody there's a lot of fun in it. I think I do it more for the fun of it ...
>
> I've never been asked this before, and as you just said to me, you must have thought about it. I like a laugh. I think if you can make people laugh and be happy—like a lot of people say I've never grown up and I don't suppose I ever have. I just get as much fun out of throwing a bunger—which sounds bloody stupid—as a kid does. I'd

Above: Jack with his rattlesnake casually draped over the driver's door.

just as soon throw a bunger or catch somebody with a bunger, give them a scare or they scare me. I can take jokes just the same as I can dish 'em out. I like to get caught myself.

I hate snakes and I have a couple of pet snakes, dummy ones, which I got from America. I paid $25 for one with lead in its tail. It's a rattler, and it looks that real it still catches me. If I put it away somewhere and I'm looking for something and put my hand on it, I just go off the same as anybody else as if it was really alive. I like getting caught myself with jokes. A lot of my mates play jokes on me, and I play them back on 'em. I think I do a lot of the things for the lot of good fun in them. I can get a laugh out of it.

CHAPTER ONE

'A truly popular win'

The REDEX trials thrilled Australians. The papers were full of praise for the achievement of the 1954 REDEX win:

> Jack and Bill Murray did a miraculous job bringing their Ford all the way round with not a single point lost, for which they deserve the highest possible credit, particularly as Jack, as usual, treated the thing in a delightfully light-hearted way, and managed to take a bit of time out for clowning here and there. (*Australian Motor Sports Spotlight*, August 1954)

Or again:

> Jack and Bill Murray, who have been good losers in the past, were that rarer-yet phenomenon, good winners—and deservedly so. Theirs was a truly popular win in the big Ford, made all the more creditable by the fact that they were only two-up. (*Australian Motor Sports*, August 1954)

The papers reported that Jack was the ripe old age of 44, while Jack himself offered 42. In reality he was just over a month shy of his 47th birthday when he drove into Sydney Showground that winter evening in July 1954. As he said:

> I suppose it's a case of the old dog for the hard road. I'm 42 and the average age of drivers was about 38. There were youngsters in the field but they did not have either the breaks or the experience or the physical reserves to stick it out. (*Truth, Souvenir REDEX Trial Feature*, 25 July 1954)

The REDEX trials opened up the country and also opened up the thinking of our people. Everyday people in everyday cars saw that their country was an opportunity waiting for them to explore. The same feature commented:

> *Outback Roads Are Menace to Nation:* One thing the REDEX Trial proved is that Australia will never march to war quickly on its roads … In peace the roads would help open up a vast country which is in

the doldrums of neglect. Australians would have an opportunity to visit the fabulous outback. Defence, Tourists, Commerce.

It was a different era, a time of innocence—now gone.

The REDEX trials left at least two lasting legacies—a nascent tourist industry whereby Australians started to explore their own land and an Australian icon who had exploded into public consciousness with a big V8, a cheeky grin and a 'give it a go' attitude—'Gelignite' Jack Murray.

As I came to fully appreciate in writing this biography, my father's involvement and success in motorsport was truly legendary. He loved motorsport and the camaraderie that came with it. He competed in everything he could, in any vehicle—if it had four wheels 'Gelignite' invariably wanted to drive it and race it—hard.

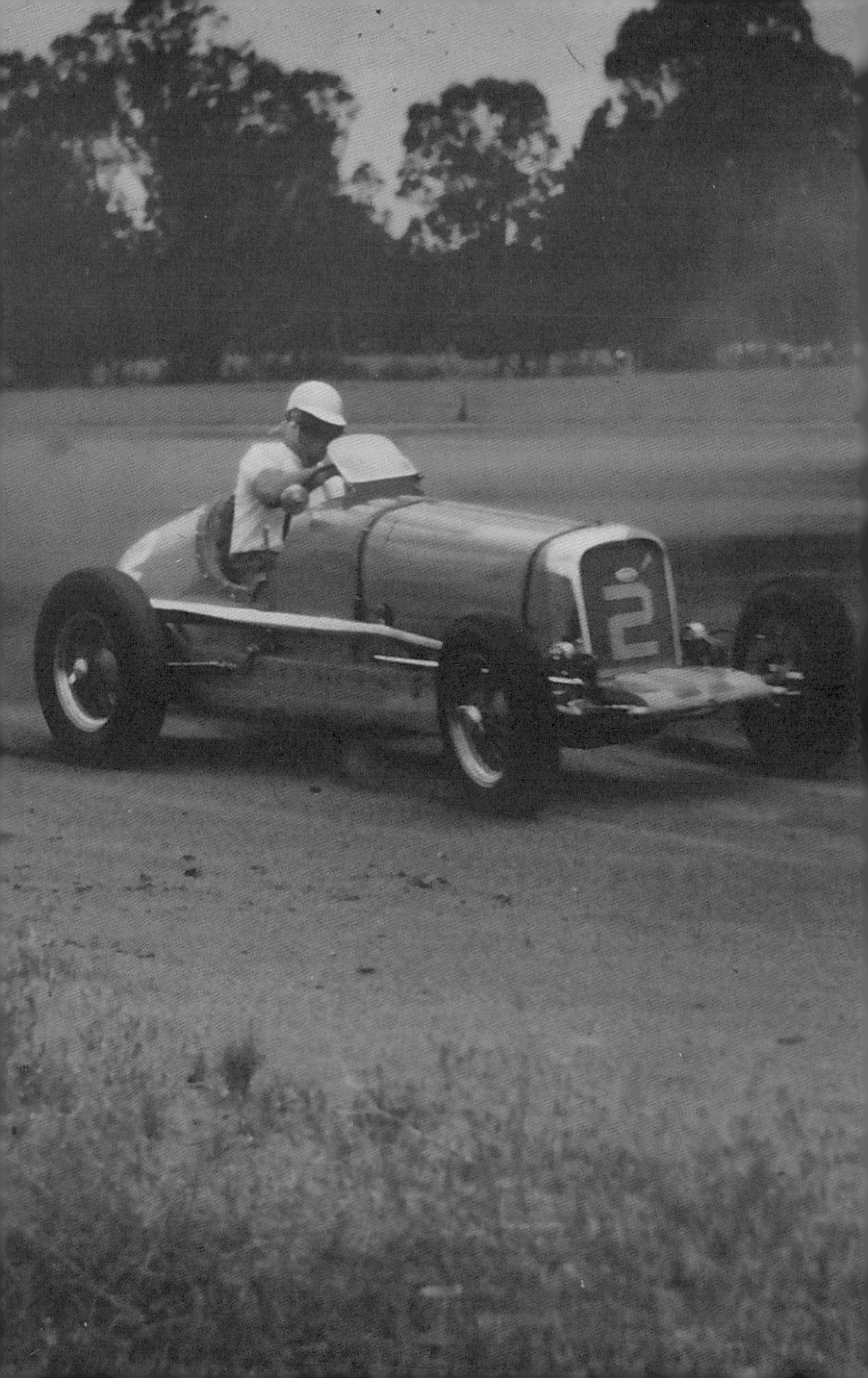
2

CHAPTER TWO
BEHIND THE WHEEL

The Early Days

Ask most older Aussies what the first Australian-built car was, and they probably recall that famous picture of Prime Minister Ben Chifley standing proudly beside Holden No 1, a '48-215' as it rolled off the production line at Fisherman's Bend, Victoria. I know I did. The date was post-World War II—29 November 1948 to be exact. Most of us would be surprised to learn that the first Australian car was actually built before the war—the *first* World War. Well before.

Historians credit Karl Benz, of Mercedes Benz fame, with producing the first car available to the public. That was in 1884. Barely a year later, an Australian agricultural mechanic named David Shearer designed a steam-driven car using principles borrowed from a tricycle and a stump-jump plough. In 1897, he applied to Adelaide City Council for approval to run his tiller-steering car on public roads. The steam-puffing beast could run at 15 mph (25 km/h) and it is reported that the Shearer machine covered several trips over 90 miles (150 km).

Steam then began to give way to petrol. Harley Tarrant gave us his Tarrant, Australia's first petrol-driven car. Harley was a surveyor who had teamed up with W. Howard Lewis to run an engineering works. In 1899, the Tarrant was offered to the public with a two-cylinder 6 horsepower motor with a three-speed gearbox and four-seater tonneau body. For ten years, eight to

Left: 'Gelignite' and the Day Special.

Above: Australian Prime Minister Ben Chifley and the first Holden. It cost £733, about two years' wages.

ten cars were produced each year—hardly mass production. But companies were transitioning and changing as technology developed. Lewis had been a bicycle importer. James Holden, way back in 1856, had established a leather and saddler business before moving in 1910 into trimming motor vehicles and then in 1919, motor body manufacture. From bicycles to motorcycles and then motor vehicles was the evolutionary path down which development raced.

But the horseless carriage was still seen as a rich man's toy, a plaything, maybe an alternative for a doctor to a horse and buggy. Then around 1898 Herbert Thomson and Edward Holmes did something astonishing: they decided to go on a road trip. Setting out from Bathurst, the adventurous pair drove the Thomson Steam Car on the first interstate overland trip, covering the 493 miles (793 km) to Melbourne in nine days, averaging on the 'roads' of the time an impressive 8 to 9 mph (14 km/h)—rather like today's commute from Sydney's western suburbs into the CBD.

In 1904 a young man named Harry James, a future Dunlop executive, had an idea. He decided to organise a 'sporting demonstration'. Why not race these contraptions? Harry, together with the just-formed Automobile Club of Victoria (ACV) organised the first competitive events and later first reliability trials ever run in Australia. Harry James is the father of Australian motorsport.

In 1905 he organised the fourth long distance reliability trial run in the world: 572 miles (920 km) from Sydney to Melbourne. What an adventure, spread over five days! There were 23 starters, including famous Australian Mark Foy; a woman driver from Adelaide; Syd Day, who was to become a famous race driver; and a poet who was later to enjoy success—one A.B. 'Banjo' Paterson. In the first Australian reliability trial we see the amateurs, the eccentrics and the professionals. The only one missing was the 'professional eccentric'—but he was to come. In 1906 the ACV organised its first race meeting, three 5-mile (8 km) handicap events on a banked gravel track built inside the Aspendale horse track southeast of Melbourne.

The year 1907 was a significant one for long distance motorsport, in more ways than one. From 10 June to 10 August 1907 the 10,000-mile (16,000 km) Paris to Peking motor race was run. Unlike race events held in Europe, 'points' on the Paris to Peking were lost for lateness. Losing points—now there's a concept that has a familiar ring destined to echo into 1950s' motorsport in Australia!

Maybe it was the Paris to Peking event that signalled the start of the long distance reliability trial. Perhaps it was the race fumes, wafting 15 miles back to South Melbourne from that first meeting at Aspendale. Who knows? Whatever the reason, barely three weeks after the engines fell silent in the Paris to Peking race, on 30 August 1907, one John Eric Murray entered the world via South Melbourne. During the years that lay ahead, little John Eric would grow into Jack. And as we all now know, 'Gelignite' Jack would definitely 'give it a go', meaning Australian motorsport would never be the same.

1920s

The name Francis Birtles (1881-1941) and the four-cylinder, two-seater, 14 horsepower vehicle known as the Sundowner Bean became famous in 1920s Australia. The car earned its name from Francis' habit of turning up at country homesteads just before the evening meal. This was a time of epic journeys. Birtles established overland routes and set speed records using both bicycles

CHAPTER TWO

Above: Melbourne, 1928. An estimated 10,000 people welcomed the Sundowner back to Melbourne. In this picture the car was mobbed by the crowd.

Below: The Sundowner Bean.

and motor cars. Based in Worcestershire and Staffordshire, Bean Cars, a small English manufacturer, commissioned Birtles to promote their product.

In 1926 Birtles set the Darwin to Melbourne record, completing the 5500 km journey in just eight and a half days. From October 1927 and into 1928, in an incredible display of ability, determination and sheer willpower, Birtles drove his trusty Sundowner from London to Melbourne, a distance of 26,000 km, in just over nine months. This was a record-breaking feat, which was not surpassed until 1955. Today the Sundowner and the Francis Birtles' story are to be found inside the National Museum of Australia in Canberra.

While we will never know for sure, perhaps amid the well-wishers was a twenty-year-old Jack Murray, looking on with admiration, inspired by Francis Birtles, the first Australian motorsport 'professional eccentric'. What we do know for certain is that in 1928, young Jack met his very first love—motorsport. It was a romance that would span six decades.

In his 1976 interview with Neil Bennetts for the National Library of Australia, Jack tells of his less-than-encouraging first motoring experience and his early motorsport days:

> **BENNETTS**: Could you tell us what was the first car that got you interested in trial racing cars?
>
> **MURRAY**: Yes, that would be a Chrysler. Going back before that, as I stated earlier ... my first job was working in a bike shop in Melbourne, building pushbikes and playing round with motor cars, a sort of what they call an 'improver', who helps the motor mechanic. I stayed there for two or three years ... and there was an old Model A Ford [*sic*: Model T]. I could drive it but I hadn't got a licence and the boss said, 'Take it over and deliver it to the dairy.' I tried stopping it and starting it a dozen times before I got there, and when I got there I drove it through the front window. Which was no joke! I had to pay for the window and fix it up.
>
> The first car that I actually got really interested in was this 1928 72 Chrysler. It belonged to J. Aubrey Jones—I think he died about ten years ago. I used to do the work on the car and he used to drive it, but not that much, and he said, 'What about going in a hill climb in it? You drive it and see how it goes.' I went in the hill climb; it was

one of the Light Car Club trials. This particular Chrysler was a 72 model, they called it, actually in years a 1928, and by all the motoring standards it was quite a fantastic car, seven bearing crankshaft and quite modern by today's standards. It had twin breaker points on the distributor, internal expanding hydraulic brakes—beautiful brakes on it. It had rubber shackles where later on they had steel and brass bushes and all that sort of stuff, and the clutch plates, single drive plate. Quite a lot of good features, and they made special heads for them. We had a 'redhead', as they called it; it was a 9 to 1 compression, a high compression head, and in those days we used Super Plume petrol which was about 80 octane. It wouldn't be as good as our standard fuel today but the car was in good trim, a roadster. They did 85 to 90 miles an hour, not bad for a 1928 model. A very pretty car, as a matter of fact. It won the prize in America of Car of the Year, and they went very well here.

In 1929 Jack entered his first reliability trials as navigator to Aubrey Jones.

1930s

Jack's personality, his penchant for fun and his driving ability did not seem to develop as much as explode on to the trial and motorsport scene—right from the beginning. It was in the early 1930s that groups of 100 or more trial drivers, co-drivers and officials would descend on pubs in places such as Moss Vale or the Hydro Majestic in Sydney's Blue Mountains for a weekend of motorsport. Never a drinker, Jack entertained himself and others with antics that included food fights; rearranging any and all shoes that had been left outside hotel rooms for cleaning; filling rooms with trees and saplings; and unscrewing door hinges and unbolting beds. Many an overindulged, under-the-weather competitor fell foul of tee-totalling Jack Murray's pranks. Even during these first steps into motorsport Jack was accompanied by his trademark 'bungers'. Firecrackers secreted in logs in fireplaces often startled unsuspecting drinkers relaxing or passed out beside the Hydro's open fire.

With the fun came success. In 1931, Jack is said to have run second in a 24-hour motor trial from Sydney to Melbourne. [Note: I have been unable to verify this result.] The 1920s and early 1930s saw the heyday of the era of intercity speed record attempts, where 'daredevils' (as they were called), raced to establish the fastest times between capital cities. Clearly there were no police radar guns back then—and besides, the country police had no hope of catching the vehicles. Post war, Jack also tried his hand at stock car racing and came to hold a swag of stock car speed records, from a quarter mile up. [Again, I have been unable to verify these records.]

It was in the early 1930s that Jack, aged 24, made the move from Melbourne to Sydney and motorsport became a passion. As he related to Neil Bennetts:

> And then I left Melbourne and came to Sydney. That would be just about the time they opened the Harbour Bridge. I'm not sure of the date [19 March 1932, during the Great Depression], but that's when I arrived here. 1932, I think was the date of the opening of the Bridge. I remember I was walking across with a girl at the time and she only walked halfway over, and she went back. She said, 'It'll never stand the weight of these people,' so I never did get across the Bridge, only got halfway and we came back again!
>
> From there on I worked in garages, worked for Chrysler, and I was a tester there. I wasn't bad; they gave me a trip to America. I went to Detroit and stayed there for two weeks and the Americans really treated me terrific, took me round all the motor places, specially the Ford place. I remember the museum, I think it was at Dearborn out of Detroit there.
>
> Then I came back and I opened a garage at Bondi in Gould Street. Then my brother Ray came over from Victoria. In the meantime, he had been a panel beater. We joined forces and we stayed together for 30 odd years. We worked on taxicabs and we bought taxicabs, ran cabs and owner/operated them for over 30 years, belonged to the cab company and got on the board of the cab company, and our main source of income was from taxicabs. We rented the garage in Gould Street but then there was one offering round in Curlewis Street and that is the garage that we kept for the 30 years—or it could have been more than that.

Early motorsport was very different from the way it is today. Circuit racing consisted of mostly handicapped events, and trials involved a combination of disciplines and the testing of vehicles. Jack explains:

CHAPTER TWO

We used to have the flying half mile in the main street of Canberra. They used to allow it and it was quite a big day up at Canberra, and they had a hill climb combined with it. What trials in those days combined was a weekend trial; there might be 50 cars in it and different classes. They'd have a slow running test. You'd be in top gear and get back practically to walking speed. Then they would have an acceleration test. Then they'd have a standing quarter: it might consist of a petrol consumption test. The car had got to be very versatile. You can tune it to go fast but it's no good for a petrol consumption test. You got an all-round result; that's what they were looking for. Everybody was really keen and enthusiastic. We'd stay at a pub, the Hydro Majestic or the Hotel Robertson, and it was a good weekend all round.

Hill climbs, acceleration tests, flying half miles and reliability trials were all run by the New South Wales Light Car Club (NSW LCC), which existed from 1929 to 1940.

Controlling Motorsport

The administration and control of motorsport within Australia has always been controversial. There has been a lot of rancour and division over the years—particularly in 1957 and 1958. At the beginning of the war, the NSW LCC had folded. After the war, the Australian Sporting Car Club (ASCC) was established, the organisation which was to run the REDEX trials of the 1950s. From 1937 to 1953, the Australian Automobile Association (AAA) controlled motorsport. It then gave up national control of 'the sport of automobilism' and together with other state-based clubs came under an umbrella national organisation. On 1 February 1953, the Confederation of Australian Motor Sport (CAMS) came into being and continues today as the governing body of motorsport within this country. Since 1958, CAMS has been the Australian national sporting authority (ASN) delegated by the Fédération Internationale de l'Automobile (FIA), the governing body for world motorsport and the federation of the world's leading motoring organisations.

Jack's involvement in motorsport grew throughout the 1930s. A young Jack was more often than not a driver of a 2867 cc De Soto owned by Mr C.E. Hillier and later Mr J. Price. Presumably these were older and wealthier motorsport enthusiasts who had the cars but maybe not the ability or youthful nerve of the young Jack. Events during the 1930s included several contests at places like Avon Dam, Wiseman's Ferry, Robertson, Bulli, Kurrajong, Waterfall, the Blue Mountains and Richmond.

Jack managed a number of wins and top-three-placegetter positions over the years. The sheer variety and different skill sets demanded by these events provided him with a grounding of experience that would later prove invaluable.

On 26 November 1932 in the *Sydney Morning Herald*, one such event is described:

> The Light Car Club of NSW held a contest to Avon Dam. It included a hill climb (100 pts), quarter mile acceleration (75 pts), quarter mile flying (75 pts), half mile acceleration (75 pts), half mile flying (75 pts) and reliability (50 pts), making a possible total of 450 points. A new condition has been adopted empowering the committee to require any of the competitors to wear crash helmets, and under this, those who have nominated exceptionally speedy cars have been directed to do so. 22 cars competed. J. Murray was the driver of J. Price's 2867 cc De Soto (Class C) and performed well.

It is interesting to read that only those drivers with exceptionally speedy cars had been nominated to wear crash helmets. Pity the poor driver of a less-than-speedy vehicle that happened to become inverted and require head protection! Safety in motorsport has, thankfully, come a long way since 1932.

For fun, so-called Mystery Trials involving instructions written in 'ancient text' were also thrown into the mix. On 1 October 1934 in *The Motor in Australia and Flying*, one such trial is the focus:

> An excellent course was chosen, taking in Bulli Pass, Albion Park, Jamberoo Mountain, Robertson, Bowral and back to Sydney, a total distance of 200 miles, which included all types and varieties of road conditions. An innovation was a water splash event. An 'observed' section with hidden officials was introduced and drivers lost points for noisy gear changes, stalling of engines, etc. Braking tests and a 'stop and start' test were also incorporated. But there were no speed events and this made this trial very different—a style of event popular

in England. Lunch was held at Robertson. The contest started on a novel and an appropriate note—with the issue of that unique map. It finished the same way—with the checked (finishing) flags in the bathrooms at the clubhouse.

Jack, who always revelled in the fun and social aspects of motorsport, was from the beginning a serious racer, as shown in one report: 'An average of 86.5 mph over the flying quarter mile by the Hudson 8 sedan driven by J. Murray ... were a few highlights of the Light Car Club's annual mountain contest last weekend. This was the best time of the day, a new class record and fastest time of the whole year.' Jack was described in press reports as 'one of the most consistent of LCC drivers'.

A Day of Tragedy

Monday 13 June 1938 was a dark day for Australian motorsport.

The date holds a great deal of significance for a particular car and its future owner, one Jack Murray. It was then that the Mackellar Special (Type 37A Bugatti, fitted with a side valve Ford V8 engine) crashed at Penrith, killing two small children and their grandmother and injuring 39 others. A horrific video of the crash can be seen on YouTube: 'Tragic Speedway Car Crash In Australia (1938) British Pathé (The Mackellar Special)'. The crash occurred while the car was driven by Wally James accompanied by a co-passenger, and was the subject of a coroner's inquest. The Mackellar Special was eventually to be owned by Jack, who paid £1000 and painted her vivid red, later selling her to his good

Above: 17-18 August 1935, 24-Hour Trial, first event of its kind held by the NSW Light Car Club. From left to right: G. Morris, Wolseley, Winner of the under 2,000 cc class. W.A. McIntyre, Terraplane, outright winner of Trial. G. Reed, Hudson, winner of over 2,000 class.

mate Bill McLachlan.

In one of his first tests on a measured mile at Engadine, Jack reached 122 mph (almost 200 km/h) in the Mackellar.

'Gelignite' Jack Murray and the Grey Ghost are inextricably linked in the public's mind from the days of the REDEX trials. But there were at least four other vehicles of historical significance in Australian motorsport that Jack also owned.

Two of these were the Mackellar Special and the Day Special. The background and significance of these unique vehicles, and the part they would play in Jack's life and Australian motorsport during the 1940s, 1950s and 1960s, is worth explaining.

The Special Cars

Today motorsport is big business. Those of us who grew up in the late 1960s and 1970s eagerly anticipated the annual October clash between Holden and Ford at Bathurst. Tribes formed around these two dominant marques: you were either a Holden man or a Ford man when it came to Bathurst. There were even rules which limited the racing modifications that could be made to production vehicles, including a rule specifying the minimum number of units that had to be sold to the general public (around 500) before a car was eligible to be entered in the Bathurst event. Of course, in the 21st century, the corporatisation of

Above: Jack in the Mackellar Special, Marsden Park, 1947.

CHAPTER TWO

motorsport is now complete, with manufacturers spending millions to feature the name Mercedes, Subaru or BMW on a podium.

But this sort of high dollar branding was not always so, particularly in Australia.

Individual drivers would often modify and intermix parts and engines from various sources and cobble together vehicles for racing. Clearly, the main objective was not to advertise or promote a particular manufacturer. Rather the objective was a true racer's goal: simply to go faster than the competition.

These were the first true 'hybrid' vehicles, not because they could run on petrol or electricity, but because they used bits and pieces from various makes of vehicle. The Formula Libre (Free Formula), in place until the late 1950s, encouraged this sort of innovation. These cars were known as the Specials, and often the name preceding the term referred to the driver who had built or originally owned the car. Perhaps it also referred to the original marque of the vehicle that formed its base.

Jack was famously associated with two of these: the Mackellar Special and later the Day Special. Damian Kringas' 2012 book *The Gelignite Bugatti*, tells the story of these cars and that era of early racing in Australia. It has been well researched and I recommend it as a must-read for any motoring enthusiast interested in the history of Australian motorsport.

In 1925, five Type 39 Bugatti racing cars would be built, two of which eventually made their way to Australia.

Bugattis are famous. Ettore Bugatti combined art and engineering when he founded his company in 1909 in the French town of Molsheim. It was the rigidity of the Bugattis, along with other fine touches, that gave them marvellous handling qualities, displaying what became known as 'the Molsheim magic'. A Bugatti has always been a much-sought-after item for any automotive collector. Like all Grand Prix Bugattis, the Aussie T39s became sought-after by collectors and enthusiasts alike—but while one was preserved, the other would have a Ford flathead V8 fitted. Jack Day, an enthusiast and engineer, campaigned and then sold this car to larrikin racer Jack. This vehicle was known as the Day Special, the 'Gelignite Bugatti'.

In 1925 the Bugatti factory constructed five Type 39 sports cars. They were modified versions of the famous Bugatti Type 35 Grand Prix racing cars. All five were identical with aluminium bodies attached to a steel chassis. Fitted with mudguards, lights and a special crankshaft to reduce the engine capacity to 1493 cc, they complied with the rules for 'Voiturettes' (small cars, sports cars under 1500 cc). The previous year, 1925, two of these Type 39s first appeared in the Grand Prix de Tourisme at Montlhery, coming first and third. Three months later at the Grand Prix held at Monza, in Italy, where the Voiturettes were combined with the Grand Prix cars, one of these type 39s came in third outright and the car destined to become the Day Special finished fourth in the Voiturette class. These two cars were imported into Australia in 1926.

Before the early 1950s, Grand Prix racing in Australia involved a handicap start system, as opposed to the grid starts adopted today. There were four classes of motor vehicle based on engine size, and drivers were often accompanied in the car by a second person in the passenger seat, referred to as a 'travelling mechanic'.

Veteran of Australian motorsports Jack Day, with his engineering works in South Melbourne, also had an interest in racing boats. In 1933, both Australian Bugattis suffered engine damage, and as technology advanced, both cars—while described as elegant and works of art—were becoming less competitive. Faced with repairs, 4607 was put up for sale and bought by Day.

It is hard to resist the appeal, the power—and even the idling burble—of a Ford V8 engine. Day eventually fitted a Ford V8 to the Bugatti. After the war, it's said as his engineering business became increasingly busy stress took its toll. Day suffered a heart attack and was bed-ridden for several weeks. Towards the end of 1946, he advertised his Special for sale in *Australian Motor Sports*. The car was subsequently sold to Jack Murray and would, from then on, be based in NSW.

A comment in *Australian Motor Sports,* September 1947, in the *Spotlight* column highlights the fact that Jack owned another Bugatti prior to purchasing the Day Special. This was the super-charged Ford V8 powered Bugatti T37A fitted by Ron Mackellar in the Bugatti chassis and hence known as the Mackellar Special. A Ford truck radiator was fitted to solve the ubiquitous Ford Special cooling problem. The car featured a belt-driven McCullough super-charger and was the first car in that early post-war period to clock over 100 mph in a flying quarter mile, run by the NSW Sporting Car Club.

By 1947, Jack owned both cars simultaneously. As reported by John Barraclough in the *Australian Motor Sports Spotlight* column, 'Jack Day, after holding out for so long, has sold his Day Special in which Reg Nutt made fastest time at one of the Lobethal races before the war, to the other Bugatti-Ford owner, Jack Murray, from NSW. Murray flew down one night, bought the car and was back in Sydney the next night.' He used the Mackellar Special for various hill climbs and sprint events in NSW. The gearshift lever was set in a slotted gate H pattern on the dash panel, and Jack had hydraulic brakes fitted, similar to the Day Special. He became known for presenting his cars polished to a mirror finish and thoroughly tested mechanically.

The Mackellar Special was a twelve-year-old racing car with a reputation as a 'devil car'. The fitting of the V8 had changed the car's handling characteristics and it was difficult to control. The rigidity of the front end had been compromised, and there was a series of crashes. Everyone who drove it met disaster and, as noted previously, in 1938, as Car No 1 driven by Wally James, it crashed at Penrith. Jack needed all his strength and athleticism to overpower the unpredictable beast. At Bathurst in 1946, Jack and the Mackellar Special scored fastest time in one race and came fourth in another. Jack split the £55 prize money between the Bathurst and Woolloomooloo Police Boys' Clubs in order to retain his amateur sportsman/wrestler status.

Jack made a number of modifications to the Day Special and success finally came. In 1948 it was present for the first meeting at Mount Druitt Motor Racing Circuit. Competing in the over 1500 cc handicap, Murray posted a first and fastest lap of 1 min 30 sec. Bathurst 1949 saw Jack top 118 mph (190 km/h) down Conrod Straight, but he would fail to finish. Results like this

Above: The Day Special in 2016. The author is behind the wheel with Rob Rowe, owner, motorsport historian and racer, supervising.

highlighted the ongoing problem Jack faced—the Day Special overheating.

In early 1951 he purchased a new Allard J2, red with red interior, and a 331 cubic inch Cadillac V8. The Allard J2 was another car of historical significance owned by Jack. He later sold the car to his friend Bill Firth, in February 1957.

By the end of the 1950s, Australian motorsport was changing and was adopting stock production cars and controlled formulas. Brabham would soon introduce Formula One to Australians in a big way, and in 1967 the GT Falcon would be created to beat the iconic Bathurst circuit. The era of the Specials had passed.

In 1964, Rob Rowe, at the time a 21-year-old working at the Sydney Speed Shop, heard that the Day Special was for sale. With £280 in his pocket, he raced to Jack's Garage. It was the young man's dream to own a Bugatti. But, like Bugatti historian and enthusiast Kent Patrick, he would pass on the sale since he realised there was not enough Bugatti left for restoration.

Today the Day Special has historical significance beyond an original Bugatti. It took Rob just over 50 years, but he finally purchased his dream Bugatti, and took it to Newcastle, NSW.

THIS PLAQUE COMMEMORATES THE OCCUPANCY OF THE UNITED STATES ARMY SMALL SHIPS SECTION IN THIS BUILDING FROM MAY 1942 TO JANUARY 1947.

DURING THIS PERIOD OVER 3,000 AUSTRALIAN MEN AND BOYS WERE RECRUITED TO MAN THE SMALL SHIPS WHICH SUPPLIED AMERICAN AND AUSTRALIAN SERVICEMEN WHO WERE FIGHTING THE JAPANESE IN THE NEW GUINEA CAMPAIGN 1942 TO 1944. THESE MEN AND BOYS WERE AGED FROM 15 YEARS OF AGE TO OVER 65 YEARS OF AGE.

THE MEN AND BOYS OF THE U.S. ARMY SMALL SHIPS LATER SERVED IN THE PHILIPPINE ISLANDS LANDINGS, OKINAWA AND THE OCCUPATION OF JAPAN.

THIS PLAQUE IS ALSO DEDICATED TO THE MEMORY OF THOSE MEN AND BOYS WHO DID NOT RETURN

CHAPTER THREE

THE WAR

As the 1930s drew to a close, war came to Europe. With the bombing of Pearl Harbour on 7 December 1941, Australia too was threatened, and all thoughts turned to war rather than sport. The Australian Grand Prix, for example, was not held from 1941 to 1946.

With the Japanese Imperial Army moving south, motorsport would have to wait. The dark clouds of the war hung heavily over the dawning 1940s.

The Small Ships

In 2012 my wife Rhonda and I stayed overnight at the Grace Hotel in the Sydney CBD. The Grace is a beautifully restored and refurbished Art Deco building of the 1920s originally built by Grace Bros, the Australian department store chain. The grand old lady rests on the corner of King and York Streets.

As we waited in the lobby for the lift to descend to the foyer, I noticed various plaques attached to the wall. During World War II, the Grace Bros building was headquarters for the US Small Ships Section, a unit of the United States Army Transportation Corps. During the war, according to the plaques, the US Small Ships contracted over 3000 Australian men and boys to work as civilian employees. They were based overseas, providing logistical support and undertaking any necessary repairs to boats, machinery and equipment in general.

Left: One of the plaques in the Grace Hotel, Sydney, commemorating the 3000 Australian men and boys who served with the US Small Ships.

CHAPTER THREE

Jack was one of these men. He served with the US Small Ships for approximately twelve months, during 1944 and 1945. He was posted to the Finschhafen area of New Guinea, based on an ex-Liberty ship called the *Half Rufus*.

Where I stood in the foyer of the Grace Hotel, Jack had stood nearly 70 years earlier, filling in his forms, signing a contract and joining the US Small Ships. He had originally planned on joining the Australian Army but had been rejected, since he had a hernia.

Jack said, 'So I thought OK ... and so I went into hospital. I think it cost me £70 to get it fixed up.'

With typical Murray spontaneity, his plans changed the day a Bondi Surf Club mate came into The Garage and announced that he was off to join the US Small Ships.

'Where are they?' Jack asked.

'New Guinea ... come down with us.' And so he did. In 1944, he found himself a passenger aboard the Dutch merchant ship *Swartenhond*, bound for New Guinea. He recalls signing on as an engineer, but the records list him as a carpenter. No doubt in time of war and need, skills were interchangeable and every man contributed as best he could.

Jack worked for Port Command in Finschhafen aboard the *Half Rufus*, which was anchored close to shore in deep water. The story of the ship is interesting. It was a Liberty ship called *Rufus King*, which in 1942 ran aground near North Stradbroke Island. Liberty ships were American mass produced cargo ships, weighing over 14,000 tons and 135 metres in length.

The bow section of the *Rufus King* was salvaged and taken to Brisbane to be fitted out as a floating workshop. The stern section was scuttled. After an initially unsuccessful attempt, during which the Captain's leg was broken by a loose anchor, the *Half Rufus*, together with two other barges, was towed to Milne Bay in New Guinea and subsequently to Finschhafen. At the time, the tow was the longest, by distance, by the longest combination of vessels, ever attempted. Jack was assigned to the *Half Rufus* in Finschhafen and also Milne Bay.

The Half Rufus

On the *Half Rufus*, the lifting of heavy gear was achieved using the original derrick and winches from the Liberty ship. Electrical power was supplied by a Bellis and Morecombe steam engine. Steam was supplied from a vertical boiler

THE WAR

Above: The *Half Rufus*.

located in the No 3 hold, which was fitted out as a machine shop. It contained lathes, shapers, milling machines and a wellequipped blacksmith's shop. The machines in the workshop were all new and of the highest quality. The ship was also used as a coalbunker, but when the winches were turned on to load coal they took so much power that machining in the workshop had to wait until the coaling was finished. (Bill Lunney and Ruth Lunney, *Forgotten Fleet 2*)

When I was a teenager, Jack kept me enthralled with stories of his war years in New Guinea. A couple of popular TV comedies at the time were *McHale's Navy*, starring Ernest Borgnine and *Sergeant Bilko*, starring Phil Silvers. Jack's wartime adventures could just have easily been called *Murray's Navy*, because they read like scripts from these series.

Here are some of his stories:

> I had a big, bushy black beard. I used to get about with no shirt on and a WAAC's cap [Women's Army Auxiliary Corps; they wore a large baseball-style cap] covered with different insignia, bits and

pieces. When I walked in the mess hall I'd always yell out to the top bloke 'G'day General' and he'd always yell back 'Hello Jack' and everyone used to think 'Who's that bloke, didn't salute the General? What rank is he? Must be pretty important.' They all knew me. Cause I didn't drink, they always trusted me with the grog, so I got to know all the top blokes.

Jack was a contracted civilian and thus had no official military rank. A magazine article once claimed he was a major, but I do not believe this was the case. However, the matter needs clarification. Men were sometimes given nominal rank in case they were captured. I confirmed the issue of Jack's rank with friend and naval historian Ian Pfennigwerth, who advises as follows: 'They had no rank in a military sense ... but some did in a professional sense—Master, Chief Engineer.'

There must have been some money to be made as Jack told me he used to keep a locker under his bed with a big padlock attached and lots of cash inside. I remember him saying he was bunking near an American guy at one stage. When Jack's cash disappeared one night, although he had his suspicions, he could not prove anything. That suspicion certainly did not do much for American-Australian relations at the time! He also told me:

> One time they gave us this boat, to fix the engine. They asked, 'How long will it take?' We said at least a week while we fix it and then test it. Well, we worked on it that afternoon, got it going and went around the other side of the island. We spent the best part of a week fishing, trying to ski ... had some real good fun.

How good can be seen by the picture.

Jack's wartime experiences provided me with more than just a few laughs and anecdotes. The war also provided me with what is probably my favourite photo of my father. On the roof of the cabin of a boat, surrounded by his mates, we see Jack bare chested, fit and tanned, arms and fists raised in the air. At 37, he seems so full of life—the sheer joy of living. It says everything about who he was, and who he was about to become, after the war.

Above: Of the many to choose from, this is my favourite photo of my father.

'Let him figure that one out'

Jack was taken aback by the sheer scale of the war and its waste. Finschhafen was a large natural harbour that was used as a staging post, resupplying and repairing vessels supporting General Douglas MacArthur's amphibious repulsion of the Japanese through the island chain all the way to the Philippines. Jack told me:

> You'd be unloading a brand new bulldozer, and the cable would break or twist or something and the dozer would go straight in the drink. The first time I said, 'Shit, what happens now?' The guy unloading said: 'Nothing ... happens all the time. Don't worry about it—we'll just order another one.'

CHAPTER THREE

Then again:

> I was standing on the shore one evening. The harbour was filled with ... I dunno ... dozens, maybe 100 ships, and they are all playing their own movie on board. Well, on each ship you can only hear your movie, but on the shore you hear all the movies. What a noise! I'll never forget that.

Another story:

> There was this American sergeant, big arrogant **. Well, he had this jeep and it was his pride and joy. No one was allowed to drive his jeep and because he had a car, he used to get dates with all the sheilas. Had a big chain and padlock. When he parked it, he put a big chain through the steering wheel and round a tree. So one night we see him pull up to pick up a girl, chains up the car and in he goes. Well, I've got a spanner to take the nut off the centre of the steering wheel ... and I've brought along another steering wheel. When he comes out, there's the chain, unbroken, still attached to the steering wheel but the jeep's gone. Let him figure that one out.

Adolf Hitler: 'a little guy who was all pomp'

Jack had two interesting connections with the war in Europe.

In 1937 he undertook a world trip over a period of seven months, accompanied by his brother Ray and two good friends, Peter Roach and Tom Mills. The boys departed Sydney aboard the *Esperance Bay* on 6 March 1937. The National Archives of Australia National Reference Service confirm Ray had ticket 14,157, Jack had ticket 14,158 and Tommy Mills had ticket 14,159. Ray (aged 31) and Jack (aged 29) both listed their occupations as 'mechanic'. Jack's diary from 1937 remains with the author to this day, and is the most extensive work remaining written in Jack's own hand.

While on holiday, Jack crossed paths with a little Austrian bloke named Adolf Hitler. Jack related the story in his National Library interview with Neil Bennetts:

> Reminiscing back on our trip to Europe: when I was in Berlin I went to the Avus racetrack there, which was really something, a circuit shaped something like a dumbbell, down two miles, then fly into a

Above: Jack, at right, wearing a pith helmet. Eccentric headwear seems to have been an integral part of his war.

saucer, then come back again practically alongside of the road going down and go into another saucer. The cars that were racing were built under subsidy of the German government; they were built by Auto Union, beautiful looking things, far superior in looks to anything of today. Even then they were doing 180 miles [290 km/h] an hour.

I had a tag on my camera, which I'd had at Brooklands, and the Nazis—they called them Brownshirts—they were about 6 ft 6 in big Germans, and they were hunting everybody off the track. But I just held the camera up; they couldn't read the tag on it and they thought

Location unknown. Given that the man in the foreground is wearing a uniform, it is likely that this photo was also taken in New Guinea. And the motive for Jack doing a handstand in such a precarious position? Either he's nuts, or just because he can—probably both.

THE WAR

I was a press official, so I sat on a brick bridge there and the cars were racing about 15 feet away from me. They hunted everybody away and I was sitting up there on my own, and the other three guys that were with me, they got put on the side and couldn't see anything—but I had a grandstand seat.

That was the best racing I have ever seen in my life. These cars, when they were coming past you, you'd see them, you'd look straight ahead and see the car come past in a flash and you'd get the sound about four to five seconds after. They were sort of beating sound, and you'd hear this terrific roar and the car was about 300 yards away, further than that—going like a shell. Those were the days of Nuvolari, the fantastic Italian, Hermann von Stuck, he won the event [*sic:* Hans Stuck.] All the well known racing drivers of Europe were competing at Avus. Hitler came over and presented the prize. I was surprised how small he was, a little guy who was all pomp and what-have-you, all the salutes. I had to put my hand up in the air,

Above: 1937 Auto Union and Mercedes *Silberpfeile* (Silver Arrows).

Above: An Auto Union Streamliner 1937. Auto Union was comprised of four car marques—hence the four combined rings, which evolved into Audi, now a subsidiary of the Volkswagen Group.

too, otherwise I'd have got thrown off the course. *Sieg Heil* (laughs). But the racing there was really something.

I did see this car later on in Paris, at the Paris Exposition, in a glass case there, painted silver, and they looked out of this world aerodynamically—oh, beautiful. [This was probably the Streamliner 1937 Type C.] I believe they only built twenty of them; there were only twenty in the world. I think it was a 12-cylinder and the gearbox had about eight or nine gears in it, a real engineering feat. They were never sold to anybody; they all belonged to Auto Union.

Jack's second connection with the war in Europe and the Nazis was even more personal. As a teenager, it amazed me.

Wernher von Braun: Hero or Villain?

One day when I was around fifteen, my father and I were watching television at home in Vaucluse, Sydney. That makes the year around 1969. Colour television was still five years away in Australia, and the black and white documentary we were

THE WAR

Above: German (Nazi) Aviation Museum: Jack's souvenir postcard.

watching was telling the story of the American space program, from the early days of the Mercury flights through to Apollo and the eventual moon landing.

At some point, the narrator mentioned the name Wernher von Braun.

Grainy footage showed a man dressed in a Nazi Death's Head SS uniform strolling about accompanied by Heinrich Himmler, *Reischsfuhrer SS*. Wernher Magnus Maximilian von Braun, or the once *Sturmbannführer* (Major) von Braun was a rather controversial figure. Depending on your values and your scale of personal morality, justice versus pragmatism, von Braun was either 'a Nazi war criminal who evaded justice, prosecution and possibly a death sentence by cutting a deal with the Americans at the end of World War II' or 'along with Robert Goddard, von Braun was the father of the NASA space program, a brilliant scientist and a man instrumental in the Americans passing the Russians in the space race'.

Nazi and/or scientist, von Braun featured on the cover of *Time* magazine and is arguably the man most responsible for Neil Armstrong taking those first steps on the moon when he uttered those immortal words: 'That's one small step for man, one giant leap for mankind.'

Midway through the television documentary, Jack casually remarked, 'I taught that guy to waterski.'

'What? That guy? Wernher von Braun? He's an ex-Nazi who now heads up the space program. Shit, he's one of the most important blokes in America ... And you taught him to ski?' I stammered incredulously. 'Are you sure?'

'Yeah ... that's Wernher all right. Harry, Harry Messel, brought him up the river one weekend and we finally got him up,' Jack proffered nonchalantly.

Those of us from the Baby Boomer generation well remember Professor Harry Messel and his famous 'blue book'—the science bible for my generation. Almost 40 years later, in 2007, prompted by an ABC *Catalyst* show featuring the life story of the Canadian-born Messel, I sent an email asking about Jack's recollection. Could he verify the story?

Above: Wernher von Braun.

The email reply came back from Messel:

> Phil—well do I remember your father, who taught me to waterski at Shoal Bay in the late 1950s. We met and skied many, many times from our place at Lower Portland and his spot near the ferry. Yes—absolutely true, Jack helped me teach Wernher von Braun to waterski—still have the photos somewhere. Often think of your dad, a fine, kind friend and a great guy. Kind regards. Messel

[Sadly, Messel passed away in 2015.]

Even as a teenager I was taken aback and impressed by the fact that my father had met, befriended and taught to waterski a man who was such an influential figure in 20th century world history. This was the man who largely provided the technical know-how for over 3000 V2 (Vengeance Weapon 2) rockets to rain down on London, Antwerp and Liege, killing thousands. But he was also the same man that enabled all us Baby Boomers to watch in wonder that seminal moment in our lives when Neil Armstrong took that step on the moon.

There are many websites and hundreds of pages arguing the case for and against Werner von Braun and his role in history. It is interesting to reflect on the duality of the man: was he villain or hero? It is pure speculation to guess at Jack's view of this enigmatic person. To Jack, no doubt, in his easy-going, egalitarian Australian way, Wernher Magnus Maximilian von Braun was just another mate Harry had brought up the river. Jack's nonchalance at the encounter was so typically and quintessentially Australian. His life was full of such events, people and encounters.

Wernher von Braun: Nazi stooge or genius? There is one final thing we can say about him: the Polish-born aerospace engineer who was awarded the National Medal of Science, twelve honorary doctorates and has streets named after him in dozens of small towns and several major cities throughout Germany, was lucky enough to be taught to ski on the beautiful Hawkesbury River north of Sydney by one larrikin and one scientist—two Australian icons well suited to the task.

The war in Europe ended on 8 May 1945. By August 1945, the war in the Pacific was also drawing to a close. Having contributed to the defeat of the Japanese in his own inimitable style, Jack thought it might be a good idea to head home, tune up the engines, get back behind the wheel and drive into some serious motorsport racing.

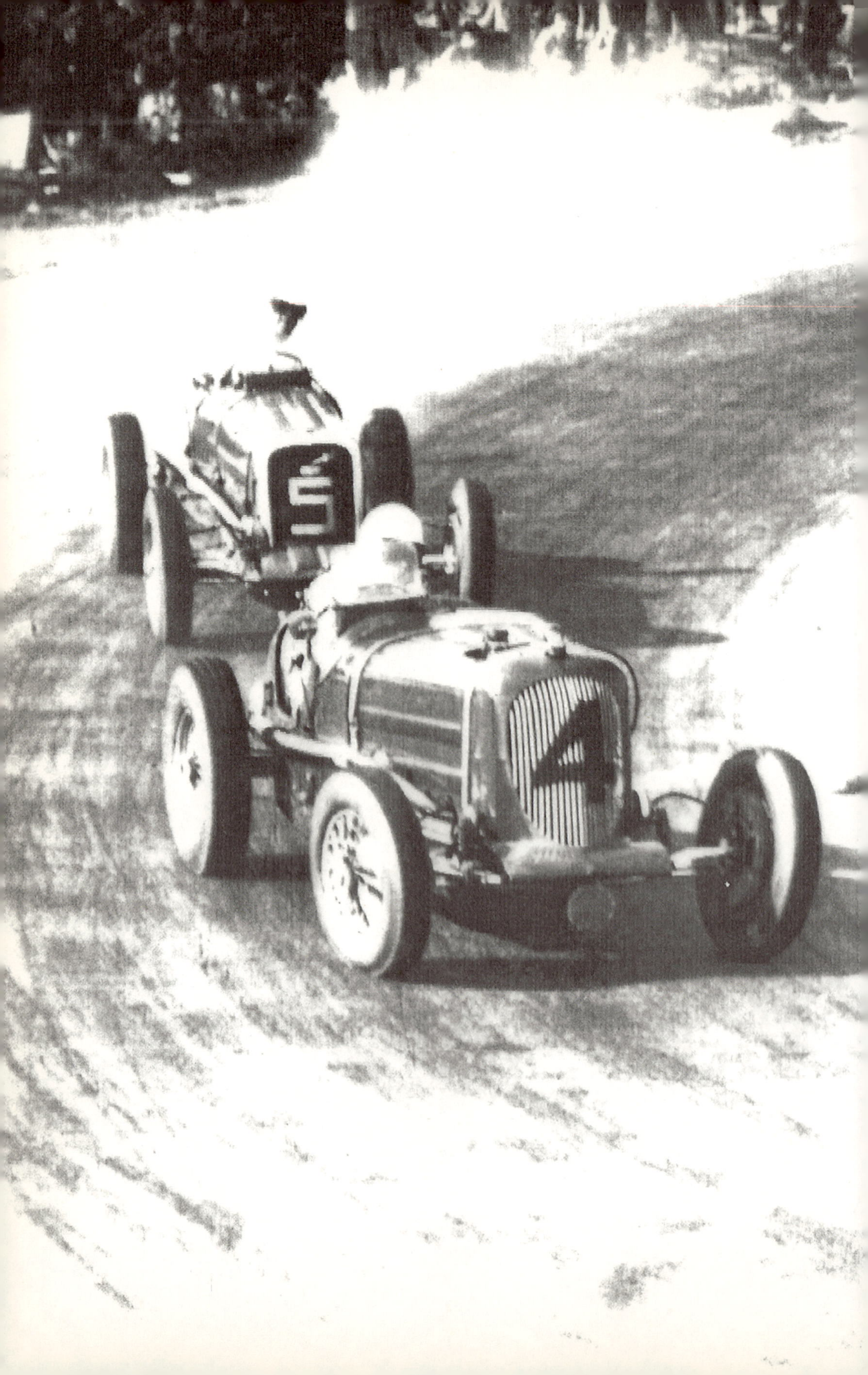

CHAPTER FOUR
CUTTING MAD CAPERS

Jack goes to Bathurst

At the end of the war Jack, then almost 38, returned to join his brother Ray at their Curlewis St, Bondi garage. The spark plugs of enthusiasm for motorsport were soon refired.

Jack enjoyed and participated in all forms of motorsport. From the end of the war and well into the 1960s, he was a regular at Mount Panorama races at Bathurst. On 7 October 1946, three races were held there, marking Jack's first appearance at the legendary circuit, at the first Bathurst races to be held post-war. As John Medley in his 1977 book *Bathurst: Cradle of Australian Motor Racing*, comments, 'Always a spectacular driver in spectacular cars, Murray was a crowd favourite.' Jack would go on to race the Mackellar Special, the Day Special, two Allards, a D-Type Jaguar and in various saloon cars on Australia's best-known and most popular race circuit.

In 1946, Jack raced the now red and chrome Mackellar Special (Type 37A Bugatti, fitted with a supercharged Ford V8 engine) and placed sixth, in a time of 21 mins 4 secs for the six laps (about 25 miles). In the New South Wales Grand Prix of 100 miles Jack placed fifth and recorded the fastest race time of 1 hr 26 mins 24 secs in the handicap event. On the fifteenth lap, Jack put in a meteoric 3:21, nearly equalling Frank Kleinig's fastest lap for the race of 3:20. Frank Kleinig and Jack Murray had an intense rivalry that over the years spanned reliability trials, circuit races and hill climbs.

Towards halfway through the New South Wales Grand Prix, both John

CHAPTER FOUR

Above: Jack Murray and the Day Special.

Crouch and Jack were repeatedly covering the quarter mile at speeds of up to 110 mph (177 km/h), these being the highest recorded during the race. They are certainly impressive for 1946, given the poor road surface after six years of war and neglect.

Bill McLachlan, Jack's good mate, also competed in the 1946 NSW Grand Prix. Video of the race can be viewed on YouTube: '1946 New South Wales Grand Prix Bathurst'.

Above: Bathurst, 1946: Jack Murray and the Mackellar Special.

In the late 1940s, Bathurst twice a year (at Easter and again in October), Marsden Park airstrip, Nowra races, Mount Druitt races and events such as the Hawkesbury Hill Climb all featured in Jack's motorsport career.

Above: 1946 Ampol advertisement: Jack Murray (fastest time) driving the Mackellar Special.

Murray versus Kleinig

At the Anniversary Day Car Races of 26 January 1947 held at Marsden Park airstrip in front of 5000 spectators, Frank and Jack again tussled. 'Kleinig and Jack Murray turned on their usual fireworks. They had a two bob bet on who would get to the corner first,' wrote *Australian Motor Sports* on 15 February 1947. Jack managed a third in the Championship Scratch Race for cars over 1500 cc and in the Long Handicap for cars of all capacities (18 laps, about 30 miles), both Frank Kleinig (twice) and Jack Murray (once) were credited with fastest lap time: 1 mins 32 secs. As described in *Australian Motor Sports* on 15 February 1947:

> Jack Murray, with the Mackellar, was next to go when the top hose blew off and the engine almost immediately seized. Jack, however, gallantly stayed with the car, although he was drenched in boiling water, and though it was cutting mad capers he managed to bring it to rest on the side of the track without endangering the crowd.

Remember, this is the same vehicle that in 1938 had crashed at Penrith, killing three spectators and injuring 39 others. The V8 powered, but the poor handling Mackellar Special needed to be tamed—and wrestler/race driver Jack Murray was just the man for the job.

CHAPTER FOUR

Above: Marsden Park, 1947: Jack 'cutting mad capers' driving the Mackellar Special.

RAAF Racing

In the 1940s, the Nowra Road Race Circuit was an interesting course made up of runways and connecting taxiways of the RAAF aerodrome at Nowra, NSW. The total lap was 4 miles 670 yards (7 km). Four races, known as the King's Birthday Meeting, were conducted during the afternoon of 16 June 1947. In the over 1500 cc Championship, Jack managed a fifth in the Mackellar V8, Car No 5. The Mackellar covered the quarter mile at over 114 mph (183 km/h). However, in the main event, the Championship of NSW over 25 laps and a distance of approximately 110 miles (177 km), Jack could only manage tenth position.

Not to be left out of the fun, Ray Murray on 13 July 1947 tried his hand at a reliability trial organised by the Australian Sporting Car Club. This was organised specifically for the 'not-so-experts'. My Uncle Ray competed in a Chrysler in the Over 2000 cc class, placing a less than impressive sixteenth. Of particular interest are the contests that were held within the trial. There were a number of sub-events. As described by *Australian Motor Sports* on 15 August 1947:

> The first of these was a rolling test in which cars rolled down one hill with a dead engine and in neutral, and got as far up the other side as they could. Ray Murray's Chrysler rolled the furthest and scored five points.

The Day Special Delivery

It was in late 1947, before Bathurst that October, that Jack acquired the Day Special, a Bugatti Type 39/Ford 3.6L. My father flew down to Melbourne one night, bought the car for about £1100, and was back in Sydney the next evening. But as reported in *Australian Motor Sports, Spotlight* by John Barraclough, Jack's trip home was certainly typical Jack—that is, not uneventful. It would set the tone for his racing of the Day Special in the years that lay ahead. *Spotlight* reported:

> Jack Murray's journey from Melbourne to Bondi in the Day Special not long ago was apparently brim full of excitement. He broke down shortly before dark and begged a tow from one of those outsize interstate transport outfits, and unable to tune in to the truck crew's mental telepathy set, was forced to continue on into the night without headlights. Eventually he fouled the rope and got the front end so hopelessly entangled that the steering linkage journal locked and the car, out of control, began to thrash from one side of the road to the other: down into the ditch one side, out again, down the other side and out again, and so on for some distance. In the end—truck driver still oblivious—the rope grabbed a post and broke, leaving Jack and his new car hanging on the end of it down a steep incline. The truck continued and was never seen again.
>
> The story improves with the thought of what the truck men must have thought when they reached their destination. Probably as abusive as hell that Murray had pinched their rope, I should think. And he didn't even thank us.

On 6 October 1947 the Australian Grand Prix was held at Bathurst, Mount Panorama. The Formula Libre race had 22 starters and was held over 38 laps of

CHAPTER FOUR

the circuit, for a total race distance of about 241 kilometres. It was the twelfth Australian Grand Prix and the first such race to have been held after the end of World War II. Bill Murray, who would later be Jack's co-driver and navigator in both the 1953 and 1954 REDEX trials, won the 1947 Australian GP, driving an MG TC. Formula Libre, the form of automobile racing allowing a wide variety of types, ages and makes of purpose-built racing cars to compete head-to-head, can make for some interesting match-ups, and provides the opportunity for some compelling driving performances against superior machinery. The only regulations typically govern basics such as safety equipment.

Disappointment: the 1947 Australian Grand Prix

For this race Jack drove the newly acquired Day Special, a Monoposto, single seat race car. After a steady drive, he was forced to retire Car No 9, having completed 29 of 38 laps. The car went well during practice sessions despite the bumpy ride from Melbourne, but squirted oil all over him during the actual

Above: Australian Grand Prix, Bathurst, 1947: Jack driving the Day Special.

Above: Jack (in background, left) watches on as Dick Bland is wreathed for second place in the 1947 Australian Grand Prix. His mechanical problems must have been disappointing, since Jack had been tipped as favourite by the *Sydney Morning Herald* prior to the race.

Above: Jack driving the Day Special, Car No 9, in the October 1947 Australian Grand Prix.

race. Naturally, the Day Special, during preparation for the race, had been given the full Jack Murray red paint and chrome treatment.

'The bends straightened out in fear'

Bathurst, Mount Panorama saw Jack Murray and the Day Special return on 29 March 1948 for the popular Easter meeting. In the Over 1500 cc Short Handicap (6 laps, about 25 miles) Jack placed third in a field of fourteen. The Day Special, Car No 5, recorded 117 mph (188 km/h) on Conrod Straight. In the NSW Hundred (25 laps, about 100 miles) Jack placed ninth in a field of 33. The race was characterised by the overheating problem that would continually plague the Day Special.

Jack caused excitement with a wild spin while pitting for more water. Jack was never one to do things in half measure. My father was a risk taker. His racing style was to go hard and go fast. He would rather 'give it a go' and have a car overheat or breakdown than nurse a vehicle home and in so doing settle for a place finish.

Jack's cars were well prepared—but they needed to be. The NSW Hundred of Easter 1948 was no exception:

> An observer in the S bends during practice said of 'Superman' Jack Murray that they distinctly had the impression that the bends straightened out in fear when they saw him coming to let him through and then snapped back into shape again when he passed. I believe his pit stop caused much excitement too. Apparently he belted into the pits with steam squirting everywhere, spun around backwards on the gravel in a high spirit of abandonment and leapt out roaring with laughter in chorus with his pit team, who were shouting jubilantly 'Thar she blows' and 'Whoa-emma'.
>
> Jack's competitiveness even extended to the racetrack car park: Apparently the Bondi rivalry between Murray and Jack Jeffrey for the most powdered and perfumed car reached a climax when Jack's white Jaguar roadster achieved a plaited leather steering wheel polished to perfection, but Murray's yellow silk racing cover, which appeared on race day fitting snugly over the scarlet Day Special, sent Jack J into a state of severe jealousy neurosis, they tell me. (*Australian Motor Sports, Spotlight* by John Barraclough, 15 April 1948)

I can just hear Jack's voice now repeating a phrase he used often: 'There is no lair like an ol' lair.'

The Battle for Supremacy

Armed with the Day Special, Jack had a new weapon with which to challenge his old sparring partner, Frank Kleinig. The venue that provided the opportunity was the Hawkesbury Hill Climb No 2 held on 16 May 1948:

Jack Murray had the Day Special and is reported to have vowed that he will not rest content this sprint season until he has succeeded in doing Kleinig (Frank); on his first run he did 62.38, which also broke the existing record, of course. Later in the day he got his time down to 60.19—second fastest of the day. Kleinig held the Day Special at bay. (*Australian Motor Sports*, 15 June 1948)

The results were: Racing Cars Over 1500 cc (best times): First F. Kleinig (4168 cc Kleinig Hudson) 58.84 (fastest time of the day and new hill record); Second J. Murray (3622 cc Day Special) 60.19.

Finally Jack had his revenge. The Hawkesbury Hill Climb Championship held on 8 August 1948 gave him his long-sought-after victory over Frank. Fastest time of the day honours went to him, a best time of 60.95 secs, beating Frank Kleinig by 1.07 secs.

But the following month, the tables turned again. The Hawkesbury Panorama Hill Climb No 3 held on Sunday 19 September 1948 resulted in Jack coming second overall in both the Over 1500 cc Class and overall time (60.2 secs), beaten only by Frank Kleinig (58.0 secs).

After competing on the Hawkesbury Hill Climbs, Frank and Jack then took their battle to the Mount Druitt circuit. In the late 1940s and 1950s the Australian Sporting Car Club ran a series of races at Mount Druitt Airstrip, near Penrith.

Murray and Kleinig battled for supremacy at Mount Druitt on 4 October 1948 (Eight Hours Day), the first meeting to be held there. The results speak for themselves, one for each: Event 6, Scratch Race for Cars Over 1500 cc (Open)

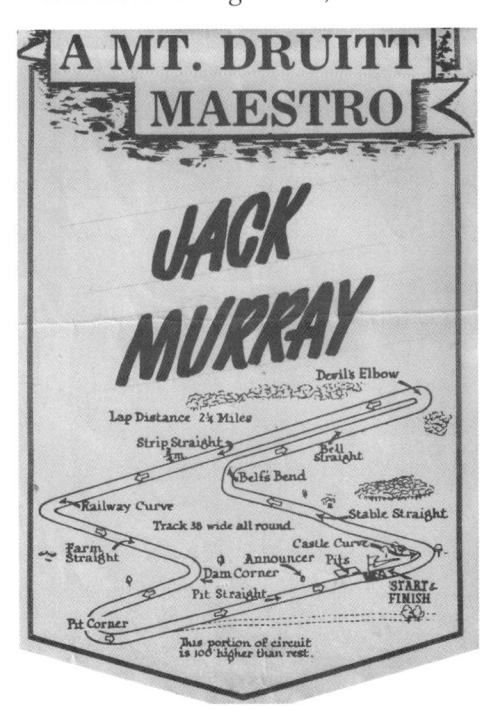

Above: One of the place mats used during a 1980 reunion of some sixteen former Mount Druitt circuit race drivers.

CHAPTER FOUR

resulted in Jack in the Day Special placing second to Frank Kleinig. Event 9, 10 Lap Handicap Over 1500 cc (Open) was won by Jack. The race was a triumph for Jack Murray in the Day Special, who was lapping consistently at 1 min 30 secs—possibly fastest lap of the day. (*Australian Motor Sports*, 15 October 1948)

With an improving Day Special, Jack continued to impress at Mount Druitt. *Australian Motor Sports*, 15 February 1949, describes events on a program shortened due to rain. The meeting was held 31 January 1949:

> ... the immense supremacy of the Day Special over other Ford specials ... Murray proved unassailable and steadily moved away from George Reed to win by 13 seconds. Murray's fastest lap of 1:29, equalling his previous record, works out at almost 73 mph (117.5 km/h) for the 1.8-mile (2.9 km) circuit. This is quite a stout effort when the lack of adhesion on the loose surface is considered, and will probably remain unbettered for some time.

In Event 5, Over 1500 cc Scratch Race, Open (5 laps, about 9 miles), Jack won again. In Event 11, Over 1500 cc Handicap, Open (10 laps, about 18 miles), he placed second, but the fastest lap of the race was his: 1 min 30 secs.

In 1949, the Easter meeting at Bathurst, Mount Panorama was held on 18 April, a sharp clear autumn day. Cool days always suited a very speedy but frequently overheating Day Special.

In the Over 1500 cc Short Handicap (6 laps, about 25 miles) Jack in the Day Special placed second by 7 seconds in a field of twelve, despite overheating and oil leak problems. In the All Powers Long Handicap event over 25 laps, the Day Special boiled its way into retirement from the race on lap 9.

The Sun newspaper reported on close mates having a lot of fun:

> Old rivals Billy McLachlan and Jack Murray, driving similar Bug-Ford cars, were started together and kept the large crowd on its toes as they battled and chased each other around the course. Bathurst 1949 saw Murray top 118 mph (190 km/h) down Conrod Straight, but he would fail to finish. Results like this highlighted the ongoing problem Murray faced—the Day Special, Car No 5 overheating. Jack and good friend Bill McLachlan had a £50 wager between

themselves on the race. MacLac (Quote: 'a charmed life has this laddie') crashed on the sixteenth lap and Murray overheated!

As reported by *Spotlight*:

The inimitable Murray came to the line with a fine stream of water shooting out of the radiator cap which, with a 'cop this' he took pleasure in squirting to enormous altitude by revving the engine. To never take life seriously would be the theme of Jack's existence ... Jack Murray, too, drove with (I quote), 'his usual verve and a bit more finesse, fairly throwing his car through the corners'.

Early motorsport offered little in the way of safety. The drivers were brave men, taking extraordinary risks at very high speeds—and many of them paid

Below: The boys at play: Jack in the Day Special, Car No 5, chases good friend 'Wild Bill' McLachlan in the Mackellar Special, Car No 4.

the ultimate price. Tragically, driver Jack Johnson died after his TC turned over in practice during the 1949 Bathurst Easter meeting.

Frank Kleinig and Jack Murray resumed their battle on 13 June 1949 at the Hawkesbury Hill Climb No 5 meeting. Frank won this round, setting a new hill climb record of just 57.6 secs. Each car had three attempts after practice from 9am to 11am. Gravel washed across the road. Bill McLachlan (Mackellar V8 s/c), Gavin Sandford-Morgan (Nutt-Bug), Jack Murray (Day Special) and Bill Ford (Hudson 6 Special) all improved during the day—Jack Murray indeed gatecrashing the select band of under-the-minute men. The Fastest Ten saw Murray listed as third, 59.3 secs.

The war of the machines continued on Sunday, 10 July 1949 at Mount Druitt Airstrip Records Day (Quarter Mile Standing Start), with 66 vehicles participating. The day was organised by the Australian Sporting Car Club (ASCC).

In the Over 3000 cc racing class, Kleinig's best northerly run in the Kleinig Hudson was 15.2 seconds, while Jack Murray did 15.6 with the Day Special. In the southbound runs, the Day Special had trouble with its pre-selector gearbox, first gear being practically useless.

In the southbound runs, no fewer than 58 of the 66 cars did slower times than they had in the opposite direction. The reason for this is not clear. Jack did 15.9 secs southbound while Kleinig did 15.1. After the standing quarters had been run off, Frank and Jack were timed over a flying quarter. In spite of the inadequate run-in and the loose surface, they clocked 118 mph and 116 mph respectively.

Murray Unassailable
My father's last motorsport event for the 1940s was held at Mount Druitt on Six Hour Day on Monday 3 October 1949. As reported by *Australian Motor Sports*, it was a day of triumph for the Day Special and Jack.

In Event 5, the Over 1500 cc Scratch Race (five laps) eight starters, Jack came first. 'At the drop of the flag, Ewing (Buick Special) was first away, but Murray (Day Special), who had made a bad start, soon had his heels and was then unassailable.'(*Australian Motor Sports*, October 1949)

Event 7 was a relay race involving three cars: an 1100 cc to do half a lap, a 1500 cc to do one lap, an over 1500 cc to do two laps. 'Coming down the straight for the last time it seemed that Monday might just make it for his team, but Murray found the accelerator just in time and popped him on the line—and it was over.' (*Australian Motor Sports*, October 1949)

In Event 8, Over 1500 cc Open Handicap ten laps, eight starters, 'scratch man' Murray had to pursue the bunch. Fastest furlong was Murray's 112 mph, a good speed on a fairly loose 0.9 mile straight with slow corners in and out. The distance was too short for Murray to catch the leaders.

For Jack, Mount Druitt was a successful finish and a great way to bring the curtain down on the 1940s, a decade that had provided him with a thorough grounding of experience, know-how and toughness in many different forms of motorsport. These skills would see the young man who 'crashed a Model T Ford into a dairy window' in the 1920s race into the 1950s and place fourth in an Australian Grand Prix, win a REDEX trial, and become the victor and placegetter in numerous circuit races, hill climbs and long distance events, to become one of Australia's best known motorsport heroes.

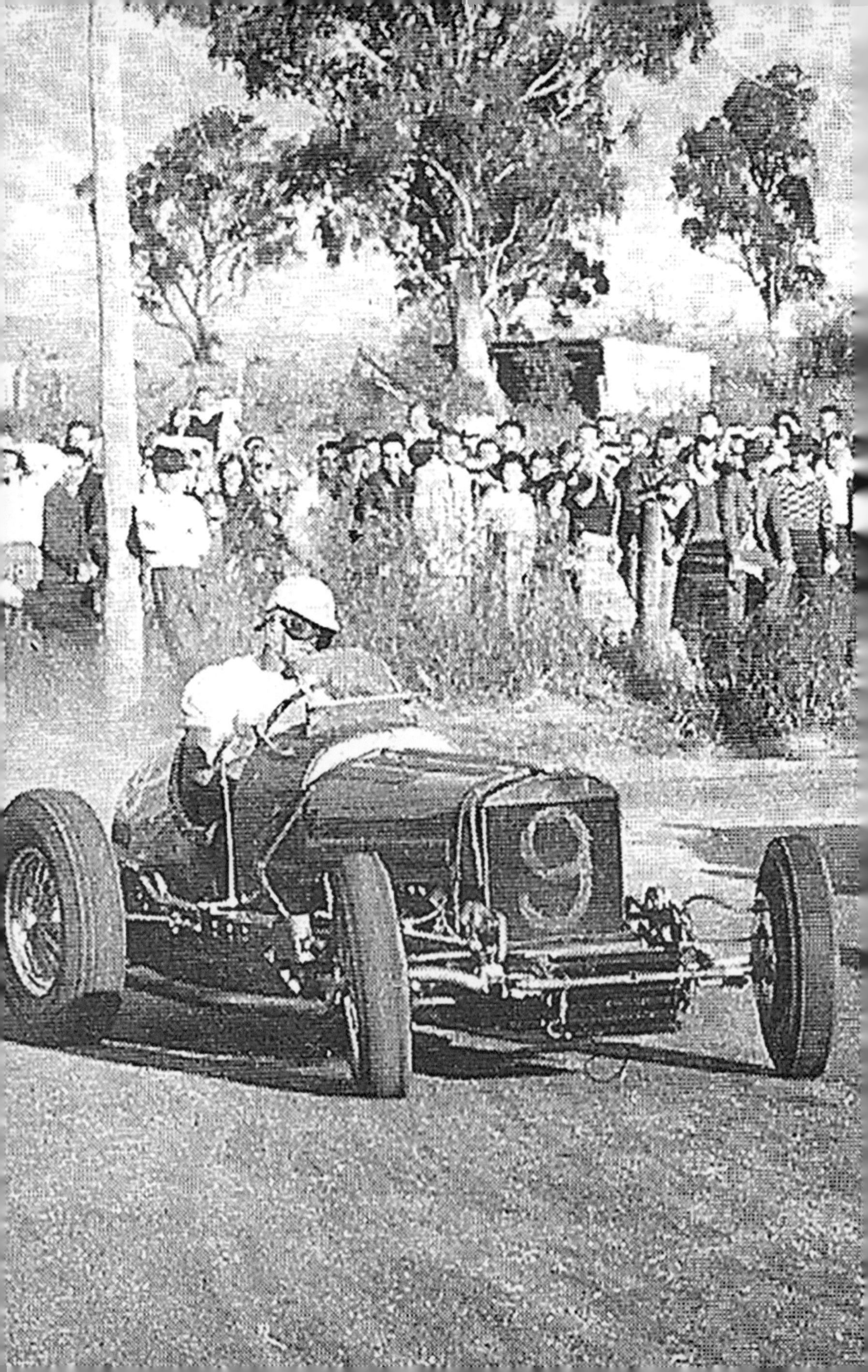
9

CHAPTER FIVE

A DECADE OF WINS

The 1950s would be the decade Jack Murray came of age, earned his moniker 'Gelignite' and led to his place in the Confederation of Australian Motor Sports (CAMS) Hall of Fame almost 60 years later, in March 2016.

As the 1950s dawned, Jack was entering his 40s. He certainly was not a young gun during this decade, but it would prove to be the period of his most prolific successes, the one in which he reached the zenith of his

Above: Celebrating the 1954 REDEX win. Jack's Allard J2, sign displaying Murray Pilot Car, leading the Grey Ghost.

CHAPTER FIVE

motorsport career. A wealth of motoring experience, a body toughened and conditioned by amateur wrestling and a non-drinker, non-smoker's dedication to physical fitness were the foundation of Jack's motorsport success. But coupled with that physical and experiential preparedness was his natural inclination to take risks and push both himself and his cars to the very limit. When the machines managed to survive, Jack was a very hard man to beat behind the wheel.

On 26 January 1950, Mount Druitt Airstrip Races saw the Kleinig versus Murray battle continue into the new decade: ' ... racing was of quite a high standard, and one of the surprises of the meeting was Frank Kleinig's defeat by Jack Murray, driving the Day Special, now equipped with crash bars round its tail.' (*Australian Motor Sports,* February 1950)

In the Over 1500 cc Scratch Race of 5 laps, Jack won and beat out Kleinig in the Kleinig Hudson.

In the Relay Race, for teams of three cars, Jack came second with Dick Cobden and Ken Tubman (the future winner of the 1953 REDEX).

In the All Powers Handicap Race over three laps, Jack placed third.

Some very unusual match-ups occurred on 19 March 1950 at the next Mount Druitt Airstrip Races. This was a combined meet, jointly held by the Australian Sporting Car Club and the Motor Cycle Racing Club of NSW. Over 50,000 spectators turned up on a rain-soaked day to watch the meeting, which included car versus motorcycle match racing. Jack and his good mate Bill McLachlan carried the banner for the car supporters in the match racing.

Modern Motor, May 1950, described the tussles:

> On the same day there were two similar match races. The first was between 'MacLac' McLachlan and his Bug-Ford and Les Slaughter on a 350 cc Velocette. The result was a dead heat. The other match race, after two false starts, resulted in a win for Jack Murray in his newly-engined Grancor Day Special, from Harry Hinton riding the double-knocker Norton. With the score at one each, it would appear that the subject of racing car versus racing motorcycle is not yet decided. From the spectators' reaction to the match races, there should be more.

Betterperforming Cars

Jack constantly sought better performance from his cars:

> Among the competitors was Jack Murray in his re-engined Day Special, looking as immaculate as ever. The new Grancor V8 engine, reputed to develop nearly 200 horsepower and based on the standard Ford block, had just been installed and should mean a great improvement in performance. ['Grancor' stands for Granatelli Corporation of Chicago, Ill. USA, manufacturers of speed and racing equipment, especially for Fords] (*Modern Motor*, May 1950)
>
> Jack Murray's Day Special, now with Grancor engine, spat back at Mount Druitt and ignited his ignition leads. (*Australian Motor Sports, Spotlight*, April 1950)

Evidently due to the fire-damaged ignition leads, Jack appears to have been unplaced in the six-event program.

The Castrol Trophy 24-Hour Trial (1000 miles) held in June 1950 proved to be more successful. As *Wheels* (October 1953) put it: 'Jack Murray navigated for Bill McLachlan and, pushing a 1947 Ford in non-stop rain, the good mates won. Bill and Jack cleansheeted.'

One report mentioned 'sharpshooter Jack Murray, armed to the teeth'. Jack was a keen shooter and guns and cartridges were far more commonplace than today. As to why weaponry was required to accompany the boys on a trial is unclear, but a 1958 Ampol Trial

Above: Jack, pistol in hand, speaking to an official during the 1958 Ampol Trial. Obviously Jack intended to take strong measures if too many points were deducted. Photo: Peter D'Abbs.

CHAPTER FIVE

photo (see previous page) seems to indicate Jack was a very keen negotiator when it came to official rulings.

Easter Monday, 10 April 1950, meant one thing: Bathurst Mount Panorama. Jack's main focus was the 25 mile Handicap event.

Damian Kringas' *The Gelignite Bugatti* quotes the *Sydney Morning Herald*, pre-Easter 1950, which reported:

> Jack Murray will drive the Bugatti-Ford plus Edelbrock motor which he steered last year. He spent £1000 importing a Grancor engine from America to fit into his car for the race. He found it unsatisfactory for the Mount Panorama course, as it has a three-speed gearbox. A four-speed gearbox is essential to give the required ratio for the steep grades of Mount Panorama. Murray has supertuned his Edelbrock motor, increasing its compression ratio, and fitted it with a special racing cam imported from America.

Doug Whiteford would win the 100 Mile Race (1950 Australian Grand Prix) but Jack's focus and preparation for the 25 mile Handicap would certainly pay off.

In Event 2, the Over 1500 cc Handicap (6 laps, 25 miles) Jack, driving the Day Special, won in a race time of 19 mins 18 secs. Jack and Doug Whiteford would post equal fastest lap time for this race of 3 mins 08 secs and both cars would be timed at 119 mph (192 km/h) on Conrod Straight. Bill McLachlan driving the Mackellar Special was third. The field consisted of sixteen starters.

In the NSW Hundred, Jack driving the Day Special (Bugatti-Ford V8) placed fourth in a field of 48. In Car No 9 Murray put in the fastest lap of the race in his last lap, passing George Pearse to come fourth: fastest lap: J.E. Murray 3 mins 08 secs (71.5 mph). 'Whiteford figured in one of the most exciting duels ever seen on the course when Jack Murray crossed the line only four lengths ahead of him in the Over 1500 cc Handicap of 25 miles,' wrote Damian Kringas in *The Gelignite Bugatti*, again quoting the *Sydney Morning Herald*.

Kringas continues:

> There's little doubt Murray had an affection for the Day Special. However, he did have trouble, especially on the long distance races

A DECADE OF WINS

Above: Jack at the wheel of the Day Special, engine cowling removed to reduce overheating. Jack even tried fitting a 'surge tank' in front of the aero screen to help with his overheating problems.

such as Bathurst. The major issue seems to have been with the Ford V8, like many of the flathead specials, overheating ... Murray would be forced to race with the side panels removed, even at times, the entire engine cowling.

Bathurst Quarter Mile Times: third fastest, J.E. Murray (Ford Special) 119.2 mph (191.8 km/h), timed on Conrod Straight.

The wettest Bathurst races at Mount Panorama—ever!—took place on 2 October 1950 at the Six Hour Day Road Races. The rain was so extreme that distances were shortened on the day. But this meeting, as well as rain, also heralded the winds of change. The innovation that occurred was the introduction of production cars, Jack driving both a sedan and the Day Special in a race for sedan cars and another for sports cars.

In Event 1, the Closed Car Handicap (6 laps, 25 miles) Jack, driving a 3622 cc Ford Pilot supplied by Hastings Deering, placed sixth in a race time of 29 mins 50 secs. [Harold Hastings Deering, from 1935, had a Sydney Ford Distributorship of trucks, cars and tractors]. Car No 7 posted the third fastest quarter mile time.

'Immaculate! Type 39 Bugatti with Ford V8 power, all of it given the Jack Murray red paint and chrome treatment. Rebuilt as a Monoposto pre-war by Jack Day, the Day Special never looked better than this,' wrote George Reed.

Above: Car No 9 and Jack, Bathurst, Easter 1950.

By driving in Event 1, Jack drove in the first saloon car race to be held at Bathurst. It was described as 'a completely successful experiment and one most interesting from the public's point of view.' (*Australian Motor Sports*, October 1950) It would eventually give birth to the era of Holden versus Ford and later the V8 Supercar Series we have today.

In Event 4, the Over 1500 cc Handicap (12 laps, 50 miles) Jack occupied the front row driving the Day Special, Car No 5, and placed sixth in a field of nineteen. He was narrowly beaten by his good friend Bill McLachlan.

Quarter Mile times: J. Murray (V8 Pilot) 88.67, 90.44 and 89.9 mph (approximately 145 km/h) and J. Murray (Bug-Ford) 95.23, 108.4 mph (174 km/h). These were fast times on a wet Bathurst track in 1950.

A Bunch of Allards

Technology and motor cars were advancing at a rapid rate and at Easter 1951, for Bathurst Mount Panorama, Jack decided to buy a new car, one he had spotted at Bathurst in October the previous year. In early 1951, Jack purchased a new Allard J2 that had been shipped to Australia on 26 January 1951.

According to Damian Kringas:

CHAPTER FIVE

Above: Jack at Hell Corner, practising in the Day Special, October 1950.
Below: Jack and the Day Special.

A DECADE OF WINS

The car was imported by Rube Gardiner from Gardiner's Motor Service, red with red interior and with Murray fitting a 331 ci (5½ litre) OHV Cadillac V8. Gardiner drove the first J2 to the October 1950 Bathurst race where it was on display and sold it to legendary racing driver Stan Jones. That's when Jack saw the Allard J2 for the first time and so at the same meeting Murray committed to buying one from the next shipment.

For Easter at Bathurst in 1951, as John Medley noted, a bunch of Allards were entered—for Jack Murray, Stan Jones, Harry Monday and Ron Ewing. These J2 models with swing axle front end, de Dion rear, coil sprung all round, in-board rear brakes and V8 power were new to Australia and the Murray/Ewing/Monday trio was entered by NSW Allard distributor, Gardiners' Motor Service.

In Event 2, the Over 1500 cc Handicap (6 laps, 25 miles, start 11.20am) J.E. Murray for R.A. Gardiner Cadillac-Allard J2 placed third in a field of over 30 entries.

In Event 4, REDEX 100 (26 laps, about 100 miles, start 4.20pm) in a field of eleven cars, Jack drove the Allard J2 for R.A. Gardiner, Car No 29. While Jack

Above: Bathurst, Easter 1951, REDEX 100 showing 'ostentatious' Jack Murray at the start.

CHAPTER FIVE

Above: Jack's Cadillac-Allard J2.

did not finish (DNF) the race, he did manage to post some fast speeds over the timed quarter mile. Bathurst Quarter Mile speeds, REDEX 100, J. Murray (Allard J) reached 107.71 mph, 108.4 mph (174 km/h).

The eighth post-war meeting on the Mount Panorama circuit was held on 1 October 1951 (Eight Hour Day) and organised by the Australian Sporting Car Club. Jack drove a Cadillac-Allard.

In Event 1, H. and E. Morton P/L Over 1500 cc Championship and Handicap (6 laps, 25 miles, start 11am) Jack placed fifth in the Cadillac-Allard Car No 6 in a field of 22 entries in a race time of 19 mins 41 secs. 'Feltham (Alta), faltering at the start, was rammed by Murray (Allard), who was rammed in turn by McLachlan (Bugatti-Ford), but they sorted themselves out.' (*Australian Motor Sports*, October 1951)

In Event 2, Ira L. and A.C. Berk Invitation Scratch Race over three laps,

Above: Bathurst 1951, showing Hell Corner at the end of Pit Straight.

held at noon, my father placed fourth in a small field of eight.

Event 3, REDEX 50 mile Championship and Handicap, involved 40 starters. Jack retired in lap 9.

Driving the new machine, the Allard J2, Jack was about the sixth fastest over the electronically timed quarter mile near the end of Conrod Straight.

The Allard got another outing on Monday 28 January 1952 at the Parramatta Park Races, again organised by the Australian Sporting Car Club. Not many people are aware that Parramatta Park was a popular venue for motorsport during the 1950s. There were seven races held that day, both scratch and handicap classes by capacity. The course was roughly two miles to the lap and had only one straight of any length. Jack registered to compete in three races driving his Cadillac-Allard.

Unusually, he appears not to have placed in any of his races that day.

CHAPTER FIVE

Above: Jack in his Cadillac-Allard corrects his drift on a fast corner. 'Jack is a real crowd pleaser as he always drives to the limit,' said *Australian Motor Sports,* February 1952.

The Grand Prix Returns

Easter 1952 was very special, since it saw the return of the Australian Grand Prix to Bathurst Mount Panorama for the first time since 1947. Race day was 14 April 1952.

In the 1952 Australian Grand Prix (38 laps, about 150 miles) Jack, driving the Cadillac-Allard J2 Car No 5 placed fourth. Bill Murray, the 1947 Australian Grand Prix winner at Bathurst, made his first (and last) reappearance there since 1947. In 1952, in the seventeenth Australian Grand Prix, Bill Murray, driving his Alfa-Alvis, placed an impressive third, one ahead of Jack. Bill McLachlan placed thirteenth. [See YouTube: '1952 Australian Grand Prix Bathurst']

The 1952 Australian Grand Prix was a Formula Libre motor race and featured 43 starters. The race, which was the seventeenth Australian Grand Prix, was won by Doug Whiteford driving a Talbot-Lago T26C Formula One car. It was Whiteford's second of his eventual three Australian Grand Prix victories (1950, 1952, 1953). This was the last meeting at Bathurst to be run by the Australian Sporting Car Club—the end of an era.

A DECADE OF WINS

Above: 'First corner first lap of the Grand Prix, as Jones' Maybach takes the lead followed by Feltham (Alta), Whiteford (Talbot), Murray (Allard) and a bunch of Cooper 1100s,' said *Australian Motor Sports*, May 1952.

Above: 'Terry Healy (left) and Mark Jansen (right) behind a rare Allard J2. This car was recently sold [late 2011] by Oldtimer Australia and has a unique history, having finished fourth in the 1952 Australian Grand Prix with 'Gelignite' Jack Murray behind the wheel.' (*Just Cars*, January 2012)

CHAPTER FIVE

Jack in the Cadillac-Allard was recording speeds of 108 mph (174 km/h) over the timed quarter mile. *Australian Motor Sports*, May 1952 refers to 'Joe Murray in his Cadillac-Allard' [Jack's nickname of 'Joey' dated back to before 1937. The earliest reference I can find to 'Joey' is in a letter dating around 1937.]

Jack wins 1952 Australian Sprint Championships

Airstrips usually make great motorsport race venues. Even if not ideal due to runway or taxiway configurations, at least they can provide a long straight and a chance to open the throttle. On 1 June 1952, the Vintage Sports Car Club of Australia held the Australian Sprint Championships at the Castlereagh Airstrip. Jack won this championship.

As *Australian Motor Sports*, June 1952, described it:

> The class for sports cars over 3001 cc brought four XK-120 Jaguars to the line, but none of them could come within sight of Jack Murray's Cadillac-Allard J2, hard though they tried. Jack Murray's two runs were quite astounding ... in the open class, Jack Murray started going faster as a sports car than he did as a racer, clocking his fastest run in a most exciting looking 14.67 as a sports car.

The results over the quarter mile were:

In Event 1, Sports Cars 3001 cc and Over: Winner J.E. Murray (Cadillac-Allard) 15.05, 14.67, 14.86 secs (average).

In Event 2, Racing Cars 3001 cc and Over: J. Murray (Cadillac-Allard) 14.86, 14.84, 14.85 secs (average).

The BTD REDEX Trophy and £25 went to J.E. Murray (Cadillac-Allard) 14.85 secs (mean).

Twenty Thousand see Jack Win at Parramatta Park

The Queen's Birthday weekend on 9 June 1952 saw 20,000 spectators gather around the 2-mile circuit at Parramatta Park to witness a six-event Road Race Program organised by the Australian Sporting Car Club. Jack fired up the Day Special for the Parramatta Park event and found success.

The results were:

In the Five Lap Handicap Race over 10 miles: Winner J.E. Murray (Bug-Ford).

A DECADE OF WINS

Above: 1952 Australian Sprint Car Championships. 'Jack won the Championship with his 5.4 litre Cadillac-Allard which wagged its tail every inch of the quarter mile,' said *Australian Motor Sports*, June 1952. Photo by John Stoney.

In the Scratch Race for Cars Over 1500 cc over 10 miles: Third, J.E. Murray. Murray and H. Monday swapped places two or three times in the last lap.

In the Ford & MG Specials Race, *Australian Motor Sports*, July 1952, reported:

> As the schedule was well under control, an extra race was squeezed in—or rather, two races in one, the Ford Specials and the MG Specials. Fords left the line first, followed after 10 seconds by MGs. Bill McLachlan dived into the garden at the Main Gate hairpin in the last lap but his competitors courteously waited for him and they crossed the line abreast. Murray, Monday and McLachlan dead-heated.

An extra race, and clearly the boys enjoyed the fun of it all and decided to have a three-way dead-heat finish. Sounds like a perfect end to a perfect day's racing.

Mount Druitt was another airstrip utilised as a motorsport venue. On 29

CHAPTER FIVE

Above: Jack, Bugatti-Ford, Parramatta Park 9 June 1952. Photographer: John Ryan, Autopics.

June 1952, the Australian Racing Club (ARC) held an event there. In the Sports Car, Over 1500 cc event, Jack managed a third driving his Cadillac-Allard, according to the *Sydney Morning Herald*, 30 June 1952.

Pipped at the Post

The Parramatta Park Road Races organised by the Australian Sporting Car Club on 6 September 1952 also included motorcycle racing:

In the Scratch Race Over 1500 cc, Jack driving the Day Special came fifth.

In the Handicap Race Over 1500 cc, Jack improved and came second. 'Joe Murray went very well in the Day Special but was pipped almost at the post.' (*Australian Motor Sports*, September 1952)

The Invitational Scratch Race over three laps saw Jack and the Day place fourth.

To wind up the program there were three group handicap races. 'Finally came Division C. Laurie Oxenford and Joe Murray both had their cars die under them and the race was won by George Pearse in a convincing manner.' (*Australian Motor Sports*, September 1952)

Such is motorsport.

> **MOTOR CAR RACING**
>
> 14 RACES.
> 1ST RACE 11 A.M.
>
> THE POSTPONED MEETING OF OCT. 5TH
> WILL NOW BE HELD ON
> SATURDAY, 11th OCTOBER
>
> **PARRAMATTA PARK**

Above: Parramatta Park Races advertisement, *The Sun*, 10 October 1952.

Glamour Driver

On 11 October 1952, Parramatta Park Races saw the biggest meeting ever. Ninety-six entries were received for the fifteen-event program. Race successes were followed by the Day Special's usual problem of overheating. Jack always pushed the Day to her limits.

The results were:

In the Group Handicap over ten laps, Jack (Bug-Ford) came second.

In the Invitational Scratch Race over three laps he managed a third.

The Scratch Race Over 1500 cc over ten laps saw Jack come second and third was Bill Murray.

In the Group Handicap over ten laps: Winner, Bill Murray, second Jack. 'Bill Murray won fairly comfortably from Jack Murray, the Alfa-Alvis showing itself to be a very fast item of equipment,' commented *Australian Motor Sports*, November 1952.

The Parramatta City Council Handicap was the feature event of the meeting.

The *Cumberland Argus* of 15 October 1952 wrote:

CHAPTER FIVE

Glamour driver, amateur wrestler Jack Murray was forced out of the event in the latter stages when his car blew boiling water in his face out of the turn into the straight near the railway viaduct. Murray's Bug-Ford looked like coming to grief as it spun in a slow turn; however, although blinded by escaping steam, Murray fought it to a standstill to safely pull off the circuit.

1952 REDEX 1000 Trial

Jack had the ability to readily transition from circuit racing at places like Bathurst or Gnoo Blas at Orange or on former airstrips such as Nowra, Mount Druitt or Castlereagh, into trial driving. Jack loved the variety and differing challenges of all motorsport.

The REDEX era was about to dawn, with the 1000 Mile Trial, under the auspices of the Australian Sporting Car Club, taking place 18-19 October 1952. This was the first time this event was run. Twenty-four starters lined up for scrutineering and bonnet sealing. A secret route was used. Sponsored by REDEX, the event was planned and organised by Norm Pleasance and Alby Johnson.

Results: Class C (1201-2400 cc Open, 1501-2400 Closed) Second J.E. Murray (Ford Consul), with 80 pts lost. The outright winner was D.H. (Peter) Antill (Mercedes Benz), with 40 pts lost.

Tremendous Acceleration of the Day Special

More circuit racing followed on 15 November 1952 with Parramatta Park Races organised by the Australian Sporting Car Club, featuring thirteen races and including motorcycle events. The race meeting was a highlight of the City Council's Civic Week celebrations.

The combined car and motorcycle meeting was held on a very hot Sydney November day. Despite the weather, which exacerbated the Day Special's tendency to overheat, Jack drove with great success once again, entering four races for two wins, a second and a third.

Commented *Australian Motor Sports*, December 1952:

> The humorous side to the morning was Jack Murray's going around confiding in people he would do over George Pearse. After blowing up his Ford 85 motor chasing George at the last meeting he had

Above: Parramatta Park, 15 November 1952. 'George Pearse (MG TC s/c) and Jack Murray (Day Special) accelerate out of railway corner.' (*Australian Motor Sports*, December 1952)

fitted a bored and stroked Mercury of about 5 litres and around 200 horsepower output. Possibly the worst kept secret ever as it was known generally two weeks earlier and even to handicapper Frank Klein. [sic: Kleinig] The tremendous acceleration of the Day Special, instead of being astonishing, was more or less expected.

In the Fair Deal Car Sales Handicap of five laps, Jack was second following a minute's penalty along with George Pearse, both drivers breaking from the line at the start. The boys were eager to resolve who would 'do' whom and both received a wrap over the knuckles! Third was G. Pearse.

In the Reliable Rubber Co. Handicap of five laps Jack dominated the rest of the field, winning in the Day Special. There were five scratchings due to mechanical problems, and a small field of three.

In the Invitational Scratch Race of three laps, Jack won from six competitors, after a rolling start. 'With a final burst of acceleration Murray just got up to win from Pearse with Hirst a very close third.' (*Australian Motor Sports*, December 1952)

The Marshall Motors Handicap of ten laps saw Jack place third. This was the main event for cars, with eleven starters. The *Cumberland Argus*, 19 November 1952, reported, 'For the first five laps, it was a battle between Pearse, glamour boy Jack Murray, driving his superb Bug-Ford, and Bill Ford, in his oversized Hudson Special. Murray drove [in] his usual devil-may-care manner.'

Nowra Triumph for the Day Special

Nowra was another airstrip that had been converted for motorsport. The circuit was in the shape of a left-handed boomerang and was 1.8 miles (2.9 km) in length, made up of roads adjacent to the airstrip and hangars. The main airstrip was not used.

Support from the Navy and HMAS Albatross made for a wonderful two days when the Australian Sporting Car Club organised an event on 6-7 December 1952. Nowra was a triumph for Jack and the Day Special. He won three of the four races he entered, only a burnt piston preventing a clean sweep.

Australian Motor Sports, January 1953, reported the results:

> The Over 1500 cc Handicap (fifteen laps) was won by Jack Murray. Coming nose to tail on the fast right hand sweep on the back leg of the circuit Ford commenced a dreadfully slow slide in front of Murray. Onlookers held their breath for what seemed 10 minutes as somehow Murray dodged and scraped past. Then, on the last lap, as Murray was following Adams through the northern hairpin, Adams spun tight in front of him and another bloodless mêlée commenced. After this, Murray scored his well-deserved win.

Jack also won the Group 'A' Handicap over fifteen laps.

In the Championship Scratch Race over three laps, with a rolling start, he was also successful. *Australian Motor Sports,* January 1953, wrote:

> Griffiths did an immense loop in the middle of the tightly packed field. Cars dodged in all directions ... Murray (Day Special) broadsided out of the way.

The All Powers Handicap of 30 laps was the longest race of the day. 'Murray went particularly well for twenty laps, [but] suddenly dropped out ...' Cause: a burnt piston. (*Australian Motor Sports,* January 1953)

Lap Record at the New Gnoo Blas

On Anniversary Day, 26 January 1953, a new race circuit was opened for business: Gnoo Blas at Orange. Anniversary Day was a term that had been previously used for Australia Day. The Anniversary Weekend Races were organised by the ASCC.

This was the first meeting on a new triangle-shaped, 3.8 miles (6.1 km) circuit, 177 miles (285 km) from Sydney. Even so, 15,000 spectators were attracted and 39 competitors. *Australian Motor Sports*, February 1953 declared:

> The official lap record was set by Jack Murray (Day Special) in 2 mins 32 secs for the 3.75 miles (approximately 90 mph or 145 km/h).

In the Canobolas Handicap of ten laps, J. Murray (Day Special) retired with universal differential (i.e. mechanical) problems. *Australian Motor Sports*, February 1953, reported on a very amusing and slapstick Ophir Handicap over eight laps:

> What a strange and comical race. The event was really meant for the slower cars but due to running troubles both Murray (Day Special) and Oxenford (Alvis-Mercury) found themselves in the field. They were wolves amongst sheep. In this race, Jack obtained fastest lap of the day, the lap record and then the world's slowest wheel change as a casual conversation in the pits between Jack, who had a blown tyre, and Peter Lowe led to Lowe's wheel being transferred to the Day Special. After this very casual changing of wheels Jack was off again—about four laps behind the field. The spectacular Jack Murray was dogged by tyre and radiator problems throughout the day.

The Edward Hargreaves Handicap of five laps was a general scramble of the day's fastest cars. In a field of eleven, no less than five cars crashed or went off the road, Jack being one of them. He ended his race amidst straw bales, down a ditch at Mrs Mutton's Corner, having tried to correct a slide by giving full power to the Day Special. No damage was done and no one was hurt. Of the fastest quarter times recorded at Orange, Jack clocked 114.03 mph (183 km/h).

CHAPTER FIVE

Confederation of Australian Motor Sport

Motorsport was growing and reorganising so that it could be enjoyed Australia-wide. On 1 February 1953, the Confederation of Australian Motor Sport (CAMS) became the new body controlling motorsport, taking over from the Australian Automobile Association.

In the early 1950s, due to growing conflict and disagreement between motorsport organisations and Bathurst Council, Orange was developing as a viable alternative to Bathurst Mount Panorama. On 6 April 1953, an Easter Meeting was held at the Gnoo Blas circuit.

Commented *Australian Motor Sports,* April 1953:

> The Gnoo Blas circuit at Orange has already established itself after two meetings as the major road racing circuit in New South Wales … other notable performers were Jack Murray (Day Special) and Bill Murray (Alfa-Alvis) who were both evenly matched and lapped consistently at around 90 mph (145 km/h) … Although entries were not large, 21 racing cars in all, every race was a grim battle at very high speeds that tensed everyone from start to finish. Fast circuit racing has at last arrived.

Above: Orange Car Races, 6 April 1953. 'Jack Murray (Day Special) chases Larry Humphries (Austral-Union) into the corner at the end of the main straight.' (*Australian Motor Sports,* April 1953)

A DECADE OF WINS

Wheels, May 1953, added:

> Sulman (Maserati 4C), Jack Murray (Bug-Ford) and Bill Murray (Alfa-Alvis) each had a very good day, running first, second and third in nearly every race. Tom Sulman [57-year-old grandfather and Australia's oldest competitor] in his Maserati 4C won five races from five starts at the Easter meeting.

In the Canobolas Handicap of ten laps Jack was unplaced in the top three. He took a quick pit stop at lap 6 with a thrown tread on a rear tyre.

In the Orange Handicap of four laps for cars Over 1500 cc, Jack was victorious.

> Lowe held his lead for two laps while fast catching up all the time were the two Murrays in the most hectic dice of the day. W. Murray never had enough steam to get past J. Murray, and after a couple of laps of tail nudging decided to get past on brakes at the slow corners. With absolutely nothing between them the two cars screamed along the Bloomfield Straight to Brandy Corner, J. Murray (Day Special) left braking to the last possible minute, pouring into the corner with smoke streaming off all four wheels. At that moment W. Murray got his Alfa-Alvis to the front and gave the stoppers a nudge and slowed to about twice the speed at which the corner should be taken. Things got very interesting for a long minute, what with J. Murray cornering almost too quickly and W. Murray trying his hardest to swap ends in front of him. When it was all over J. Murray was 200 yards in front and disappearing down the long straight.

In the Major Mitchell Handicap of six laps, Jack was second, as he was in the next race, the Ophir Handicap of eight laps.

In the Edward Hargreaves Handicap of five laps, the Day Special was withdrawn with a broken universal. (*Australian Motor Sports*, April 1953)

In Quarter Mile times from the Orange races, the fastest was Vennermark (Maserati 4CL) 129.5 mph, second Bill Murray (Alfa-Alvis) 122.5 mph, and third J. Murray (Bug-Ford) 120 mph (193 km/h).

CHAPTER FIVE

The Duckhams
On 21-22 March 1953, the Duckams Reliability Trial was held. Duckhams motor oils and greases was an English-based company, sponsoring drivers and events to promote their various machine lubrication products. They were eventually taken over by BP in the late 1960s. The 1953 Duckhams provided an impressive win for Jack's good mate, 'Wild Bill' McLachlan. Like many trials to follow, there was much argument about the wording for some sections and protests were lodged. The Duckhams was rated as the hardest short trial in NSW: the 350-mile route retired eight out of the fifteen starters. Bill McLachlan (Ford Customline) won, many points down, but still 200 in front of his runner-up. The trial presented competitors with a very difficult navigation exercise, according to *Australian Motor Sports*, May 1953. It is unclear if Jack competed in this event.

1953 REDEX 1000 Trial
On 2-3 May 1953, the REDEX 1000 Mile Trial was staged by the Australian Sporting Car Club, sponsored by REDEX. Routing that year was generally west and southwest of Sydney, 952 miles (1532 km), running time 22½ hours. *Australian Motor Sports*, June 1953 wrote:

> Run for the first time late last year, the REDEX 1000 Mile Reliability Trial has proved a welcome addition to the competition calendar. As opposed to the Duckhams and Castrol Trials, which are noted for their bad roads from start to finish, the REDEX is run over good roads at a fairly high average speed.

The results were: Class A: Winner J.E. Murray (Ford Customline), with 395 pts lost.

Outright and Class C Winner was D.H. Antill (Ford Consul), 305 pts lost, his second successive win.

During this trial, at one stage Jack became lost. *Australian Motor Sports*, June 1953 wrote:

> Still no track, and then salvation. A swagman was strolling down the road towards them. Firing a few questions at him and then sweeping him into the back of the Customline, Murray slid the car into the

Above: Jack in 1954, standing outside the Homebush Ford factory with a new Customline.

Above: He drove Ford Customlines in a number of events and promoted the cars, as seen here.

bush at the pointed out place and commenced a fearful dice down to the control. Their at-first willing passenger became petrified in the rear. As the car slithered to a halt at the control the swagman was out like a flash and into the scrub.

Only in Australia, and certainly only back in the 1950s, would a swagman ever come to the navigational rescue of a competition trial car.

The Castrol Trial

The Castrol Trial held 11-12 July 1953, run by the Australian Sporting Car Club, provided another opportunity for Jack to hone his trial driving skills for the REDEX events to come. Nineteen starters faced weather conditions that played havoc with the event.

The results were that Peter Antill in his Mercedes Benz 170S was the winner for the third successive year.

The trial was called off at Oberon due to snow, rain, fallen trees over narrow forest tracks and impassable rivers and creeks. By then only Antill and two others remained. The remainder of the field were bogged, smashed or lost.

CHAPTER FIVE

Australian Motor Sports, August 1953 wrote:

> Jack Murray was next, a few minutes later, charged his De Soto into the bog, got sideways, and stuck, blocking the road. Nothing would budge the car. There was no purchase for a block and tackle, chains were useless, and the frantic efforts of Murray and crew only got it deeper and more immovably stuck.

1953 REDEX Trial

Sunday 30 August 1953 saw the start at Driver Ave, near Sydney Showground of the first REDEX. Two weeks later, on 14 September 1953, the survivors returned. A substantial entry fee of £20 was applied in order to 'keep out any who were only desiring publicity'. As we have already heard, Jack's first long distance REDEX trial ended with a rollover in Queensland.

The Orange Grand Prix

Partly due to the deteriorating relationship between Bathurst Council and the Australian Sporting Car Club, there was no car racing at Bathurst's Mount Panorama circuit in 1953.

On 5 October 1953, however, a race meeting was organised by the Australian Sporting Car Club at the Gnoo Blas circuit at Orange. These particular races aroused a lot of ill feeling and resignations. The reason? Like golf, sailing and even races such as the Stawell Gift, whenever handicaps are involved, as surely as day follows night, controversy, angst and arguments are not far behind.

The NSW Grand Prix was run over 100 miles (161 km) as a handicap event, but also with an award for the fastest time. A compromise had been reached.

In the KLG Handicap of 20 miles, dead-heat equal third were J. Murray (Day Special) and L. Humphries (XK-120 Special).

In the REDEX Invitation Scratch Race: J. Murray in the Day Special was second to Jack Brabham in his Bristol-Cooper.

Mount Druitt Races

Mount Druitt Car Races, organised by the Australian Racing Drivers' Club (ARDC), took place 25 October 1953.

Australian Motor Sports, November 1953 wrote:

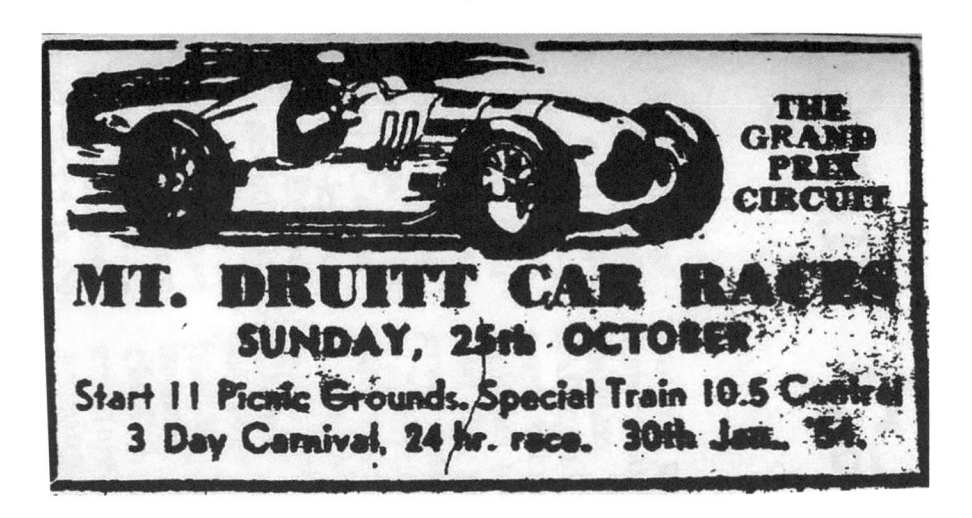

Above: Mount Druitt races advertisement, *The Sun* newspaper, 15 October 1953.

There was some new blood at Mount Druitt No 14, notably Jack Murray, who competed with the Bug-Ford (sometime Day Special, but people seem to have given up calling it by this name) for the first time on the new circuit and seemed to enjoy his day.

In the Stars' Scratch Race over 6¾ miles (10.9 km), Jack driving the Day Special was second again to Brabham's Bristol-Cooper. *Australian Motor Sports*, November 1953, reported on the excitement:

> ... best display was David McKay's with the red MG which spectacularly disembowelled itself in a cloud of smoke on the hairpin after Dam Corner, spewing oil all over the track. In the oil, Jack Murray spun round and round, Tom Sulman went nearly out of control ...

The DJ Collings-Power Reliability Trial

On 23 January 1954, the DJ Collings-Power 600-mile Reliability Trial was held. It was a 24-hour trial conducted by the Australian Sporting Car Club over first and second class roads in southeast NSW. Problems arose, as they are wont to do in trials, but Jack, always inventive, often came up with innovative solutions. *Australian Motor Sports*, February 1954, described one:

CHAPTER FIVE

Cars were being bogged and banked up at the Lachlan River. J. Murray sized up the situation and spied a tractor conveniently left by the body who do things to roads. Quickly hauling the Riley out, he towed his own car across. Leaving the tractor with engine ticking over, Murray disappeared off down the road.

Results were, in the General Classification, third J. Murray (Ford Mercury) 175 pts lost and in the Over 2500 cc Class, second J. Murray (Ford Mercury) 175 pts lost.

1954 REDEX 1000 Trial

On 27 March 1954, the REDEX 1000 offered a short trial, in effect a warm-up or practice for the longer 1954 Trial to come. Jack and Bill Murray won this short event, a portent of things to come later that year.

Bathurst Mount Panorama 1954

Easter Monday, 19 April 1954, saw racing return to Bathurst Mount Panorama, organised by the Australian Racing Drivers' Club (ARDC). As a symptom of the fractured nature of administration then operating within motorsport, both Orange and Bathurst hosted motor race meetings that Easter Monday. The ARDC was the new so-called 'upstart' club and the Australian Sporting Car Club (ASCC) the older, 'official' body. It was the ARDC's first meeting at Bathurst, and it was the final appearance of the sparkling Day Special being driven by Jack. Cars and motorsport were moving on and the Day was becoming less competitive.

The results were:

In the Group A Scratch Race over three laps, J.E. Murray Car No 30 was listed as an entry but Madsen, Pearse and Murray excused themselves. Jack said that he 'would rather watch the race'.

The Bathurst Hundred (26 laps; about 24 entries) was the main event of the meeting for racing cars of all powers. The start was by handicap. Jack placed seventh on handicap in his Bugatti-Ford Car No 30. He placed fourth on scratch. 'Jack Murray, who for once had been almost inconspicuous, came in not far behind Cobden,' wrote *Australian Motor Sports* of May 1954.

In the Bathurst Flying Quarter Mile Speeds: J. Murray (Bugatti-Ford), 111.8 mph (180 km/h) was ninth. The winner was doing an impressive and

Above: Bathurst, Easter 1954. 'Jack Murray's Bugatti-Ford in the pits. This car was always very well turned out.' (*Australian Motor Sports,* May 1954)

significantly quicker 136.3 mph (219 km/h).

Bathurst, Flying Quarter Mile speeds taken during practice and the meeting (*Australian Motor Sports,* May 1954):

First was R. Cobden (Ferrari), 136.3 mph (219.3 km/h), 2 litre, supercharged V12 producing 250 horsepower.

Fourth was J. Brabham (Cooper-Bristol), 130.3 mph (209.6 km/h).

Ninth was J. Murray (Bugatti-Ford), 111.8 mph (179.9 km/h).

In a lead up trial before the long distance 1954 REDEX, an unusual result occurred. On 22-23 May 1954 another Duckams Trial was held. Jack won the trial, but so did four others! Five cars placed equal first: Neville Vale (Mercedes Diesel), Ken Griffin (Holden), Ken Tubman (Peugeot), Jack Murray (V8 Ford) and Arthur O'Shea (Citroen). Perhaps this result alerted the REDEX organisers who, fearing a multiple and confusing tie for first place, promptly instituted 'horror' sections to separate the field and produce a single unequivocal winner.

A few months after the May 1954 Duckhams Trial, the name 'Gelignite' Jack Murray was coined. Jack reached the zenith of his motorsport career in

CHAPTER FIVE

July 1954, when he and Bill Murray won the 1954 REDEX Trial. No points were lost. This was an extraordinary accomplishment and one that was not to be repeated.

Murray versus Brabham

On 29 August 1954 at Mount Druitt Races, the now famous 'Gelignite' Jack raced head-to-head with that other famous Australian driver—Jack Brabham.

Brabham dominated this event with two wins, a new lap record and a spectacular and talented save of his Cooper-Bristol at 110 mph (177 km/h) when a steering tie-rod broke. The ARDC described Brabham as 'one of the most outstanding drivers in the world'. The ARDC would prove correct in their assessment as Sir Jack Brabham went on to become three-time Formula One World Champion, in 1959, 1960 and 1966.

In Group A, Racing Car, Scratch Race over three laps, Jack in the Day Special was third to Brabham in his Cooper-Bristol.

'It's a Grudge Match'

On Monday 4 October 1954, the two Jacks again competed at Orange's six kilometre long Gnoo Blas racing circuit. Nine races made up the program at this meeting. 'Gelignite' Jack drove both the Day Special and a saloon car at this meeting.

In the Cafes' Handicap of six laps, Jack was second in his Bug-Ford. 'From the start Brabham went to a comfortable lead and won from Jack [Murray] by a minute in a time of 14 mins 47 secs.' (*Australian Motor Sports*, October 1954)

Part of the program was set aside for a special match race between Bill Murray (Alfa-Alvis), Jack Murray (Bug-Ford) and Harry Monday (Mercury Special). Said *Australian Motor Sports*, October 1954:

> As the three cars were being marshalled into position for the rolling start, and the drivers were being cautioned against rough tactics, a dull thud in the middle distance announced the inevitable charge of gelignite. They did a lap in formation behind the pace car, a Jaguar Mk VII, started well, then swapped places for a couple of laps until they crossed the line with Bill Murray ahead of Jack, and Monday third man.

A DECADE OF WINS

Above: 'Rolling start of the grudge match race. Jack Murray (Bug-Ford) leads out Bill Murray (Alfa-Alvis) and Harold Monday (Mercury Special).' (*Australian Motor Manual*, 1 November 1954)

Below: An advertisement for the match race, *The Sun*, 1 October 1954.

IT'S A GRUDGE MATCH!
Jack Murray (Bug. Ford)
v
Bill Murray (Alfa Alvis)
v
Harry Monday (Mercury Special)

The Murrays argued all round Australia over the merits of their cars—now Monday says he can beat both!

See this race of the season at—
ORANGE CAR RACE MEETING
6-HOUR DAY, MONDAY, OCT. 4

This Meeting is being organised by Australian Sporting Car Club Ltd., on behalf of Orange Cherry Blossom Carnival Committee.

CHAPTER FIVE

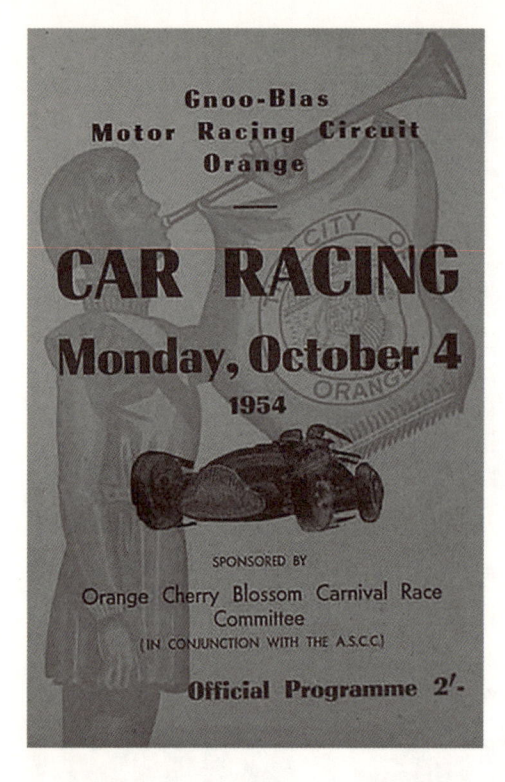

Jack led the first lap but Bill eventually won by a length, with Jack second and Bill Monday a length and a half behind.

'In 1954 ... Brabham and Murray would duel it out at a race track in the country NSW town of Orange—the iconic Gnoo Blas circuit that encircled the local mental asylum.' (*The Gelignite Bugatti*, Damian Kringas) In the REDEX Scratch Race of twelve laps, Brabham in his Cooper Bristol won with Murray second in his Ford Bugatti.

The KLG All-Powers Handicap, over twenty laps, was undoubtedly the most interesting race of the day. Jack won in a Lancia Aurelia. The huge field comprised almost anything over two litres in sports cars and every available car in the racing division. *Modern Motor*, December 1954, wrote: 'The race was won by REDEX Trial victor Jack Murray, who drove D. Jamieson's Lancia Gran Tourismo 2500, liberally handicapped for its first appearance.'

Above: Mount Druitt. 'Jack Brabham in the REDEX Special Cooper Bristol runs outside Jack Murray in the Day Special. Jack's Bristol was super competitive due to some special modifications.' Photo: George and Lesley Liebrand.

In the final race of the day, the Airzone Email Handicap for sports and saloon cars, Jack was third in the Lancia Aurelia.

Australian Grand Prix 1954

The nineteenth Australian Grand Prix was held 7 November 1954 at the Southport Road Circuit near Southport in Queensland. Jack was forced to pit driving his Cadillac-Allard J2 5.3L. A fuel line burst and high octane racing petrol was pumped into the cockpit. Chemicals were burning his skin, so he pulled into the pits and stripped off to his underpants. His nylon underpants had been reduced to three loops of elastic. *Australian Motor Sports*, November 1954 wrote:

> Jack Murray, bouncing across the apron to his pit, leaping out and tearing off his trousers—a broken fuel line had filled the Allard's seat with fuel. It was a moment before Jack's pit crew could stop laughing long enough to tell him the seat was dissolved out of his nylon shorts, upon which he disappeared hastily into the Ecurie Corio pantechnicon, to appear as hastily in a borrowed suit of overalls,

Above: Jack driving his Cadillac-Allard J2, 1954 Australian Grand Prix.

leapt into the car and off again ... Jack Murray drove his usual fiery race, but luck was not with his Cadillac-Allard.

South Pacific Road Racing Championships

On 31 January 1955, the Gnoo Blas Circuit at Orange was the venue for the South Pacific Road Racing Championships held by the Australian Sporting Car Club Ltd. Naming rights and disputes gave rise to the rather unusual title for the event. The race meeting attracted 30,000 spectators who enthusiastically lined the 3¾-mile (6 km) circuit. Prince Birabongse of Thailand, in his two Maseratis, joined Jack and competed in the championship event.

Jack, driving his Cadillac-Allard Car No 56, placed outright fourth and a second (some reports say third) on handicap in the 27-lap South Pacific Championship for Racing Cars, which was sponsored by the business houses of Orange. Clearly, the boys had a lot of fun. As *Cars*, April 1955, reported:

> Best dice of the race was between Murray in the Cadillac-Allard, Robinson in the Jaguar Special and Wilcox in the Ford Special.

In 1955 officials took a dim view of advertising on cars. This seems almost comical in the motorsport world of today, driven and funded by the advertising dollar. *Australian Motor Manual,* February 1955, reported on the misdemeanours:

> Jack Murray and Stan Coffey aroused the ire of CAMS by appearing with their respective cars marked 'Henderson Springs Special' and 'Dowidat Spanner Special' and were requested by the Chief Steward, Mr Lex Denniston, to cover the offending names, which they did with masking tape.

Murray Missed Death by Seconds

Safety in the 1950s, both for drivers and spectators, left much to be desired. The meeting was marred by the tragic death of Ian Mountain of Victoria, who crashed his car through a wire cable fence and was killed instantly. A spectator, James Young, was also killed and six others injured. Jack commented to Neil Bennetts in his National Library interview:

> I've been in quite a few car crashes, but I've never been hurt. The worst injury I've had from cars is the odd grazed knuckle when a spanner has slipped.

At Gnoo Blas in January 1955, like most race drivers at some time in their career, Jack definitely rolled the dice. As *Modern Motor, Sportlight*, March 1955, wrote:

> In an earlier race REDEX Trial winner Jack Murray missed death by seconds when his car caught fire. Officials flagged him off as flames enveloped the petrol tank. The fire was put out just in time to prevent an explosion.

Bathurst Mount Panorama 1955

In Easter 1955, tragedy would again darken Australian motorsport.

The meet was full of mechanical problems for Jack. In practice sessions, his Cadillac-Allard had troubles and the car failed to make it to the start line on race day.

There was a terrible crash involving driver Tony Bourke in the Alfa-Alvis previously owned by Bill Murray. Coming over the last hump on Conrod Straight, Bourke lost control and the Alvis plunged into the crowd. The resulting spectator carnage saw one killed outright, one fatally injured and twenty injured. Bourke was in shock but unhurt.

The End of the REDEX Era

Later that year, in June, the 1955 REDEX 1000 was run as a precursor to the third Round Australia REDEX Trial. As in the 1953 Round Australia REDEX, Jack again had 'rollover' problems. *Motor Manual*, 1955, wrote:

> Jack Murray, winner of the 1954 REDEX 1000 and 9600 miles trials, overturned in his Ford V8 near Merriwa, in the Hunter Valley, but pressed on. Murray's Grey Ghost, in which he won the two trials, slid on a grassy bend and toppled over. Before the car could be righted another vehicle skidded into it. The result—a battered front, dented doors, crushed boot and smashed windows. Jack and his crew of three pushed the car back on its wheels and reached the

CHAPTER FIVE

next control only five minutes late. But he got lost twice and finished the trial 990 points down. Forty-nine cars were entered, 39 started, and only sixteen finished.

The 1955 REDEX Round Australia Reliability Trial ended in confusion, disaster and protest. It was a public relations nightmare, and the end of an era.

An Ailing Allard
Saturday 1 October 1955 saw a one-day meeting take place at Bathurst Mount Panorama. We can only guess, but Jack's Cadillac-Allard must have had troubles at Bathurst, as it had earlier in the year at Easter. The car again failed to reach the starting line.

Mobilgas Economy Run and the Battle for Control
From 7-9 December 1955 an event that was both unusual and significant in terms of Australian motorsport took place. The Mobilgas Economy Run would influence racing for years to come. Originating in the USA in the early 1950s, the event focused solely on fuel consumption. The route over 1010 miles (1625 km) was set from Melbourne to Sydney and the run was conducted under strict supervision. All cars were stock. No coasting was allowed and four passengers had to be carried in each car. Results were worked out on a ton-miles-per-gallon basis.

The results for Class B: 1301-2000 cc, Ford Consul, W. McLachlan and J. Murray, were not good. The boys appear to have come a distant last (seventh) in their class, according to *Australian Motor Sports,* January 1956. Clearly, saving fuel and economy driving were neither Bill's nor Jack's forte.

More significantly for the future of Australian motorsport and 'Gelignite' Jack, the Mobilgas Economy Run event and an Ampol Trial caused my father and 30 other drivers to be banned, Jack for two years. He had competed in event(s) not sanctioned by CAMS—hence the licence ban.

A battle for control and administration of motorsport was raging within Australia, and the drivers were caught in the middle. The Trials Clubs of NSW broke away from CAMS following a dispute about the allocation of rights to a Round Australia Trial for 1956. The dispute centred around sponsorship by either Ampol or Mobilgas and a power struggle between CAMS and NSW clubs. It affected drivers throughout 1956 and 1957. *Wheels, the Sport,* April 1956, wrote:

We believe that those who drove in spite of CAMS' warning in the Mobilgas Economy Run were harshly treated and that this has been the main cause of the unsightly squabble between the majority of NSW clubs and CAMS.

Once again, conflict, disagreement and protest were, unfortunately, an integral part of motorsport.

In 1956, the Mobilgas Round Australia Trial was held in an event that covered over 14,000 km. VWs made a clean sweep of outright placings and, as a result, public interest waned. The winner was Eddy Perkins. Jack did not compete in any Mobilgas Trial due to the CAMS dispute. He seemed to be aligned with the Ampol events, which competed with those licensed by CAMS.

Ampol Round Australia Reliability Trials

On 26 August 1956, a 14-day Reliability Trial commenced.

Mechanical problems were starting to plague an ageing Grey Ghost that had seen so many hard roads with Jack behind the wheel. *Australian Motor Sports*, September 1956, reported Jack's woes:

> One of the favourites, Jack Murray, broke a kingpin on his 1948 Ford V8 and reached the control 70 minutes late, to lose 70 points. Murray won the 1954 Round Australia trial in the same car but ran into trouble continuously this year.

Navigational errors added to the problems. But as always, Jack made light of misfortune. As *Australian Motor Sports*, September 1956, wrote:

> The 1954 Trial winner Jack Murray took the road into the Mary Kathleen Uranium mine and reached Cloncurry 87 minutes late. He denied he'd got lost. 'I've got shares in that company,' he said, 'I just wanted to see how it was getting on.'

Another driver called Jack Murray came third and won Class 2-3 litres in a Holden. This 'other Jack Murray' was a transport operator from Minto. To avoid confusion, he was often referred to as 'Minto' or 'Milko' Murray, due to his sponsorship deal.

Above: From left to right: Bill McLachlan, Terry Byrne and 'Gelignite' Jack at the start of the 1956 Ampol Trial.

The winner was Allen Taylor driving a Peugeot 403. Despite their problems, Jack and Ray Murray finished eighteenth in the Grey Ghost out of a starting field of 113 cars.

The 1956 Ampol Trial reminded all competitors, yet again, of the dangers and risks associated with their chosen sport. Tragically, Les Slaughter and Bill Mayes were flung into an icy stream and died when their MG ran over a cliff.

The D-Type Arrives

As motorsport advanced, Jack needed to upgrade his racing cars in order to remain competitive. To the list of his vehicles—the Mackellar Special, the Day Special, the Grey Ghost and the Cadillac-Allard J2—we can add the D-Type Jaguar.

The D-Type was purchased in late September or early October 1956. As detailed by the online Jaguar registry:

Above: Jack advertising U-Grip trousers in his D-Type Jaguar racing car. Photo: Jack Hickson, State Library of NSW, 02778, 1957.

D-Type Jaguar Chassis No XKD532 Red, was purchased by Australian Jack Parker, while visiting England, direct from the Jaguar works. Despatched on 12 October 1956 and shipped to Sydney as deck cargo on a freighter, arriving early 1957. Purchased for famous rally driver 'Gelignite' Jack Murray to race and use as a road car by owner. Maintained by Murray at his Bondi garage.

And what of Jack's celebrated Cadillac-Allard? Damian Kringas wrote:

Murray sold the Allard J2 to friend and neighbour John William (Bill) Firth in February 1957. One of six sold new in Australia, under Firth's ownership the car is said to have run a 'very fast' quarter mile in the 1960s. With only two owners and low mileage, the Allard was sold in late 2011.

CHAPTER FIVE

On 7 July 1957, the 6000-mile Ampol Trial commenced at Bondi and finished there two weeks later. There were 78 starters. The clockwise route went to Melbourne, Maree, Mt Isa and Mossman before returning to Sydney. Jack and navigator Neville Vale competed in a Fiat 1100. A broken axle, having just left Birdsville, put an end to their campaign. Jack walked back into town and when questioned replied that he was 'testing some new type of shoes'.

Once again, Jack was competing in an event unsanctioned by CAMS. Jack's very close mate, Evan Green, was linked with Ampol. It was a difficult time for all involved.

Australian Motor Sports, September 1957, wrote: 'A previous Round Australia winner, 'Gelignite' Jack Murray, retired at this point with a broken back axle in his Fiat.' Jack drove Car No 67, a Fiat 1100 plated JM 456, with navigator Neville Vale. With the administration dispute still unresolved, Jack did not compete in the 1957 Mobilgas.

The Ampol Trial 1958

This event might be described as the most significant trial in Jack's long list. More significant than the 1954 REDEX win? How could that be? Well, the 1958 Ampol was the event at which Jack would meet a budding young real estate agent, 24 years his junior, named Dorothy Rosewell. Neither of their lives would ever be the same again. And as we shall learn, Dorothy's Ampol Trial took a decidedly dangerous turn.

Once again CAMS was licensing Ampol events. Calmer heads had prevailed and peace had broken out. With 148 starters, the 7000-mile event focused on eastern Australia. *Australian Motor Sports*, July 1958, wrote:

> Jack Murray was only six points down, but during the next day's stage to Adelaide a misread signpost took him 30 miles off course along a bush track, and the howling rainstorm mingled with his tears at Burra, where he shed a whole 75 points. At Port Augusta he was seen chasing navigator Dave Johnson with an axe.

In early 2016 I attended a Southern Cross Rally Fiftieth Anniversary get-together and chatted at length with Jack's great mate and fellow Rally Hall of Fame inductee Dave Johnson. I can report—thankfully—that Dave was too quick for an axe wielding Jack back in 1958.

In Car No 82 Fiat 1100, Jack and navigator Dave came thirty-third overall, but third in class, with 109 pts lost. The 1958 Ampol Trial was directed by Evan Green.

Jack did not compete in the 1958 Mobilgas Trial, but there were no shortage of Murrays who did. There were two Chrysler Royals in the 1958 Trial: Car No 3, Bill Murray from Crossmaglen and Car No 54 'Milko' Murray from Maitland. The trial was won by Eddie Perkins, VW Car No 2, repeating his win of 1956.

Jack Back at Bathurst

On Sunday 5 October 1958 and Monday 6 October 1958, Bathurst Mount Panorama was once again the centre of Australian motorsport. The 1958 Australian Grand Prix was held on Monday 6 October, the administrative dispute now over, and after a three-year absence, Jack had returned, his ban lifted. He drove his D-Type Jaguar.

The main event on Sunday was the 1958 Australian Tourist Trophy over 26 laps with 38 entries. As described by John Medley, 'Matich's C-Type Jaguar sounded sharp, but Jack Murray's smoky D-Type did not.' Jack, Car No 76, finished fifteenth.

In Event 1, Sports Car Scratch over ten laps, with 38 entries, Jack finished fourth. He did not compete in the Grand Prix on the Monday.

The histories of many Jaguar cars can be found listed online. Jack was also to become the owner of a white E-Type Jaguar. While online entries always need verification, a summary of Jack's D-Type entry is as follows:

> March 1959, Bathurst, third; also Bathurst October 1959, April 1960, October 1960 and April 1961.
>
> November 1961 sold to Bob Jane (Melbourne); restored by Jim Shepherd and repainted BRG; used for display purposes at Jane's tyre depots; 1976 car stolen and driven through plate-glass window of Sydney showroom prior to an intended suicide attempt but crashed. Repaired and repainted by Shepherd and completed in 1977. By 1980 it was reported to have covered less than 10,000 miles since original purchase: Then it was sold to George Parlby (Sydney) for a reputed $125,000. Some further restoration work done; sold to Jeffrey Pattinson, Coys of Kensington, UK, then it was sold to Allen Lloyd (UK).

CHAPTER FIVE

Above: Jack in his D-Type Car No 76 at Mount Panorama, 1958.

In reading about the lives and times of many of the sporty Jaguars, it is sobering to read how many were ill-fated and killed their enthusiastic, but perhaps unskilled owners.

Jack's D-Type Jaguar had another outing at Bathurst Mount Panorama in Easter, March 1959.

In Event 4, Sports Car Scratch over six laps with 36 entries, J. Murray Car No 76 Jaguar D-Type, was fourth, his fastest lap 3:04.1.

In Event 7, Sports Car Scratch over ten laps, Jack in his D-Type placed third, his fastest lap 3.04.8.

Fast Lap Despite the Rain

In October 1959, Bathurst Mount Panorama, took place on Saturday 3 and Sunday 4. On race day, in what some said were the worst conditions in living memory at a race meeting anywhere in Australia, the rain bucketed down. (John Medley, *Bathurst: Cradle of Australian Motor Racing*) Events involved racing cars, sports cars and sedan cars. Jack drove his D-Type Jaguar.

In Event 4, NSW Road Racing Championship for Sports Cars of thirteen laps, with 37 entries, in Car No 76, Jack placed fourth, his fastest lap 3:18.

In Event 7, Sports Car Scratch over six laps with eleven starters, it was almost dark, and only the truly committed remained. Headlights on, the starters contested this final event, six laps for sports cars, duelling through the rain.

Motorsport Morphs

As the 1950s drew to a close, motorsport in Australia was changing yet again.

The era of the open top race car was drawing to a close and sedan racing was in its infancy, but beginning to grow in popularity. Motorsport itself was morphing as enthusiastic amateurs saw the first appearance of manufacturer-backed teams and the growing involvement of advertisers, as in other sports.

Fun was still to be had, but motorsport was becoming increasingly professional—and very serious business.

POSITIVELY
NO ADMITTANCE
TO WORKSHOP

WELCOME
GOODB
"JELL"

MURRAY'S OWN
"HOW I WON REDEX TRIAL"
WIRY JOE

CHAPTER SIX
THE GARAGE

'Gelignite' Jack and Ray Murray's motor vehicle repair workshop was a Bondi landmark. Like the Grey Ghost it housed, Jack and Ray's place of 'business' over the years developed a character and personality all its own. Ever since I was a boy—and as far back as the 1930s—it was always known as The Garage.

It was a place of memories for me. The Garage is where Uncle Ray taught me as a young boy to ride a pushbike. I remember thinking he was still balancing

Above: Young ladies were always welcome at The Garage to view Jack's 'toys' and oddities.
Left: Jack points out some of his trophies, collectibles and skulls— human and otherwise.

CHAPTER SIX

me by grasping the seat, but he had in fact let go and I was bicycling on my own for the very first time.

If ever a building or location was to be a representation or a physical manifestation of a man, The Garage was for Jack: eclectic, historic and overflowing with Aussie humour. The Garage was a comical museum crammed with an amazing collection of souvenirs, cartoon-decorated walls, memorabilia and toys the two brothers and their friends had collected over the years. Occasionally, mechanical repair work was also undertaken.

And the address? Like its larger-than-life and eccentric owner, The Garage had a duality of its own. In his 1976 interview with Neil Bennetts, Jack gives the address of The Garage as No 92 Curlewis St, Bondi. Two years later, as Roger Climpson drives beneath the roller door to film *This Is Your Life*, we read No 94 beside the entrance—on the eastern side at least. Council, Sydney Water and the Office of State Revenue all refer to The Garage as No 94 Curlewis St. Freshly painted in 2015, No 92 Curlewis St now adorns the entrance.

At just over 12 metres wide, the property is certainly not wide enough to cover two blocks of land—and it doesn't. Lot 23 Section 3 in Deposited Plan 747, comprising the whole of the land contained in Certificate of Title Folio 23/3/747, is a single block of land. I was a Registered Land Surveyor—but even I am confused! 92? 94? 92-94? Even Google Earth offers little help. Local councils

Above: Uncle Ray with a backdrop of the hundreds of girlie calendars, which passed as wallpaper in The Garage. Rob Rowe, current owner of the Day Special fondly remembered these decorations from a visit as a 21-year-old.

allocate street numbers and Waverley Council refers to the site as No 94.

Regardless of all this confusion, it has always simply been known to all and sundry as The Garage.

There is a certain ironic consistency that a man whose very birth date(s?) were shrouded in mystery all his life should own a property whose very street number seems arbitrarily to change over the years. But truth is stranger than fiction.

'A social call on the Marx Brothers'

Kym Bonython once remarked that this is how his visits seemed.

The best description ever written of The Garage—and describing it is a challenge in itself—is Evan Green's, from his 1966 *Journeys with Gelignite Jack*:

> I went to see Jack Murray at Bondi. He and his brother Ray ran a garage there, servicing their own fleet of taxicabs. The Garage was in a long, barn-like building flush with the footpath. A couple of kerbside petrol pumps were used to refuel the cabs. No other business was encouraged. The footpath outside The Garage entrance was rarely busy, as most locals walked on the other side of the road. Especially the womenfolk. Sound came booming out of the cavernous interior and the occasional burst of vivid language was not to everyone's taste.
>
> Jack was in a far corner of the building, resting in an ancient deck chair. To reach him, I had to walk past a long and impressive collection of his 'toys'. On the left was the Grey Ghost—tyres flat, unregistered and being used as a wardrobe. Near it were two speedboats, a collection of waterskis, a collapsible canoe, the remains of a wrecked helicopter and a man-carrying kite. On the right was a 150 miles-per-hour Jaguar D-Type sports car, protected by a specifically tailored dust cover. Beside it was a new American Plymouth with high performance V8 engine, stereo record player and a collection of horns and alarms that could play the first bars of *Colonel Bogey*, moo like a cow, give a wolf whistle, ring bells or let off a shrill blast like the whistle of an express train. Then there was a cabin cruiser with twin outboard motors and his current rally car, set up with extra spare wheels, fog lights and long-range fuel tank. At the end of this exotic line of machinery rested Jack, wearing a

CHAPTER SIX

singlet, old pants, slippers and dustcoat. This garb was Jack's standard Garage uniform.

On the wall near him were posters from the Round Australia Trial days, some newspaper cuttings, the jaws of a tiger shark, the five-foot-long saw from a sawfish and the skull of a steer with an in-growing horn. Also wired to the wall were two elephant tusks, a fin from the biggest hammerhead shark ever caught in Australia, a turtle shell four feet across, the head of a large crocodile, ten feet of whale rib and one of its vertebra, the tail of a 500 pound dugong, a set of buffalo horns won from the original owner with the aid of an axe and four hours hard labour, the jaws of a dolphin, the spear from a marlin and several human skulls. All but the latter were hunting trophies, gathered by the Murray brothers or their friends ...

On the far wall hung the proudest acquisition, the Olympic flag from the 1960 Games. [Rome was in 1960. Most likely the flag was from Tokyo in 1964 and purloined by Keith Whitehead.] Jack had missed going to Rome so a friend brought him back the flag instead. The friend had souvenired it by organising a diversion and then

Above: The Garage—a home for toys and often filled with laughter—oh, and some of the language that invariably accompanies the repair of motor vehicles.

THE GARAGE

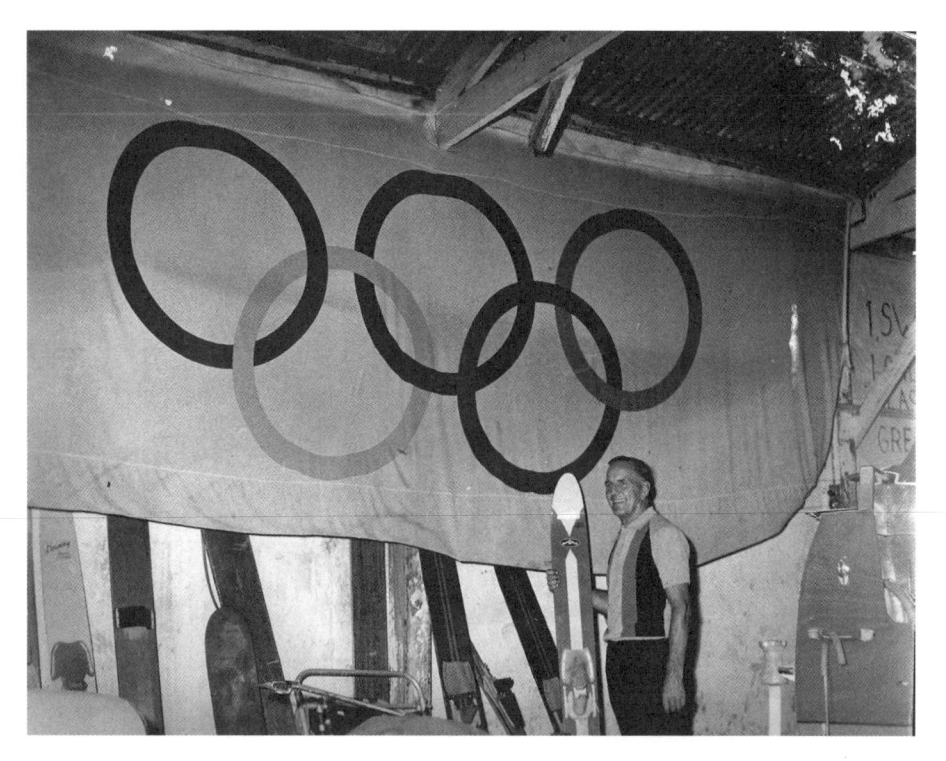

Above: Jack came close to being an Olympian, and he did manage to get a flag.

cutting the flag from the pole. A 20-foot length of white material, decorated with five coloured circles, had fallen over him and he ran, shrouded like a ghost, from the stadium. Jack had thoughtful, if unconventional friends.

Toys and Taxis

Evan continues:

> Just before I arrived, a woman motorist had stopped beside one of the pumps. Ray walked out holding a brightly shining electric lead-light. 'Sorry lady, the power's off,' he announced. Jack was laughing about the incident. 'Giving Ray a roast' was a favourite pastime. There was a rivalry between the brothers, which their friends tried to perpetuate. Sign-written in bold letters on the wall near the Olympic flag was a record of financial losses incurred by Jack and Ray during their leisure hours. On the left was Jack's list. It was compiled beneath the

CHAPTER SIX

heading *Rollem Joe*, a reference to his career as a pioneer stock car driver at the Sydney Showground, where he inverted his vehicle on 27 separate occasions. The list referred to accidents on the road, in the air, and on the water. The entries read: Plymouth £250; Hudson £300; Fiat £200; Ford £200; helicopter £500; Ski 1 (burnt) £250. There was no total, only space for more entries.

Ray's list was much briefer. Beneath the heading *Sinkem Raymond* was printed: One ship sunk £20,000. With only one entry on the wall, Ray was well in front. The item referred to the loss of a luxury cruiser, which Ray was taking from Sydney to Hayman Island for a friend. Ray was not going to be allowed to forget that disastrous voyage. Painted on the already crowded wall were a number of

Above: The impressive tally of cars, boats and an 'aquacopter' Jack had managed to destroy—all eclipsed by Ray's successful sinking of one very expensive pleasure cruiser.

THE GARAGE

Above: The Garage was at times the scene for celebrations, filming of ads, *This Is Your Life* and the launches of various trips and adventures. *Pix* Magazine launch 1967.

Above: During the war years, taxi drivers, mates and friends were often farewelled from The Garage.

CHAPTER SIX

Above: Originally proclaiming 'Murray Bros', today Bondi Garage: No 92 or No 94 Curlewis St, keen supporters in 2014 of the Eastern Suburbs Roosters.

suggested theme songs—*How Deep is the Ocean, Ebb Tide* and *Sand in My Shoes*. As though to cast doubts on his navigational ability, a compass was outlined in whitewash, correct in every detail except that east and west were reversed.

When I visited as a small boy, there was a large, open box situated near the deck chairs at the rear of The Garage. Within it lay dozens if not hundreds of bullets (cartridges, actually) of various calibres. One day I picked a particularly large and menacing cartridge out of the box, examined it and casually lobbed it back where it came from.

Jack jumped a mile and let out an expletive. Not realising it at the time, I had dropped a cartridge and if it had struck the primer of one of the others, I could have initiated a World War II simulation right there in Bondi.

The Garage had the potential to be a very dangerous place for a boy to play around in—particularly one who did not know his explosives, ammunition or guns.

Evan Green in his classic description of The Garage forgot to mention the bullet holes in the bricks in the rear wall, souvenirs from the time the place became a firing range for testing the sights in hunting guns. After almost 80 years of history, Garage stories could fill this whole book. Some at least must be told.

THE GARAGE

No Third Warning

Jack once told me the story of the recidivist taxi driver—though, as you would probably have guessed by now, Jack did not use exactly those words. This particular driver had developed the habit of calling in at The Garage around lunchtime to enjoy the camaraderie and partake of his packed lunch in one of the several deck chairs that passed for a lounge area at the rear of the cavernous building. No doubt keen for his feed, the driver invariably sped through the workshop. Jack had warned him to slow down: it was too dangerous and he was likely to bowl over one of the young mechanics. Jack had in fact warned him twice. 'Gelignite' Jack did not give a third warning.

As 1pm approached, and the arrival of Speedy Gonzales in the fastest taxi in Bondi drew near, tools were laid down in anticipation. All eyes fell upon Jack who, grease gun in hand, was calmly walking around the area where the driver usually parked his vehicle. The greasy floor was now awash with slippery ooze.

Then Jack reclined in his favourite deck chair and waited. He did not have to wait long. The rear wall of The Garage was ancient double brick, which had withstood numerous .303 bullets over the years.

The front of a careening, sliding taxicab hardly marked the flaking paint. The same could not be said of the taxi.

'Oh shit! I'm so sorry mate.' Jack never told me whether the cab was owned by the driver or the brothers. It really didn't matter to Jack. The point was that he never gave a third warning.

Never Ever Park Here

Fairly clear and unambiguous, I would have thought. For many years these were the unequivocal words that were emblazoned across the roller door shutter that separated The Garage from the normal outside world. Curlewis St locals, indeed, everyone in Bondi knew to heed that simple four-word command. Caps, huge font, it read with all the gravitas of the 11th Commandment, not handed down by God but by 'Gelignite' Jack Murray. If ignored, the consequences were likely to be more than serious.

Occasionally a stranger to the area—who else would be so foolish?—would try his luck. Big mistake. The boys would use a pair of trolley jacks and one jacked up the front, the other the rear. The startled owner would return to find his offending vehicle sitting in the middle of the traffic in Curlewis St—with four flat tyres. Beneath the windscreen wiper, a parking infringement notice

CHAPTER SIX

Above: A wall of The Garage showing the Ampol Trial of 1964. The quote from the caricature shows my brother John in the leading Car, No 93 saying to a bearded, ancient Jack in Car No 54: 'Get cracking dad. This is a tow-away area.'

would add to the pain and reinforce the message. Jack enjoyed very good relations with the local constabulary through his many years of support for the Police and Citizens Boys' Club.

Jack versus Bea
When two eccentrics clash, the results are interesting to say the least. Bea Miles was a Sydney identity in the 1950s, 60s and 70s. She could equally be described as a well-read Bohemian rebel or a troublesome ex-mental patient. She was particularly renowned for her contempt for Sydney taxi drivers and her refusal to pay her fare. Nearly all taxi drivers knew Bea by sight, in her tennis shoes, tattered coat and green tennis hat. They refused to pick her up. Stationary at

THE GARAGE

a set of traffic lights, an unsuspecting driver would often turn around to be confronted by a gesticulating Bea ensconced in the back seat demanding to be taken to her destination—free, of course. If drivers forced her out of their cabs she was known to remove doors, jump on the bonnet or provide unwanted dents by bumping against the sides.

One day she made a serious error of judgement, jumping into a cab owned by a couple of brothers from Bondi. The driver promptly delivered Bea to The Garage. She, true to form, refused to alight from the taxi. Jack asked her twice and, as we know, he never asked three times. All four doors were flung open, a large hose was dragged into position and Bea Miles was literally washed out of the cab and out of The Garage. No doubt the passing locals would have been bemused by such antics. The Garage was often a circus, complete with Jack as ringmaster.

Catastrophe

'Gelignite' Jack and his Garage were inseparable all through his life, from the 1930s. Strolling the 50 metres from the entrance to the rear, reading the walls, looking at the cars, passing the trophies and his quirky memorabilia was like walking through his life. When Ray retired in 1970, Jack acquired sole ownership.

Above: The Garage after the fire of 1 May 1981. Devastation— roof completely gone, interior gutted and many cars written off—a lifetime of memories and keepsakes gone in one night.

CHAPTER SIX

He had no intention of retiring; 'we're more or less retired now' he had said many years before. But in the early 1980s Jack was in his 70s and his health problems had increased. It was almost as if The Garage knew. It too was an ageing building.

In the early morning of 1 May 1981, there was a catastrophic fire. Jack lost three cars of his own in it, two of which were uninsured, and twenty other vehicles were also damaged. Jack's comment? 'Well, at least we've got some light in the place now.' It was this ability to smile in the face of adversity that many regarded as my father's most endearing trait.

The Grey Ghost Departs, Survives and Returns

This is a tale of how the Grey Ghost and the Murrays parted company—if only temporarily.

Following the death of Don Whitby, the letter below was forwarded to his family. It explains the circumstances that led to Jack losing possession of the Grey Ghost. Perhaps the old Ford knew something, because her temporary absence meant she survived and was not present for the catastrophic fire of May 1981.

> *May 14 1983*
> Dear Mrs Whitby, and family of Don,
>
> Sadly I just heard of Don's death this last week, when I phoned the Holy Spirit Private Hospital to have a yarn with Don. Maurice Walsh had called to The Garage to tell me that Don had gone to hospital, but as I have been out of town for the past ten days it was not until yesterday that I was able to phone.
>
> My sincere condolences to you and the family.
>
> Don was always a lot of fun, and thinking back to when I gave him the Grey Ghost it seems but yesterday, and when I last saw Don at The Garage in Bondi, he did say that he would return it to me—one day. We joked a little and he told me of his illness, but one doesn't always consider just how ill a person can be, and sadly this year several friends have died of leukaemia.

The Grey Ghost has a lot of memories, and if I can pay for any of the improvements made by Don, let's know and I would be interested to have it back, and perhaps eventually it could be used as a museum piece, as was the original idea. Meantime I could use it and enjoy the fun of driving it once more.

Our original agreement was based on trust and his using the car certainly gave pleasure to many people, especially in the last big car rally. You might say to yourselves 'why give a car to Don?'... but I liked his approach and good humour and when he proposed to give the car a revival to look like the original one in which I won the REDEX, and with the proviso that I had use of it any time when I wanted it, it's been good to know he had these pleasures. We had a lot of fun and good times together.

As you may know, tragedy hit me twice in 1981-82 when I lost my leg, then later when I lost everything in the fire at The Garage—all my cars with little or no insurance. But that's life, and I'm fortunate to still have my health and to be able to drive a car, and the return of the Grey Ghost would really be something at this time of life. When Don was leaving for Queensland he did say he was taking the car, but if anything happened I could drive up and pick it up. As we are all getting older (I'm 75) it seems a good idea to give the old Grey Ghost some new life in memory of Don Whitby.

I look forward to hearing from you, and you can phone me c/- Dorothy Rosewell, reverse charges. Let's know what's what and as I have said I am happy to fly or drive to Queensland to collect the car to drive it back to Sydney.

Very Sincerely,
Jack (Gelignite) Murray

This letter went unanswered. It may or may not have been delivered. In any event, the car was not returned to Jack Murray. At some stage Mrs Whitby stated that 'the car was left to her son in Don's will'.

CHAPTER SIX

A number of years later the Grey Ghost finally returned home when my brother John purchased the car at a Queensland auction. Sadly, Jack did not live to see his car returned to the family.

The Grey Ghost Today

I hope that the Grey Ghost will one day find a permanent home, perhaps alongside the Sundowner Bean within the National Museum of Australia in Canberra. This would offer the greatest opportunity for Australians and others to learn of the Ghost's achievements and about its famous owner. Professionally and appropriately restored to its former 1954 glory, the

Above: 2016. The Grey Ghost is currently stored in a lock-up in Petersham, Sydney. It is occasionally put on display at various motoring events around the country. The Ghost proudly still bears Jack's personalised plates, JM 456, just as it did in 1954. Photo courtesy of Tom Ryan.

Ghost would be a fitting centrepiece of a display telling the 'Gelignite' Jack Murray story.

From the Ashes

Following the devastating fire of 1981, thanks to the project management skills and steadfast determination of Dorothy Rosewell, The Garage was rebuilt. This process took many years and protracted negotiations with an intractable Council that clearly would have preferred a residential development.

In 2016, 'Gelignite' Jack Murray's No 92 or No 94 (take your pick) Curlewis St, Bondi Garage is owned by John and me and operates as a leased mechanical workshop. The bullet holes remain.

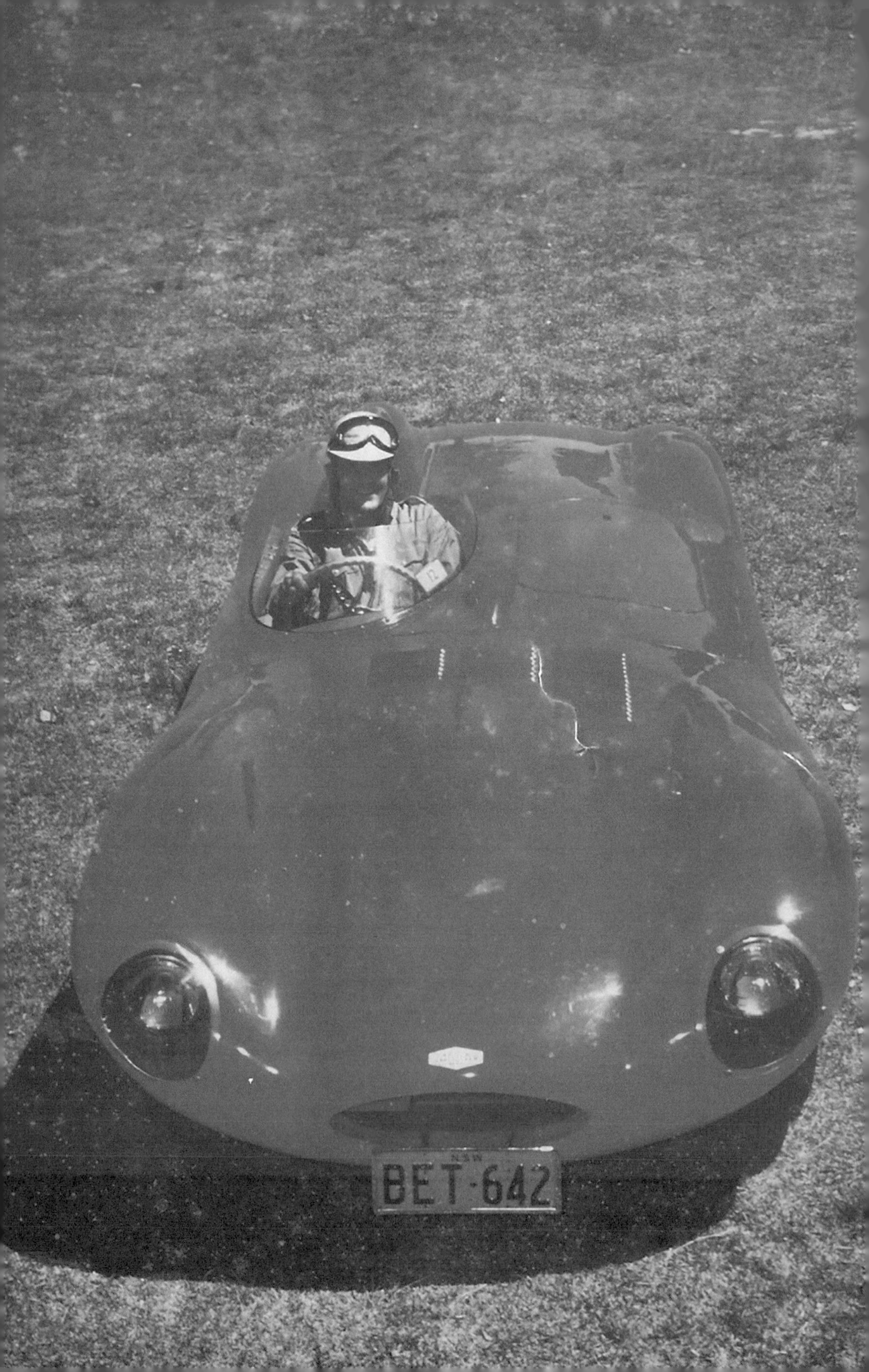
BET-642

CHAPTER SEVEN
THE SWINGING 60S

With the dawn of the swinging 1960s society was about to undergo a revolution, and so was motorsport. Bathurst Mount Panorama was held Monday 18 April 1960, with a total entry of over 120, many of the entrants in the rapidly expanding sports, sedan and grand touring fields. Jack drove his successful and competitive D-Type Jaguar.

In Event 4, Sports Car Scratch over six laps, there were 42 entries and Jack in Car No 76 came third. His fastest lap was 3:01.0 and over the timed quarter mile, 150 mph (240 km/h).

In the final event, Sports Car Scratch over ten laps, with 39 entries, he also placed third in a time of 30:59.33.

Brabham Comes of Age

The October 1960 Bathurst Mount Panorama meeting took place on Saturday 1 October and the following Sunday. Jack Brabham was coming into his own and the world champion dominated the entries, reappearing at Bathurst for the first time since 1954. In winning the Craven A International Race, he set a new lap record.

From 11am to 2.30pm on the Saturday was reserved for practice, with three races to follow, then a full day's racing on Sunday, followed by another meeting at Orange's Gnoo Blas circuit on the Monday. A busy weekend indeed.

Left: Jack's silver D-Type Jaguar from Bathurst was later resprayed red, his favourite race car colour.

CHAPTER SEVEN

In the second qualifying heat for sports cars over three laps, Jack was positioned third on grid (i.e. front row). The 1960 NSW Sports Car Championship over thirteen laps was merely a matter of finding out how far Matich would be in front.

In Event 4, Second Qualifying Heat for Sports Cars, there were fourteen entries. Jack came third in his Jaguar.

In Event 3, 1960 NSW Sports Car Championship over thirteen laps, there were 40 entries, and Jack placed fifth.

Murray Crash Confusion

In *Historic Racing Cars in Australia*, John Blanden's 1979 book, in connection with another D-Type Jaguar Chassis No XKD520 (not Jack's), he writes:

> The car was seriously damaged in late June 1957 when it crashed into the rear of a timber truck while being driven by Davey's [Jack Davey, radio and television personality] close friend, the highly regarded racing driver, Jack Murray. The car was an insurance write-off. Murray was seriously injured and required a long recuperation, which still left him with health problems.

When we read this story, neither Dorothy Rosewell nor I had heard of this incident. I never saw Jack suffer from any health issues related to a car crash. Despite numerous crashes, boat explosions and plunging from flying contraptions of various sorts, my father led a charmed life in terms of injuries. He was never seriously hurt.

I cannot confirm the story of the June 1957 crash. An online search of the Jaguar Registry of XKD520 suggests that *Bill* Murray was in fact the driver.

The Armstrong 500 1960

In these years, sedan racing was growing in popularity. The 1960 Armstrong 500 was held on 20 November 1960. This event was an endurance motor race for Australian-made or assembled standard production sedans. It was held at the Phillip Island Grand Prix Circuit in Victoria over a distance of 167 laps (501 miles).

This was the first ever event of the race later to be known as the Bathurst 1000. It would come to dominate Australian motorsport. Jim Thompson, managing director of shock absorber manufacturer Armstrong York Engineering, was encouraged by his PR man Ron Thonemann to increase its business with major carmakers, particularly Ford and Holden, by sponsoring it.

Class B was for cars with an engine capacity of between 751 cc and 1300 cc. This class featured Ford Anglia, Renault Dauphine, Simca Aronde, Triumph Herald and Volkswagen Beetle. Jack drove with W.H. (Bill) Murison and V.T. (Vern) Curtin in Car No 21, a Simca Aronde, placing: DNF or Did Not Finish, meaning it dropped out.

Above: The 1960 Armstrong 500 in which the Simca did not last the distance. (Autopics 60705)

Below: Clearly there were some major mechanical issues requiring the other 'jack'. (Autopics 60758, photo: Peter D'Abbs)

CHAPTER SEVEN

Bathurst 1961

As in the 1950s, both circuit racing and trials featured in Jack's motorsport career throughout the 1960s.

The 1961 Easter Bathurst meet took place Sunday 2 April and Monday 3 April 1961.

Practice on the Sunday concluded at 2.30pm, with four races programmed for that afternoon. Rather than one all-day race, as happens now at the October Bathurst races, this was a time of multiple shorter races.

In Event 3, Sports Car Scratch Over 1500 cc, three laps, Jack in Car No 76 came third. His fastest lap was clocked 3:05.6.

In the Sports Car record fastest lap, Matich in the Lotus clocked 2:40.1, and Jack was second.

In the main event, Sports Cars over ten laps, with 24 entries, Jack was fifth in his Jaguar D-Type.

It is difficult to compare driver abilities and car capacities over the years and in very different eras. So many factors come into play. In his 1997 book *Bathurst, Cradle of Australian Motor Sport*, John Medley took race times from various years and converted them, perhaps a little unrealistically as he concedes, into 100-mile times. In other words, for each year he identified which driver would be the fastest over the 100-mile journey. He then lists those times from 1940 to 1969. In 1946 Jack Murray is credited with the fastest time of 86 mins 24 secs for a 100-mile journey. Jack achieved this time behind the wheel of the Mackellar Special in the NSW Grand Prix over 25 laps (100 miles) on 7 October 1946. He placed fifth on handicap.

The Queen's Birthday Weekend, 10-12 June 1961, saw the Australian Sporting Car Club's annual event, the Southern Mountains Trial. Sponsored by TCN Channel 9, the event covered 1250 miles of treacherous mountain roads, often in rain and mist. The 'other Jack Murray', Minto, competed in a 1939 Chev and Jack himself competed in a Simca with B. McNabb; he came fifth. (*Racing Car News*, July 1961)

In July-August 1963 the Castrol 500 was held. This event was the MG Car Club's contribution to the NSW Senior Trials series, and twenty starters left from Ryde. Despite snow, rain and fog, fifteen cars managed to finish. Jack drove with R. Wilcock in an Elite for a fourth with 61 pts lost. (*Racing Car News*, September 1963)

The Anniversary Runs

The first of the Anniversary Runs was on 30 August 1963, exactly ten years after the first REDEX. It also happened to be Jack's 56th birthday. Jack (as the second trial winner in 1954) and Ken Tubman (the first in 1953) left Sydney Showground at 2pm. The boys were joined by a crew from *Modern Motor* magazine which included Evan Green, Scott Polkinghorne and Jules Feldman. Dr Phillida Sampson, a rally driver from England, was also part of the crew. They travelled in a Wolseley. *Modern Motor* had decided to re-enact the complete trial over the 6500-mile route. BMC supplied vehicles, a Morris 850 and a Wolseley 24/80 automatic, and Shell supplied fuel and lubricants. 'Baby' cars had not been considered capable of completing the route ten years earlier. This run included out-of-the-way places such as Arnhem Land, Ayers Rock (Uluru) and the Snowy Mountains. (*Modern Motor*, November 1963)

As sedans began to rule on the mountain, the 1963 Armstrong 500 was held

Below: Jack 'doing donuts' near Uluru. Today this would be banned.

CHAPTER SEVEN

at Bathurst Mount Panorama on 6 October 1963.

In Class B, Car No 33, Jack and Alan Edney in a Morris Elite completed 113 laps and placed fifteenth. Class B, the £901 to £1000 class, featured 1.5 litre Ford Cortina, Morris Cooper and Elite, Renault R8 and Simca Aronde.

Jack's Watch Trick

At the end of 1963, Jack took part in an advertising event designed to promote BMC vehicles. He and Evan Green were part of a larger team challenged to drive one of the new Morris 1100s for 1000 miles a day—every day for a month.

Jack and Evan travelled together, one driving while the other rested on the back seat. One of their stints involved driving nonstop from Sydney to Perth, north to Carnarvon, down to the south western corner of the continent, back up to Perth and then east across the Nullarbor to Sydney. They covered more than 6750 miles (10,863 km) and were away five and a half days. The run from Perth to Sydney took two hours less than two days. In all, the car was out for 28 days and covered more than 30,000 miles. This is where Jack invented his 'watch trick' as he told Neil Bennetts in his National Library interview:

BENNETTS: Now, your watch system?

MURRAY: Oh, the watch system, oh yes. The joke was, Evan and I, when we were driving together, we'd have three hours on and three off. And I'd say 'Oh yes,' and I'd have three hours and Evan would wake me up and I'd drive for three. He'd sleep for three and I'd drive for three, then I'd wake him up. After a while, I'd sleep for three, and I let him have about an hour. Then I'd wake him up again—and he never checked the time.

I sneaked two hours off him. In the end, he was really getting tired, because I'd cheated him out of about six hours. So this time he woke up and he was driving along. I didn't want to sleep, and he said, 'How many breaks have we had?' I knew what was coming. I said, 'Three'. He said, 'Three, well, we're driving three hours, three on and three off. It would have to be nine o'clock in the daytime. Are you sure I'm getting my full issue?' I said, 'No, I've been touching you two hours every break.' He said, 'Why—instead of having nine hours, I've had three?' I said, 'Yes, that's right.'

He's never forgiven me for that. He said, 'I never ever thought to look at my watch. I was taking your time. But I've learnt something else. Keep your own watch and hang it up on the dashboard where they can all see it.'

Evan Green was once quoted as saying, 'Behind the wheel, Jack could go and keep on going, safely and steadily for a long time.' Evan learned that to be true—but you also had to keep your own eye on the watch.

The Canberra 500

The Canberra 500, the Canberra Sporting Car Club's contribution to the Senior Trials series took place in March-April 1964 on roads between Canberra and Yass. Peugeot had decided to use The 500 as a shakedown for their cars and crews to be used in the more prestigious Ampol Trial later in the year.

Racing Car News, May 1964, reported that Peugeot had a team of three cars, the third handled by 'veteran Jack Murray with Roy Denny guiding him'. They came fifth in their Peugeot 404, with 125 pts lost.

Above: Jack and Roy Denny climbing up the winding road from the Murrumbidgee River ford in the Canberra 500.

CHAPTER SEVEN

At age 56, Jack now earned the moniker 'veteran' to go with 'Gelignite'.

Jack and Roy teamed up again for the Hardiebestos 500, part of the 1964 Senior Trial series, held March–April 1964. They came second. These events were all practice and preparation for the 1964 Ampol Round Australia Trial.

'Gelignite' and 'Cracker' Jacks

The 1964 Ampol Round Australia Trial, covering 7500 miles, attracted 200 entrants. It commenced on 14 June 1964 and ran for two weeks. This was an important trial for a number of reasons, not least of which was that 56-year-old 'Gelignite' Jack Murray would face some very special competition—namely his twenty-year-old son John, under the moniker 'Cracker Jack'. John had 'Jack Murray Jnr' written on the side of his car, and his mate Peter Barnes was the navigator.

John and Peter were young and pretty much novices at long distance trials. Neither had been in an event of this length before. In preparation for the event, the boys had entered others such as the North Shore Car Trial over 300 miles in the Sydney, Gosford and Newcastle area. In total, John and Peter together entered twelve car trials, one each weekend. My brother was no stranger to competition, having been a former placegetter in state VJ sailing championships. But 7500 miles of Australia's roughest roads would test the most seasoned trial driver and navigator.

Above: Peter Barnes washing the 'Cracker' Jack Valiant used in the 1964 Ampol Trial. (Autopics 64982, photo: Ian Thorn)

It was almost six years since 'Gelignite' Jack's last big trial, the Ampol, in 1958. The results were interesting, to say the least.

'Cracker' Jack Murray, driving a lime green Valiant sponsored by Milo lost 262 points and placed thirty-third. 'Gelignite' Jack in Car No 54C with Roy Denny as navigator placed fortieth in a Peugeot 404 Plate HYT 276, with the loss of 333 pts. The junior apprentice had 'done' the senior master!

The engines were hardly cool before the boys at The Garage called their sign-writer mate to record the momentous win by 'Cracker' Jack.

Evan 'Bluebird' Green, in addition to being a journalist, author and prolific writer, also participated in the organisation and administration of rally events. He had acquired the nickname 'Bluebird' when he project managed Donald Campbell's attempt at the land speed record on Lake Eyre in 1964. Donald Campbell and his father Sir Malcolm Campbell remain the only people to have set both land and water speed records. Donald Campbell died in 1967, trying to break the water speed record yet again. Jack had met Sir Malcolm Campbell during his 1937 world trip.

As Vice President of the Australian Sporting Car Club, Evan brilliantly directed the Bridgestone-Antill Trial, held on 15 August 1964. The trial covered a distance of 530 miles, and was part of the 1964 Senior Series conducted around Gosford, Maitland, Dungog and Stroud. Jack had direction issues, but as reported in *Racing Car News*, September 1964, he did earn the thanks of some other competitors: 'This error [navigation] cost Jack Murray any chance he may have had ... it was here that Jack Murray proved himself the complete sportsman when he retired to tow Gerry [Crown] home.'

Senior Trials Championships 1964

Jack and his good friend and navigator Dave Johnson competed together in the Senior Rallying Championships throughout 1964. The Simca 12/12 Mountain Rally was held 22 August 1964 but Jack, driving a Peugeot 404, was unplaced. The following month, September 1964, yielded a better result. The Thornleigh 500 was run by the Thornleigh Car Club as part of the Senior Championships, attracting 43 teams for the 500-mile run. Jack and Dave placed third with 62 pts lost. (*Racing Car News,* November 1964)

The Southern Mountains 700 was run by the ASCC at the end of October 1964 as the climax of the seven-event NSW Senior Trials series. Jack and Dave again came third, with 107 pts lost.

CHAPTER SEVEN

This meant that the overall Senior Trials Championship results for 1964 were: Drivers: Second Jack Murray; Navigators: First Dave Johnson. An impressive Barry Ferguson, as driver, won the title for the fourth consecutive year.

Trials and Tribulations

Jack focused on trial driving in 1964-65 between Bathurst events at Easter and in October. He was never one to let the wheels stop turning or the engine cool down for very long.

March 1965 saw the Canberra 500 run, Round 1 of the 1965 NSW Trials Championships and was organised by the Canberra Sporting Car Club. The many state-based motoring clubs were the backbone of motorsport during this period, providing organisation and staffing for many trials. The route was mainly west of the ACT, and was designed as a reliability trial, demanding three-point reliability of car, driver and navigator. In their Peugeot 404, Jack and Dave came eighth, with 141 pts lost.

The 1965 BP Rally, a five-day event covering 2000 miles throughout Victoria, was Jack's ideal motorsport event—providing challenging driving conditions, a win and a chance for a lot of fun. Jack and Dave won Class C with 185 pts lost.

As *Racing Car News*, June 1965, reported:

> 'Gelignite' Jack Murray gave others a hand lighting several double-bunger crackers. The bang of one, dropped behind a radio reporter taping an interview with a driver, was replayed the following day in the interview on the local radio station.

Saturday 12 June 1965 saw the running of the Rothmans Southern Mountains Car Trial, attracting 25 starters over 1000 miles. It was organised by the ASCC and directed by Bob Selby-Wood [Jack's sometime navigator]. The trial commenced in Canberra.

According to *Racing Car News*, July 1965, Jack was well up to his usual form, as was Dave Johnson. Their passage through the field was uneventful and they were doing well. But in the true sporting fashion for which Jack is renowned, they took time out to assist other cars which were in difficulties, such as Bob Holden's Skyline and Brown's Cooper S. 'The rub came when they struck trouble themselves with a broken engine mount and there was nothing anyone could do in return.'

Comments such as the above, from both rivals and journalists, give an interesting insight into my father. Certainly Jack was competitive and liked to win, but it was always about the fun and there was always an overall feeling of camaraderie amongst the competitors, united against the course and sometimes the officials.

Another month, another trial. Jack and Bob Selby-Wood driving their Peugeot 404 managed to win the 1501 cc to 2500 cc Class of the KLG 300, which was held 24-25 July 1965. The event, always exacting for the poor navigators, attracted 212 entries.

The Antill Trophy Trial 1965

On 7 August 1965 the Antill Trophy Trial was contested, over 660 miles, with 24 starters. It began at Gosford and the winner was Barry Ferguson for the third time running. This meant that he was able to keep the trophy he was making a habit of winning. 'It was bad luck for Jack Murray/Selby-Wood in the many-miled Peugeot 404. They broke a clutch rod in the second section and went home,' wrote *Racing Car News,* September 1965.

It was just such a breakdown and an early return home that gave rise to yet another 'Gelignite' Jack story. Bob Selby-Wood related it in his unpublished book *We Build Utzon's Dream* and his son confirmed it. His father was the Sydney Opera House Project Superintendent, in charge of the entire construction from 1961 to 1970:

> After breaking down in a rally, Jack and Bob managed to limp their Pug [Peugeot] back to the Sydney Opera House where Bob had parked his Mini Cooper prior to Jack picking him up for the Trial. It was still dark, around 4am, when they got back there and Bob offered to take Jack up to the top of the biggest shell [known as A2] to give Jack a guided tour.
>
> Jack, of course, always knocked the Opera House during its construction and said that 'no silly bastard would go and see a bloody opera' and that 'it was a complete waste of money'. Bob, on the other hand, was of course of the opposite opinion. So off they went in the dark, climbing ladders to get to the very tip of the arch. By the time they got up there it was breaking daylight on a perfect Sydney Harbour morning and Bob, having not only the love of the building

but also being a direct descendant of a First Fleeter, was standing on the tip and facing the Harbour. He said with great passion,

'Look Murray, you will never get a better view of the greatest harbour in the world than this', waving his hands, acclaiming the view.

Bob then heard the tinkle of water running behind him. As he turned, he saw Jack peeing from the shell. Jack said, as only 'Gelignite' Jack would, 'If people ask me have I seen the Sydney Opera House, I'll say to them: "Seen it? I've pissed on the place".'

Piddler on the Roof is what Bob called this tale.

The Armstrong 500 1965

As October approached, another Bathurst loomed—and it would prove to be a very successful one for Jack.

It was held on 3 October 1965 at Bathurst Mount Panorama. This was the sixth running of the Bathurst 500 touring car race. Jack competed with his rally and travelling friend, Bill McLachlan. Jack and Bill were jokingly referred to as 'the two old gentlemen in their wheelchairs' by the younger brigade of drivers. But when the results were posted, they fell silent. Jack and Bill McLachlan in Car No 12, their Ford Cortina Mk 1 GT500, came fifth in Overall Position

Above: Bathurst October 1965, with Bill McLachlan at the wheel of the Cortina. (Autopics 65740, photo: Lance J. Ruting.)

and third in Class D, having completed 128 laps.

The £1301 to £2000 class featured the first of what came to be known as the Bathurst Specials, the Ford Cortina GT500 named for the race. The class also contained Fiat 2300, Humber Vogue, Studebaker Lark, Triumph 2000 and Volvo 122.

It had been nineteen years since Jack first began racing at Bathurst.

Crossroads Alice

'Gelignite' Jack enjoyed testing motor vehicles and oils, as well as travel—any opportunity or excuse where a group of mates could get together and set off on an adventure of some kind. As long as they were behind the wheel, where they were going or why really did not matter to my father. He and Evan Green frequently paired up to share the fun.

During November and December 1965 the duo undertook just such an

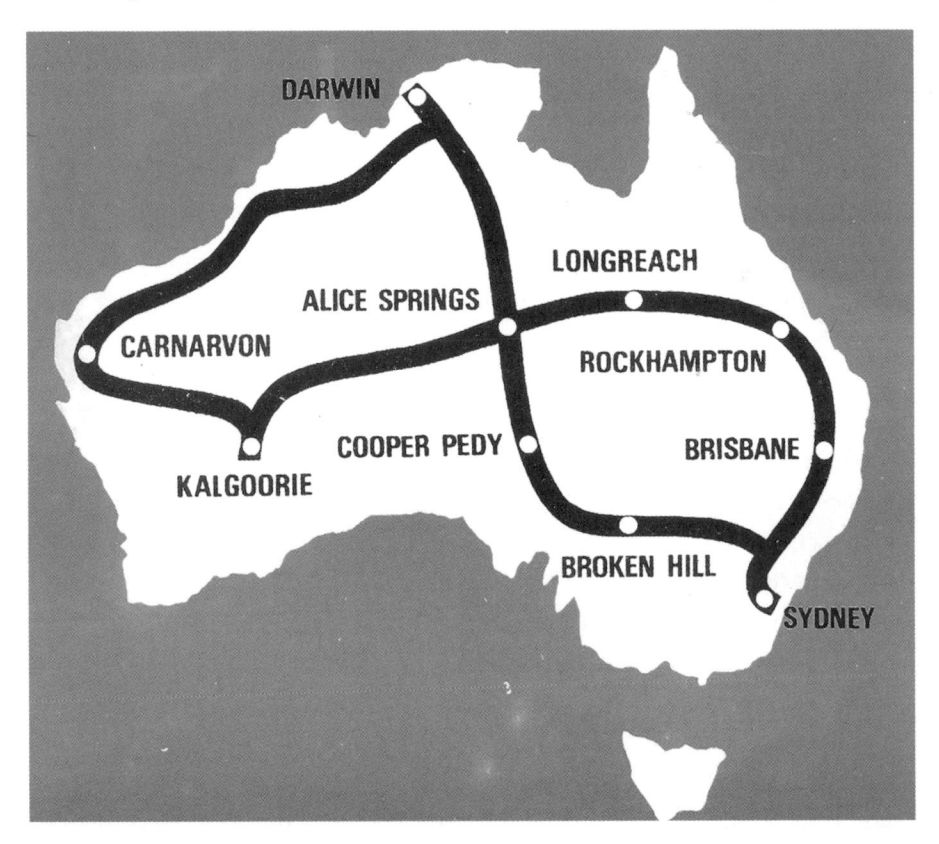

Above: The route crossed some of Australia's most barren deserts.

adventure, one that became the documentary film *Crossroads Alice*. The trip was designed as a test of BMC (Austin 1800 DYL 090 and a Morris Mini Deluxe) cars and Castrol oil. The vehicles completed a 12,000-mile (19,312 km) Figure 8 crossing of the Australian continent.

It was not all fun since Jack was quite ill for part of the trip, possibly due to sunstroke. Over the years he competed in seven round Australia trials and many adventure trips testing cars, lubricants and drivers.

Evan Green always laughed when he recalled *Crossroads Alice*. It gave him one of his favourite 'Gelignite' stories. As we shall learn later, on this particular expedition Jack was prepared to sacrifice all, even his leopard skin underpants.

NSW Trials Championship 1966

The 1966 NSW Trials Championship of ten rounds kicked off on 5 February. The 300-mile event was sponsored by Neptune [a petrol supplier of the 1960s] and organised by the Renault Car Club. The event was described as 'basically a navigator's trial with one good driver's section'. Skylines were crewed by Kennedy/Mewburn and Murray/Johnstone [*sic:* actually Johnson].

Jack and Dave in the Skyline GT came seventh.

BP Rally of Southeast Australia 1966

This was held April-May. The field of 37 entries read like a who's who of car trials in Australia. Nathalia, near Echuca in Victoria, was the gathering point for starters and a 1500-mile trial stage commenced at Albury. The event was hampered by fog, rain, dust and mud. The BP event was 'the biggest challenge any navigator can face,' according to *Racing Car News*, June 1966.

Jack and Dave Johnson came third in Class C (1501-2000 cc) in their Skyline with 393 pts lost.

The Gallaher 500 1966

On 2 October 1966 the Gallaher 500 was run at Bathurst Mount Panorama. The year 1966 marked a twenty-year span for Jack in his racing at Bathurst. The Gallaher was an endurance motor race for production cars and was the seventh running of the Bathurst 500.

It was the first time that the event had been staged under the Gallaher 500 name, [indicating sponsorship by a tobacco company]. The event was described as 'Australia's Blue Ribbon Production Saloon Car Classic'. The race rules required that 250 examples of a particular model had to be registered for a vehicle to be eligible for the race. This number had been extended from the 100 examples required in previous years.

In Class B Car No 39, Jack and Bill Ford in a Prince Skyline were sponsored by Wheelmar Distributors Pty Ltd. However, the motorsport gods were unkind this particular Bathurst, and they did not finish. Class B ($1801 to $2040) featured 1.5 litre Ford Cortina, Hillman Minx, Isuzu Bellett, Morris Cooper, Prince Skyline, Renault R8 and Toyota Corona.

The Southern Cross Rally 1966

October 1966 saw a very important event for Australian motorsport, particularly in Australian rallying history. The inaugural Southern Cross Rally, directed by Bob Selby-Wood, brought classic international rallying to Australia. It attracted 69 starters, including European stars Paddy Hopkirk and Rauno Aaltonen. The 4000 kilometre, four-day event ran from Sydney to Melbourne and return.

Jack, driving a Prince Skyline GT, Car No 33, started the rally at Roselands Shopping Centre in typical 'Gelignite' fashion: wearing a wolf's head mask and detonating a smoke bomb. After taking the lead on the second night and setting a cracking pace, Barry Ferguson and Tony Denham in a Volkswagen hit a tree only 360 kilometres from home. Victory went to Harry Firth and Graham Hoinville in a Ford Cortina GT. Placings went to Greg Garard and Frank Goulburn (Holden) and Ian Vaughan and Roger Vaughan (Cortina GT).

Unfortunately for Jack, the

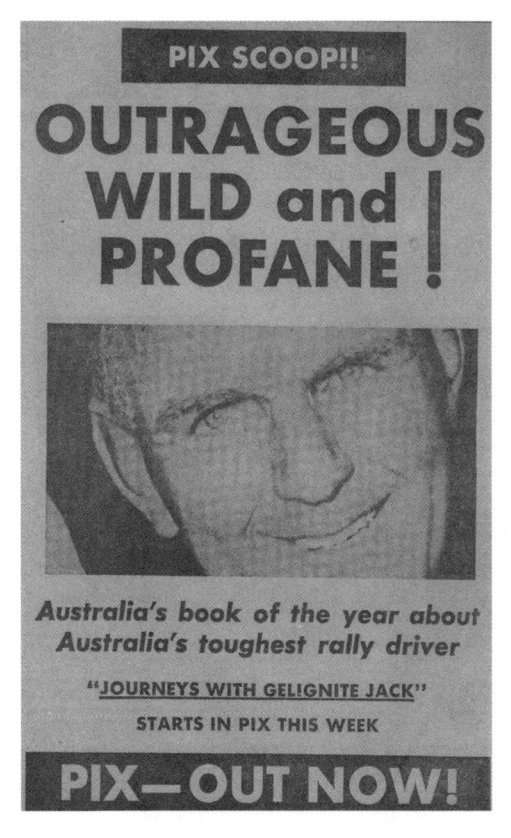

Above: *Pix* magazine serialised Evan Green's book over three weeks.

CHAPTER SEVEN

Above: Smiling and having fun: BP rally, circa 1967. Jack was by then 60. (Autopics 65918, photo: Harry Cape)

Skyline GT let the boys down and Jack posted a DNF.

With the publication in 1966 of Evan Green's *Journeys with Gelignite Jack*, Jack's fame and iconic status, and the affection many Australians felt for him, were celebrated. In early 1967 Evan's work was also published as a series in *PIX* magazine, gaining an even bigger audience.

In the 1960s, Jack's appearances at Bathurst were interspersed with trials and adventures. He competed in a Simca in a BP Rally in the mid-60s, probably the tenth BP Rally of 1967, in which 36 entrants left simultaneously from three capital cities. The event covered 1400 miles in three days.

Jack's Bathurst Record

The 1967 Gallaher 500 was held at Bathurst Mount Panorama on 1 October 1967. Although he probably didn't realise it at the time, this would prove to be a poignant Bathurst meet for Jack—his last race on the Mount Panorama circuit.

The year 1967 marked a 21-year career span for Jack racing at Bathurst. He had raced the Mackellar Special, the Day Special, two Cadillac-Allards, a D-Type Jaguar and sedans such as a Ford Pilot, Ford Cortina GT, Morris Elite and Prince Skyline.

In 1946, he had placed fifth in the NSW Grand Prix and recorded fastest overall time for the handicap race. With Frank Kleinig, he held the lap record. In 1950 Jack won an event recording the fastest lap time, reaching 119 mph (192 km/h) down Conrod Straight. In 1952, driving the Cadillac-Allard J2, Jack placed a credible fourth in the seventeenth Australian Grand Prix.

Throughout his 21 years of driving at Bathurst, Jack achieved many scratch, handicap or class placings: first (1), second (2), third (7), fourth (6), fifth (4), sixth (1), seventh (1), ninth (1), thirteenth (1), fifteenth (1) and thirty-fourth (1). Of course, race cars being race cars, there were a few DNFs and DNSs.

In 1960, in his D-Type Jaguar, he was clocked at 150 mph (240 km/h) down Conrod Straight.

In 1965, almost 20 years after first racing at Bathurst, the 'old men in wheelchairs' Jack (58) and Bill McLachlan (48) had placed fifth overall and third in class driving a Ford Cortina Mk 1 GT 500. The younger brigade took note.

The year 1967 saw the eighth running of the Bathurst 500 production car race. Cars competed in five classes based on purchase price (Australian dollars)

Above: Carl Kennedy and Jack in the Prince Skyline, Car 31C, Bathurst 1967. (Autopics 67730)

of the vehicle. In a seminal moment for the race, the first Australian-built V8 muscle cars appeared in the form of the first Ford Falcon GT.

In Class C, the $2101-$3000 class was dominated by the Morris Cooper S, but also contained Fiat 124 and 850, an automatic gearbox Ford Falcon, Holden HD X2 and Prince Skyline.

Car No 31, a Prince Skyline GT, with Jack and Carl Kennedy behind the wheel qualified in thirty-ninth position. On race day they improved, placing thirty-fourth overall and thirteenth in Class C, having completed 113 laps.

The Cross 1967

From 4-8 October 1967, Jack competed in the Cross driving a Prince Skyline adorned with his personalised plates, JM 789. In only the second time the event had been run, the Cross was rapidly developing a reputation as a major international meet. From 1966 to 1980, the rally attracted many of the world's leading rally drivers and factory teams.

Above: Jack driving, with an unknown front passenger, and rear passenger Brian 'Ginger' McEwen. (Autopics 67803, photo: Lance J. Ruting)

Car versus Plane

In early 1968, as Jack and Evan Green were preparing to compete in the London to Sydney marathon later that year, the question was: 'How could two rally tested veterans best prepare for days and nights of endless driving?' Clearly, the answer was: 'Spend days and nights endlessly driving. But why not make it interesting, and race a plane as well?' Another adventure lay ahead.

At noon on Friday 26 April 1968, Jack and Evan set off from Essendon Airport, Melbourne, to race a Morris 1100 cc 'S' against a light plane around Australia. The boys drove day and night, living in the car, and managed to circumnavigate the continent in eight days and six hours, covering around 10,000 miles (16,000 km). That was an incredible 197 hours and 40 minutes to complete a drive most of us would spend a year undertaking.

The details are a testament to both Jack's and Evan's endurance and ability to spend many hours behind the wheel. The tachograph showed 192 hours 45 minutes, which included 22 hours 15 minutes of breaks (12 per cent of time), covering 9682 miles (15,581 km) with an average speed of 91 km/h (if taken on actual driving time) or 80 km/h on average overall. Top speed between Norseman and Carnarvon reached 82 mph (132 km/h).

The light plane was restricted to flying during the day only—and to add interest and a 'battle of the sexes' component to the race, the plane was piloted by 22-year-old Anne Carter and Margaret Kelly. The plane was restricted to eight hours a day as neither pilot was licensed to fly at night. The car crossed the finish line in Melbourne only eight hours after the plane.

Jack and Evan were now confident they could tackle the challenges ahead in the London to Sydney race.

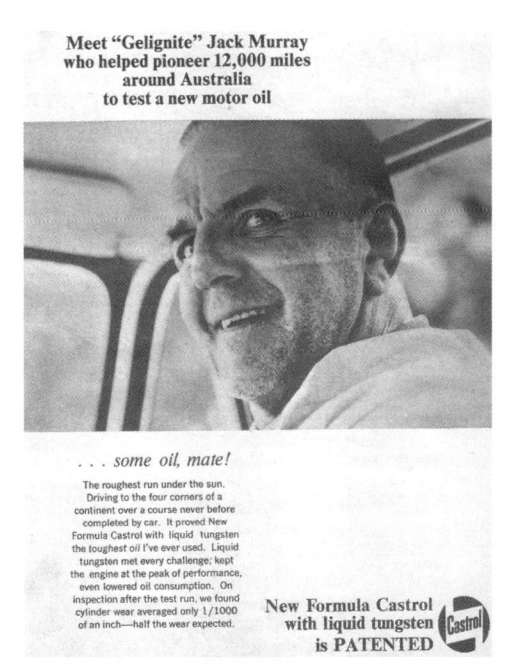

Above: Car and oil companies sold their products having been 'Gelignite' tested.

CHAPTER SEVEN

Above: Evan Green and Jack after their drive round Australia.

The London to Sydney Marathon 1968

The first London to Sydney Marathon left Battersea Park, London on Sunday 24 November 1968, with all 100 competitors planning to arrive at Warwick Farm, Sydney 23 days later, on 17 December 1968. Just over half, 56, would last the full journey.

Competitors travelled through eleven countries, from London to France, Italy, Yugoslavia, Bulgaria, Turkey, Iran, Afghanistan, Pakistan and India, then across Australia to Sydney. There was a nonstop nature to the event, with competitors eating and sleeping in their cars. There were even plans for tourists to join a Jack Murray Barrackers' Bandwagon, with Jack's mate and motor magazine editor Max Stahl as tour guide. A brochure had even been printed, but since Stahl was offered a late berth in a Mercedes, the tour didn't go ahead.

Jack and Evan were running eighth out of 72 when they arrived in Perth on the *Chusan*. After giving dire warnings to all the overseas drivers about the fearful Australian wildlife, ironically it was Jack who was the first to hit a kangaroo, just outside Perth.

As they raced across the Nullarbor and into South Australia, Murray's and Green's Car No 31 was the race leader in the Flinders Ranges stage. Then tragedy struck, as they ran fifth, only 36 hours from the finish line. An enthusiastic service mechanic over-tightened a wheel bearing, and the hub collapsed near Curnamona, South Australia. Evan commented at the time, 'But for losing a wheel, Jack Murray, George Shepheard [veteran Australian driver] and I might have won.'

The damage could not be fixed, and so the crew of Car No 31 wrote a HELP message in insulating tape on the sand. Knowing their chances of winning the Marathon were over, they stripped naked and basked in the sun, Murray and Shepheard cavorting around the car like hairy nymphs. A non-competing friend, Stewart McLeod, drove up to offer help. Too late the nymphs realised Mrs McLeod was in the car too.

Parts supplied and repairs finally completed Jack's, Evan's and George's Austin 1800 limped across the finish line in twenty-first place.

Someone working for the government's Road Safety Council in 1969 had a sense of humour. Under the headline *Drivers Push Road Safety*, Max Stahl wrote in *Racing Car News* in March 1969:

Above: London to Sydney Marathon, London start. Evan, Jack and Australia's very own Miss World, Penny Plummer.

CHAPTER SEVEN

Top 20 drivers will make appearances at the Royal Easter Show to talk of their experiences, particularly with regards seat belts and tips for young drivers. 'Gelignite' Jack Murray and Evan Green are amongst this select group of drivers. This is due to a liaison between the Road Safety Council of NSW and CAMS.

Again in 1970, Jack featured in a neat little road safety advertisement advising motorists to share the road. There is no mention of encouragement to do so by the use of gelignite. (See YouTube: 'Jack Murray road safety video 1970').

Papuan Safari 1969

Both Jack and Evan, competing in separate vehicles, ventured overseas in September 1969 to compete in the Papuan Safari. This rugged event, organised by the South Pacific Motor Sports Club, covered 800 miles in three days. 'Evan Green and Roy Denny (Austin 1800) and 'Gelignite' Jack Murray (Morris 1100 S) came eleventh and thirteenth after trouble with some of the exceedingly nasty rock outcrops, which had no regard for sump guards,' wrote *Racing Car News*, October 1969.

Above: The winners, Andrew Cowan, a 32-year-old Scottish rally driver, Colin Malkin and Brian Coyle, driving a Hillman Hunter. Andrew Cowan's skill and talent would see him go on to win the second London to Sydney Marathon in 1977.

THE SWINGING 60S

Alice Springs to Darwin Reliability Run

Jack finished off the 1960s doing what he loved to do best—sitting behind the wheel of a car with mates and driving it hard till the car or the men broke. Late in 1969 he was part of a team that drove a Morris 1500 from Alice Springs to Darwin, and then Darwin back to Alice Springs, over and over and over again. As a motoring journalist commented at the time:

> One thing you can say in favour of British Leyland executives is that they have confidence in their product. This was amply demonstrated when they recently sent forth a Morris 1500 to complete 15,000 non-stop miles in ten days (24,104 km)—equivalent to one year's normal motoring, they reckoned, in the space of the average vacation.
>
> The team of drivers for the venture was headed by BMC's urbane and skilful public relations boss and rally driver Evan Green, with support from his old sparring partner Jack Murray, broadcaster John Pearce, Ian and Leo Geoghegan, Darwin BLMC dealer Mick Nudi, BLMC service man Alan Kemp, Green's regular navigator Roy Denny, and *Modern Motor's* Technical Editor Barry Cooke. They rested the drivers, but not the car.

The run was to take the form of sixteen uninterrupted journeys up and down the Stuart Highway between Alice Springs and Darwin, with two men crewing the car, changing over at the end of each trip.

The whole enterprise got off to a bad start when the car fell off the trailer bearing it over the appalling road between Port Augusta and the starting point at Alice Springs. Fortunately, there was no serious damage. There was fairly keen competition between crews for the fastest run over the 954-mile (1535 km) journey and this finally fell to local Mick Nudi and Roy Denny: an astonishing 11 hours 45 minutes, or 81 mph average (130 km/h). The schedule allowed for a 63 mph average, but as trouble beset the car, time was lost irretrievably. At the end of the trip the average was just over 60 mph.

So the 1960s ended for 'Gelignite' Jack somewhere between Alice Springs and Darwin, amidst outback dust, good mates and a lot of (s)miles.

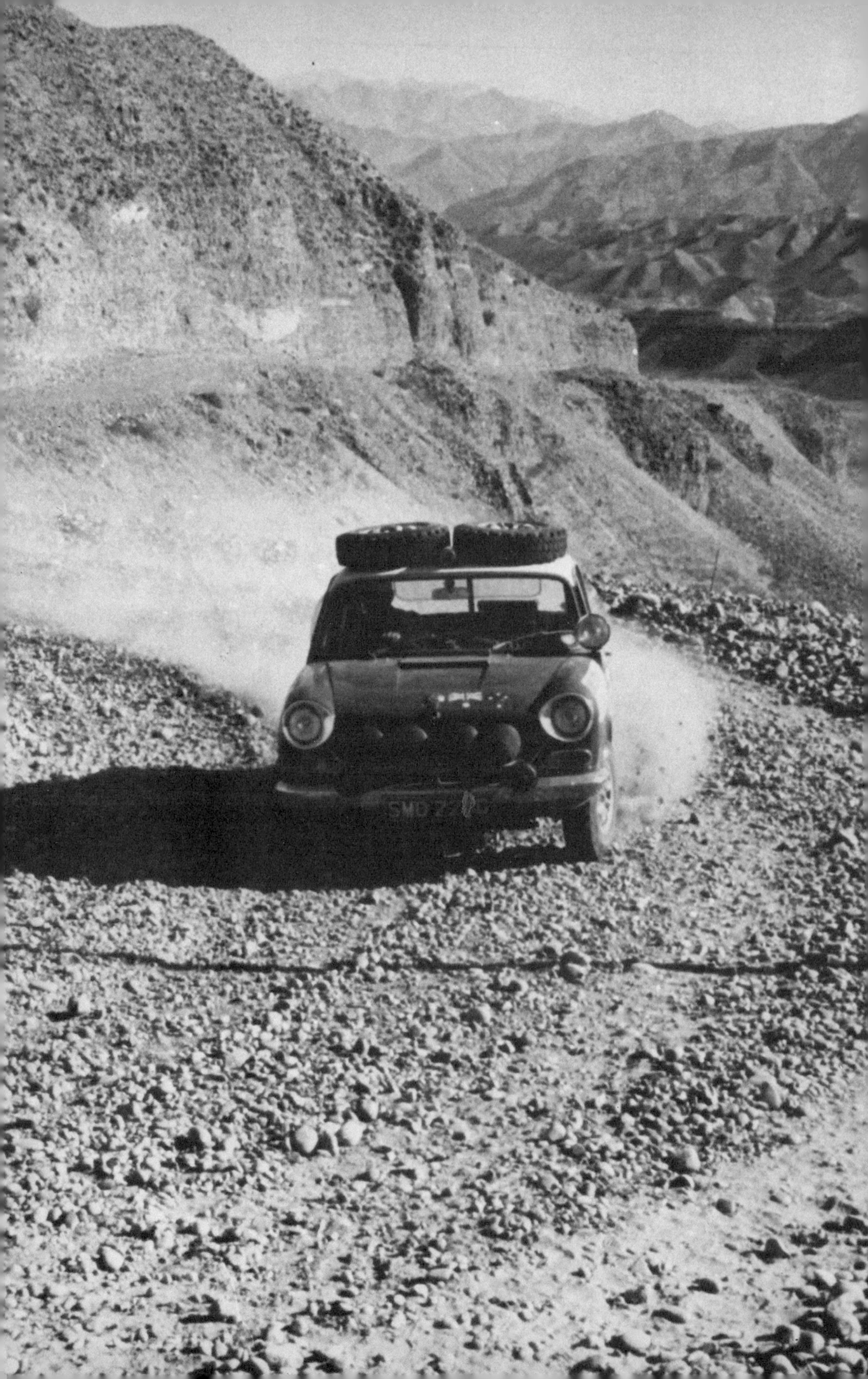

CHAPTER EIGHT
THE LONG DRIVES

The London to Mexico Rally 1970

With the new decade came a major motoring challenge for Jack. The London to Mexico World Cup Rally started at London's Wembley Stadium 19 April 1970. Five weeks later, 27 May 1970, crews were due to finish in Mexico's Aztec Stadium, four days before the World Cup Soccer Championships. The European leg of the journey covered eleven countries: England, France, Germany, Austria, Hungary, Yugoslavia, Bulgaria, Italy, France, Spain and Portugal. The South and Central American sections included a further fifteen countries: Brazil, Uruguay, Argentina, Chile, Bolivia, Peru, Ecuador, Colombia, Panama, Costa Rica, Nicaragua, Honduras, El Salvador, Guatemala and Mexico.

Only one in four of the entrants who started in London would complete the 35-day, 26-country odyssey.

On Anzac Day 1970, two old mates managed to get together in Portugal before departing for South America. Jack and Wylton Dickson, the organiser of the 1970 London to Mexico Rally and the future organiser of the 1982 Peking to Paris Motoring Challenge, went to a bullfight together in Lisbon. Many years later that day would create for me a poignant memory of my father and his love of motorsport. Following Jack's passing in 1983, while preparing his Mitsubishi Scorpion for sale, I opened the glove box to find the Peking to Paris Motoring Challenge entry form Wylton had sent my father. The race

Left: The foothills of the Lataband Pass, east of Kabul, Afghanistan.

CHAPTER EIGHT

Above: Start of the 1970 London to Mexico Rally. From left to right: Evan Green, Hamish Cardno (*Motor Magazine*) as navigator, an official, 'Gelignite' Jack Murray (arms folded) and car No 92, a British Leyland works entry Triumph 2.5 Pl.

never went ahead—but Jack was planning his next long drive right to the end.

Jack and Evan Green, as drivers, teamed up with Hamish Cardno (*Motor Magazine*) as navigator in the London to Mexico Marathon. Car No 92 was a British Leyland works entry Triumph Mk.2 2.5PI. Right from the start a blockage problem with the fuel injection system emerged. This recurring problem was later attributed to a valve guide disintegrating and shedding crumbs of metal. A crash in France in which the Triumph was driven over a cliff and hit some trees did not help matters. With Cardno driving, the Triumph left the road, rolling and spinning down a hill near Rouaine in the French Alps. Fortunately, no one was injured. The car was pulled out, hammered into shape and the boys drove on. (*The Courier-Mail,* April 1970)

It took the Andes, however, to finally put Car No 92, out of the rally. The Triumph did not arrive at the Santiago checkpoint within the time limit and was eliminated.

The flying Finn, Hannu Mikkola, with Gunnar Palm in their Escort Mk 1 won the Rally. It had been quite a journey: 5000 miles (8000 km) through Europe and 11,000 miles (18,000 km) through South and Central America. While in excess of 100 cars started the journey, only 23 completed the course.

Ampol Trial 1970

Ampol Trials, like the REDEX Trials before them, were a feature of round Australia motorsport in the 1960s and 70s. The 1970 Trial was run from 20 June to 5 July. The actual trial section of the Ampol started on 24 June 1970, competitors having driven from all states to gather in Alice Springs. Jack teamed up on this occasion with radio personality and 2GB presenter John Pearce, as co-driver, in a Morris 1500. Experienced navigator and trial competitor Roy Denny provided directions. The trial proper started from the Alice and ended in the Sydney Showground.

Above: Jack sits on the roof of the crashed Triumph, Rouaine France.

Apparently there was much fun for Jack and his mates, but not a lot in the way of success. Car No 74 was DNF.

My brother John also competed in the Trial, co-driving a 308 Holden with Max Stahl and Jim Sampson.

With the start of the new decade, Jack's brother Ray turned 65 and he decided it was time to retire. Jack was never one to consider retirement. His entire life was an adventure, not work. In November 1970, after almost 40 years in business together, the brothers dissolved their partnership and Jack purchased Ray's share of The Garage, becoming its sole owner.

The following year, 1971, Jack and his radio mate John Pearce teamed up again to undertake a Race the Train dash from Sydney to Perth. This nonstop drive took 46 hours, and the boys ended up beating the train by an easy seventeen hours.

'Wild Bill's' Legacy

The years now seemed to be passing faster than ever. On Boxing Day 1971, Jack's close friend Bill McLachlan passed away, aged 54. Ten years younger than Jack, Bill's death should not have happened. He was kicked in the chest while helping break up a blue in the Tropicana, the pub he and his wife Marie ran. The kick resulted in what was described as a 'split' in his heart. Bill put up with the pain for a day or two. Back then they only had rest as treatment, and while in hospital he wrote *The Manuscript*, the story of his and Jack's epic 'weekend' trip away that had turned into a three-week adventure all the way to Darwin and back.

After his release from hospital, sometime later, and maybe pushing himself too much, Bill's heart failed.

'Gelignite' goes Caravanning

In May 1972 Jack went caravanning. He had been offered yet another adventure, a further chance to travel Australia and revisit the outback he loved. A caravan representative, Englishman Gordon Abbey, had rung Jack to ask if he would go. Gordon was the first salesman in Australia for Freeman Caravans, which later became Winnebago Caravans. Jack said, 'Let's meet' and they did, at the factory where the caravans were made. As with all his adventures and trips, there was no money in it for Jack—but there was also nothing for him to pay. As an iconic Aussie, Jack would attract good publicity and no doubt give the trip a lot of 'bang'. Of course, he agreed to do it.

It involved 30 vehicles enlisted to promote the caravanning lifestyle in Australia. Almost 45 years ago, it was necessary to advertise caravanning. Judging by its popularity today and the thousands of grey nomads, clearly such early promotion was very successful. Jack spent four weeks and three days travelling Australia with Gordon Abbey in a 'piggy back' camper van on the back of a V8 Holden Ute.

The route went south and west from Sydney and on to Adelaide in South Australia. From there, the convoy headed north via Oodnadatta, past the Birdsville Track, Ayers Rock (Uluru) and on to Darwin. Jack met up with many old friends, including diver, seafarer and Darwin personality Carl Atkinson. Heading south, the mass of vehicles turned east at the Three Ways towards the coast, and then down the east coast of Australia. The convoy drove finally into the Caravanning and Camping Show in Sydney—the dirty vehicles straight off the track.

By 2010 Gordon Abbey was living in the same mobile home retirement village as my parents-in-law, Sid and Dot Tracey, at Morisset on the NSW Central Coast. Over coffee, Gordon laughed as he recalled some of Jack's antics. As he stood on the tailgate of the ute one morning, Jack enquired of his travelling companion, 'Gordon, can you see that brolga on my stork?' Then there was the time Jack placed a rubber snake in some hot springs to scare the women relaxing there. Gordon also remembered Jack's favourite: 'milkshakes, double malt and double ice-cream and peaches, cream and cereal for breakfast'. During the trip, Jack did the cooking and Gordon did the cleaning. Edgells tinned food was a sponsor, fortunately for Jack. Having a can opener must have added considerably to his culinary skills.

REDEX Anniversary Run

The twenty-first anniversary of the start of the 1953 REDEX Reliability Trial, the first, fell on 30 August 1974. In November 1974, *Wheels Magazine* organised and sponsored the re-run, involving Ken Tubman, winner of the first REDEX Trial and Jack, winner of the second. Both Ken and Jack drove Peugeot 504s in

Above: 'Gelignite' Jack starts amidst a cloud of smoke at the Anniversary REDEX.

CHAPTER EIGHT

Above: Clearing a BBQ site—'Gelignite' Jack style.

the re-run. Evan Green formed part of the support crew.

It comes as no surprise that there was an element of competition in the re-run. Ken Tubman won, while Jack came a close second. Tubman was a very competitive and accomplished driver. In 1974 at the age of 58, with Andre Welinski and Jim Reddiex, he won the London-Sahara-Munich World Cup Rally in a Citroen.

An Interview and a Death

On 18 May 1976, at age 68, Jack sat in The Garage with Neil Bennetts and recorded his National Library of Australia interview. Three months later, on 28 August 1976, his brother Ray, aged 71, passed away after a stroke.

Jack decided to give himself a present for his 70th birthday: the second London to Sydney Marathon.

The London to Sydney Marathon 1977

The second London to Sydney Marathon left London on Sunday 14 August 1977 and finished at the Sydney Opera House on 27 September 1977. It was sponsored by Singapore Airlines. It had been nine years since the first marathon in 1968. There had been five long distance car marathons, starting with the 1907 Peking to Paris race, followed by the 1908 New York to Paris via

THE LONG DRIVES

Alaska, the 1968 London to Sydney Marathon, the 1970 London to Mexico World Cup Rally and finally the 1974 London to Munich via Sahara Rally. Jack had competed in two of these.

At just over 30,000 km, this rally was the longest ever driven. In fact, it was twice as long as the first London to Sydney marathon, and time spent on the road would be about 30 days, with 80 starters setting off from London to travel through sixteen countries on three continents, including two major sea crossings. It was a *very* long drive. In fact, *The Long Drive* was the name given by freelance journalist, writer, professional photographer and rally competitor John Stathatos to his 1978 book, an account of the rally. Stathatos was born in Athens and educated in Switzerland, Greece and England, and had finished the London to Munich via Sahara rally in the smallest car competing.

Jack competed in the 1977 Rally as part of a three man crew driving Car No 68, a Peugeot 504TI. The other Australians were Bruce Mudd and Geoff Perry. Evan Green competed separately, in Car No 39 sponsored by Endrust Australia Ltd, and drove a Range Rover.

While showing initial promise, Car No 68 was plagued by bad luck that culminated in a crash involving a tractor and other mayhem.

There are several references to Jack and the ill-fated Car No 68 in *The Long Drive*. Not having been trained in the Classics or Greek—ancient or modern—I am uncertain whether the Greek language lends itself to expressing the difference between gelignite and dynamite. In any event, throughout his book, Stathatos consistently, but inaccurately, refers to Jack 'Dynamite' Murray. This tends to raise one's concerns as to the accuracy of other information in John's account of the rally.

However, almost 40 years after the event, the account of a published writer, author and a competitor who was actually there on the ground is surely the best source available. This is how it describes the event unfolding for Car No 68:

> As the cars underwent scrutiny and competitors met for the first time, it was seen as the strongest of the private Australian entries. Right from the beginning, however, the Peugeot 504 had problems and arrived 'booming' in Milan minus an exhaust. A local Peugeot dealer soon remedied that problem. The car performed well over a testing 15 km loose gravel stage, winding up the face of a steep cliff on the journey from Milan to Athens, with 5 mins 42 secs penalty.

CHAPTER EIGHT

But events took a bizarre turn when Car No 68 negotiated the Athens traffic in an unconventional manner, with a 70-year-old Jack perched on the mudguard, kicking the front nearside wheel to point it in the desired direction. His improvised—if unorthodox—steering technique proved successful, since 'Dynamite' Jack was at the time in twenty-fourth position, the best placed of the private Peugeots. Of the 61 crews who had made it to Athens, Evan Green and his Range Rover were in fifteenth position.

As the Rally progressed, the penalties began to mount. When several competitors, including Car No 68, on the leg from Tabas to Fariman (Iran) elected to drive straight to the Afghan border from Tehran, they avoided the desert stage, at the cost of 48-hour penalties.

Success in rallies, particularly long distance events, requires skill, endurance and thorough preparation—but also luck. *The Long Drive* tells how luck deserted Jack's Peugeot:

> Unluckiest of all was 'Dynamite' Jack Murray who had skipped the desert loop. Trying to reach Fariman via Mashhad he blew the head gasket on his Peugeot. It was tightened down but blew again. He reached Mashhad late in the morning, where the old head was removed and planed. At 7.30 that evening he left for Fariman, but then the radiator went and he had to turn back yet again. By the morning of the 24th Jack was over 30 hours behind the rally. He headed for India, hoping to catch up at Delhi.

The rally pushed on and by Bombay only 46 crews out of the starters managed to clock in:

> As for 'Dynamite' Jack Murray, the Malaysian Fiat and the Dickin-Park Mini, they had vanished from sight.

The final reference to Jack and the gallant Car No 68 tells an extraordinary tale. Jack's favourite phrase 'truth is stranger than fiction' was never more true:

First car through was probably the Peugeot of 'Dynamite' Jack Murray, who fought as hard as anyone to reach Madras [on the east coast of southern India]. Leaving Fariman one and a half days late, he had missed both Kabul and Delhi. On the morning of the 26th the Peugeot hit a tractor travelling on the wrong side of the road some 50 km south of Agra [the Taj Mahal just over the horizon]. The badly damaged car would be loaded on a truck and taken to Bombay, but in the meantime Jack was surrounded by a mob of angry villagers. Pursued by gunfire, he fled to a nearby police post, but the officer in charge threw him out again. Jack promptly flagged down a passing car. Unfortunately, in a scene by Mack Sennett [director-actor who is seen as the inventor of slapstick comedy] out of Kafka [German language writer using dark themes], the driver turned out to be the owner of the tractor and suddenly pulled out a pistol. The portly Australian driver was forced to flee through the rice paddies on foot, turning up in Madras three days later.

There is an understandable tendency for an author to embellish and employ poetic licence, in order to engage readers. But I have my concerns about the accuracy of some of the more colourful details of this tale.

In August 2015, however, I talked with Max Stahl and John Stathatos' account of events seems to be confirmed. Stahl told me, 'Jack's car ended its run in Pakistan [*sic*: India] when it hit a tractor travelling on the wrong side of the road and it seems Jack was a bit lucky to escape angry and armed villagers who chased him through a rice paddy!' Jack's words from his interview with Neil Bennetts echo in my ear: 'I say, truth would leave fiction for dead. But you tell people and they don't believe you, so I never bother telling them.'

While not the most successful of Jack's rallies in terms of result, the 1977 London to Sydney Marathon certainly challenged not only Car No 68 but also Jack—but no doubt it also offered him a lot of fun along the way.

Jack may not have finished in a car—but Andrew Cowan, driving a 280E Mercedes, certainly did. Mercedes placed first and second in the 1977 London to Sydney Marathon. Andrew Cowan had won his second London to Sydney Marathon, nine years after the first.

CHAPTER EIGHT

Star of Film and Spectacle

In May 1977, Jack and a German television crew climbed aboard a Mercedes Unimog and a 300D diesel sedan and set off on a trip to Central Australia. It was designed to follow the route of Ernest Giles, the 19th century explorer, in a film that was a joint production for Channel 7 and German television. The party of five started at Chambers Pillar, south of Alice Springs.

In July 1978, Massey Fergusson asked Jack to get behind the wheel of one

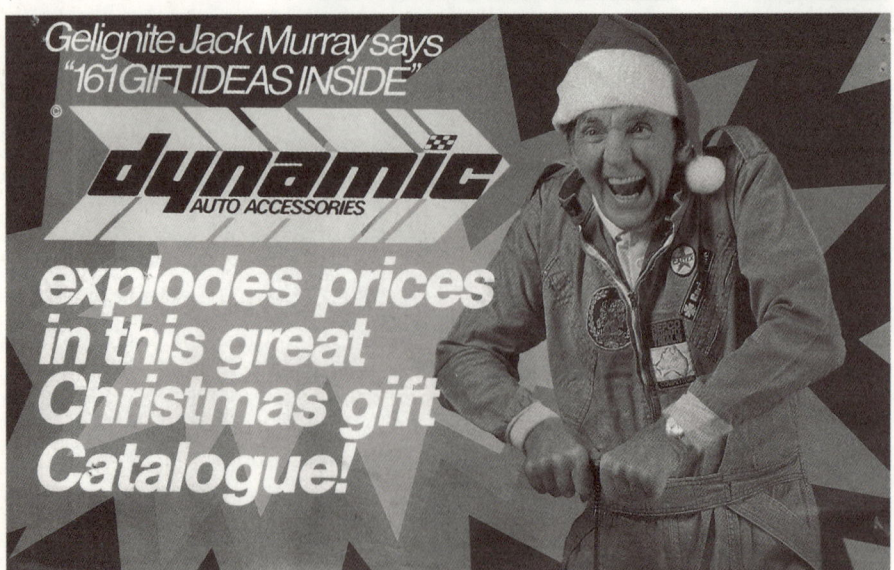

Above: A small collection of Jack's many advertising appearances.

of their tractors while surrounding tractors were blown up to the booming strains of Tchaikovsky's 1812 overture. The smoke and explosions, with musical accompaniment, were designed as a re-enactment of Napoleon's war in Russia. For participating in this onerous task, Jack was to be rewarded by Massey Ferguson with the princely sum of $3000. I reckon he would have done it for free.

Jack was always very popular with advertisers.

Repco Reliability Round Australia Trial 1979: The Last Drive

This was to be Jack's last competitive motorsport event, and he competed in it alongside his son John. Jack was scathing of this last experience of trial driving. The camaraderie and the social aspect of rallying enjoyed by teams in earlier years at places like the Hydro Majestic and during the REDEX days were no more. Tired men simply fought to keep awake. For Jack, the fun had gone.

It may have been, in his words, 'the most useless bastard event' to end his career in competitive motorsport, but the career it capped could hardly have been more stellar or varied.

As we have seen, Jack's career spanned six decades and covered all forms of motorsport. His successes and achievements were many, and the vehicles he drove to victory are significant in the history of the sport in Australia. Such an achievement in one sport would more than satisfy most men—but as we have seen, Jack has been described in numerous ways, but never 'like most men'.

He enjoyed other successes and achievements, hard fought and won, in at least another three sports. Much more of his story remains to be told.

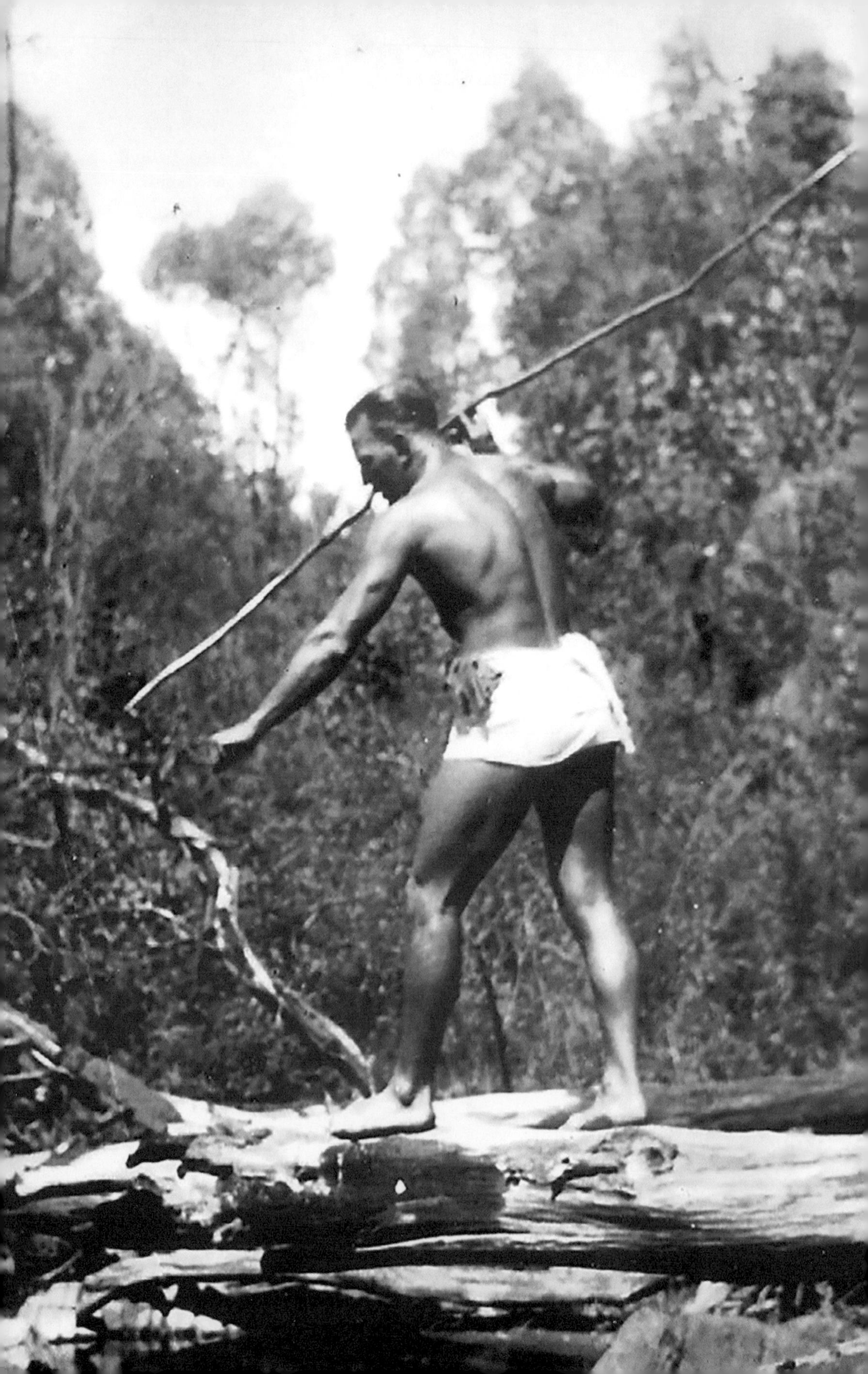

CHAPTER NINE
ADVENTURER, HUNTER, DIVER AND FIREMAN

Round the World Trip 1937

Little remains that Jack actually wrote himself: a hand written speech prepared for a Brisbane boat show, some personal letters written while on overseas adventures and a couple of postcards. There is, however, Jack's diary, a daily account of a world trip that he undertook over approximately seven months in 1937. It is the most extensive work remaining written in his own hand.

While today we accept this as a normal rite of passage for young people, a round-the-world trip was quite an adventure in 1937. At 29 years of age, how did he manage to fund such an enterprise? For a number of years my father bought and sold cars very successfully. I recollect that he won a salesmen's competition—perhaps for Chryslers. And of course the taxi business used cash. I would surmise that a pound or two that should have rightly belonged to the taxman found its way into cars, engines, boats and, in 1937, travel.

Jack recounts in his National Library interview with Neil Bennetts:

> Of course, I've done hundreds of things ... I've been for a trip round the world and all this sort of thing. Four guys together went away on the old *Esperance Bay* for nine months. I think it cost us £1200

Left: Hunting, fishing and kayaking. Jack loved the Australian outdoors and the freedom it offered.

CHAPTER NINE

each—no, it was just on six months. We bought a car in England for 12 pounds 10 shillings down in Great Portland Street, [and] the four of us took it to Europe and we went to Belgium, Brussels, and down to Trieste, Fiume, Monte Carlo, Geneva, Lugarno, Berne, Zurich and Interlaken. We put the car on the boat, took it back to England, and they said, 'You're the salesman, you take it down and sell it'... Then we caught the *Queen Mary* and went first class, let our heads go. I forget how much it was in those days, but we went to New York on the *Queen Mary*.

Jack, then aged 29, his brother Ray (31), and mates Tom Mills and Peter Roach sailed out of Sydney Heads on the *Esperance Bay* on 6 March 1937. As with most of Jack's adventures, the trip was full of events, highlights and characters, including famous sportsmen, actors, a Sri Lankan prince, racing car identities and others.

After arriving in England, the boys bought their car and travelled extensively throughout Britain and Europe. In London they witnessed the Coronation of King George VI, on 12 May 1937. In Paris, they visited the Exposition Internationale des arts et techniques dans la vie moderne. In Berlin, they

Above: On 8 April 1937, they visited the Pyramids at Giza. Jack in centre front, standing with hands in pockets, and Ray second from right is on the camel, then Peter Roach, Tom Mills and unknown.

watched racing at the famous Avus circuit and Jack shared a view of the day's racing with a little Austrian bloke named Adolf Hitler.

MURRAY: Then we came back to England and I saw the meetings at Brooklands. I met personally … Prince Bira. He was driving a Bugatti, and I shook hands with the famous English guy who got killed, Sir … Malcolm Campbell … and who else did I meet? I met a couple of guys there. The racing there was good but nothing compared to what they were doing over in Berlin. That was really something.

BENNETTS: What was your impression of Sir Malcolm Campbell?

MURRAY: A terrific guy. Yes, he would be the number one guy. He was more like an Australian than anyone I've met, actually. He was a nice guy. As a matter of fact, I had dinner with him the following day. He talked on Australia; he'd never been here, but later on he did come here … Evan Green or somebody was involved with him some time back there. The racing in England at Brooklands—of course it was an old track and out-of-date compared to Avus.

Evan was coordinator of Campbell's successful land and water speed record attempts in 1964, at Lake Eyre, South Australia and Dumbleyung, Western Australia.

Above: Sir Malcolm Campbell, then his son Donald Campbell on Lake Eyre in 1964.

CHAPTER NINE

Above: Across the USA: Tom Mills and Jack Murray in their 1936 two-door Plymouth Sedan.

In New York, Jack and Tom Mills bought another car and drove it across the USA. They then returned to Australia via New Zealand in October 1937, aboard the SS *Monterey*. Ray had returned early, since good friend Tommy Jarrett, who was looking after the brothers' Garage, was having some difficulties.

As shown by autographed photos, Jack and Ray crossed paths with the former World Heavyweight Boxing Champion, Max Baer, in 1937. But there is no mention of the encounter in Jack's diary. Exactly where and when?

Max Baer, 1909–1959, was an American boxer of the 1930s, one-time Heavyweight Champion of the World, as well as a referee, and also took an occasional role in film and television. He is rated No 22 in *Ring* magazine's list of the 100 greatest punchers of all time.

The Manuscript and the Odyssey

> Jack said: 'What are you doing on the weekend?'
> I [Bill McLachlan] said: 'I'm easy—what do you want to do?'
> Jack: 'It's too cold to ski. What about we go for a shoot?'
> I said: 'OK. Where will we go?'
> Jack: 'Just let's go … and let it develop from there.'

And so it did. Bill eventually wrote a 23,000 word, 70 page story about how two good mates from Sydney's Bondi set off on a weekend shooting trip and ended up driving a train in outback Queensland, diving for salvage on World War II wrecks in Darwin Harbour and finding time to pass themselves off as CSIRO 'fungus scientists'. A weekend shoot developed into an 8000 km odyssey across Australia. Jack's and Bill's 'weekend' would prove to be yet another great adventure providing much of the knowledge of the Ford V8, the country and themselves that would enable Jack two years later to go on and win the 1954 REDEX.

This was a time when 'a good cuppa' and 'a real good feed' would be described as 'beaut', and all the necessities two good mates needed to go away for a weekend would be thirteen guns, a compass and a coin to toss to decide which way to go. It was a time before global positioning systems, global warming and global terrorism. It was a time before the restrictions, rules and regulations of modern life cramped the style of adventurers. There weren't even any speed cameras!

'Wild Bill'

Dougald Andrew (Bill) McLachlan was a self-made man, having put himself through university and obtained a degree in chemistry. During World War II he was 'loaned' to the Americans in New Guinea to research and help with 'the extra things that grow in the tropical climate', both on the troops and the infrastructure of war. Bill was given a PhD for that research. Throughout much of that time Bill and Jack were close friends; they were both extraordinary men. Bill owned factories, which mainly produced paint, in the Sydney suburb of Campsie.

As Bill lay in his hospital bed in 1971, twenty years after the trip he described as 'the adventure of a lifetime', he decided to put pen to paper and record for posterity the events of that journey across a continent, as well as the people, places and events that were at the birth of Australian motorsport.

Bill referred to his writing as *The Manuscript* and gave it the title: *The Other Side of the Story: The Sequel to* [Evan Green's] *Journeys with 'Gelignite' Jack*.

It's a great yarn, a story that gives us an insight into the friendship of two mates and into a post-war Australia just starting to discover its full potential as a country worth exploring in its natural, if sometimes harshly rugged beauty.

CHAPTER NINE

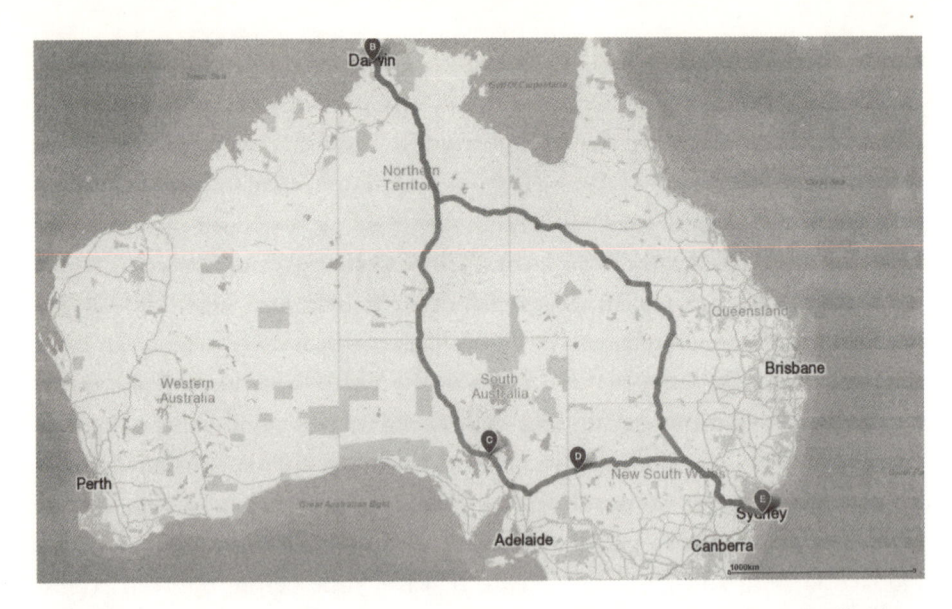

Above: Map of the 'weekend' trip route, Sydney to Darwin via outback Queensland return, taking in Alice Springs and the Woomera rocket range.

Above: Mataranka Springs, Northern Territory. Jack begins to master the dugout canoe. No worries here, since there were only freshwater crocodiles in these waters, no salties—or so Jack hoped.

'Cut off your fingers'

Rain which flooded Queensland roads caused Jack and Bill some troubles. As *The Manuscript* says:

> Then disaster; we slid into a bog. Things looked crook ... Jack said, 'Give her a good kick in the guts and she might make it.' OK—I did. There was a helluva bang and the back axle broke! No one spoke English for about five minutes. Jack's second language being profane, he made great use of it. At any rate, it eased the tension and we both sat down and had a good laugh at the situation.
>
> Jack remembered the lid of the camp oven and this worked real beaut and up she went, and Jack for some reason got half under the front of the back wheel to give it a bit of turn when the old girl started to roll forward. I said, 'Jump out quick, mate—she's rolling forward' and at the same time I grabbed the bar of the bumper jack, to try and hold the car from rolling on Jack until he got out. This worked OK and he got out, but it jammed my fingers between the screw bar of the jack and the bumper. As the car started to roll forward Jack took one look, grabbed the camp oven, ran around the front of the car and chocked the wheel so it could not roll any further. Then he came back to look at the situation.
>
> He said, 'If I let it go it will cut off your fingers and you'll look funny picking your nose with your thumb, so I had better try and lift her enough to get your fingers out.' Well, there we were, miles from nowhere and only Jack's back and tenacity and big heart between fingers and no fingers. He put his back to the car and grabbed the bumper: 'You pull your fingers out when I lift.' Well, did he lift! I reckon the car weighed about two and a half ton gross, so he was on the best part of 5-600 pounds. Anyhow, he said, 'Ready?' and I said, 'Bloody oath!' He upped his legs and the veins stood out on his forehead like bits of cord and he kept lifting till my fingers came free. I said, 'Thanks'. He said, 'Get stuffed, and put something on your fingers before they fall off.' I had some penicillin gauze, which is mighty for things like this, as there did not appear to be any broken bones. We bandaged them up and had a cup of tea from the primus ...

CHAPTER NINE

.45s on the Hips

As night fell, the boys spotted some lights and set off for what looked like a property. Bill continues:

> Things looked pretty rough: a broken axle, busted fingers and somewhere between Tambo and Blackall in real sheep country. In no time flat it was dark and things looked crook. We saw a light … so we took off. We were both in flying suits, sheepskin flying jackets, a .45 on the hip and a high powered Hornet on a sling over our shoulders, not to mention 50 rounds of ammo each and Jack sported the Zenith radio with its pressmatic keys and hydraulic aerial.
>
> About 8pm we arrived. It was a sheep station, a big one, as it turned out, one of the biggest in Queensland, a section of Reubens' property, Northampton Downs, and there were about 50 shearers and drovers shacked up there because of the rain, waiting for the sheep to get dry enough to shear. We opened the door to the mess or cookhouse and stepped in.
>
> There were about 30 blokes in there finishing off their supper and you could have heard a pin drop. As a matter of fact, the only noise was the hiss of the carbide lamp. Jack said, 'Christ, you would think we come from bloody Mars. We're just a pair of city mugs with a broken axle down the road apiece, looking for some help and maybe a feed—and we can pay.'
>
> … I remember we both had kangaroo skin rugs over our shoulders and no doubt, did look a bit odd. But Jack's honest Australian vituperation soon put them at ease and we were made most welcome.

Unshaven, kangaroo skins, .45s on the hips, rifles slung over shoulders, 50 rounds of ammo bandolier style slung across the chest—why wouldn't the mess hall came to a standstill when these characters walked through the door!

Jack's Dives

Bill may have almost lost his fingers when the big Ford rolled forward, but Jack's luck almost ran out the day Darwin legend Carl Atkinson took him diving for pearl shell. As Bill writes:

Above Left: Jack with smaller salties waiting to be skinned. **Above Right:** Bill McLachlan with large groper caught on an excursion to Bathurst and Melville Islands, north of Darwin. 'It was a whopper and turned the steelyard beam over at 560 lb. So we gutted him and I crawled inside and poked my head out his mouth.'

Above Left: Note the large growth on this huge croc's tail.

Above Right: Jack wearing a diver's hard hat.

CHAPTER NINE

The next day was a lay off, so Carl said he would take us pearling in the lugger.

The diver grabs all the shell he can and loads it into the basket and there was plenty of shell, because it had not been worked in this area since before the war. At one stage, Jack was the diver—helmet and corselet only, of course, and boots and microphone in the helmet. When called on the intercom he said he was stuck on a coral head and we would pull his airline off if we were not careful. Well, Carl was an expert and he talked to Jack and got his situation clear and it appeared that Jack had his arm entangled in the airline and his boot had jammed in a coral outcrop.

Carl eased off the main sheet and got some more slack to Jack, but not enough to tangle him further, and eased off the pressure by coming up into the wind. We got the signal from Jack over the intercom and we started to ease Jack up to the surface very slowly. Finally, we had him on deck and (no injuries) apart from a bad bruise on the arm and a solemn promise from Jack that he [had] completed both his pearl dives—the first and the f***king last. He was OK, thanks of course go to the cool and efficient action of Carl, who again showed what a practical, skilled professional he was! Also a real mate—and if you ever read this, mate, I thank you for Jack!

Above: Carl Atkinson's pearling lugger.

Above: Jack and June Dowling buffalo hunting. Note that both are carrying rifles.

I am also grateful to Carl—otherwise yours truly would not be here today! Continues Bill:

> Next day, Carl agreed and introduced us to a buffalo hunter, who would show us the ropes and, with the use of Carl's weapons carrier, we picked up our guide at the administration building. What a shock! It was a girl, June Dowling, the daughter of the administrator and considered one of the best buff shots in the area. Anyhow, by now, we were immune to surprises …

Shooting

Jack was a man of his time, enjoying the hunting and shooting that in the 1940s and 50s were seen as mainstream recreational activities and were enjoyed by many Australians.

When viewed from today's perspective, many of the native animals Jack and his friends pursued and hunted would not be killed. Today they are protected species. The control of pest species such as feral goats, pigs, foxes and even domestic dogs interbred with dingoes is a serious problem for rural, even suburban Australians. Issues surrounding their culling are hotly debated. Recreational shooters argue that they can play a role in reducing pressure on stock and grazing lands.

CHAPTER NINE

The shooting of a magnificent creature such as a wedge-tailed eagle is today not only illegal, but abhorrent to most Australians. As a young man I shot at crows and other birds with a .22, in Queensland. Today, I volunteer as a Native Animal Rescuer and researcher into kangaroo management: a one-generation transition from hunter to conservationist.

The reality is that our views and attitudes are more often than not shaped by the times in which we live. Jack lived in a time before terrorism and before gun crime was prevalent in our cities. The sport of shooting, the camaraderie of mates and the enjoyment of the Australian outdoors were all a part of his life.

Vivian Hamilton was one of Jack's best mates throughout his life. My brother John owes his middle name, Vivian, to the great friendship the two men shared.

Risk Taker

Jack was a natural risk taker. People who drive race cars, climb mountains or seek adventures where their life can be on the line all are. One of his favourite verses expressed his attitude to danger:

Above: In the Victorian high country: McMillans Lookout near Benambra, and Sassafras Gap, about 480 km from Melbourne.

Above: Viv Hamilton at left with Jack and a trophy wedge-tailed eagle.

> No game was ever worth a rap
> For a rational man to play
> Into which no disaster—no mishap
> Could possibly find a way ...

These were the words of Australian poet, jockey and politician Adam Lindsay Gordon (1833–1870). Jack would always 'give it a go', however dangerous an activity seemed to others.

Fireman Jack to the Rescue

In 1980-81, Nambucca Heads Surf Lifesaving Club celebrated its Golden Anniversary and produced a magazine to commemorate the occasion. One of its many articles was an historical feature:

> 'Sharkbait Sam' remembers ...
> On one very hot January day the brush and dead grass on the cliff at the Headland caught fire. A few of us were camped at the Headland Park and we rounded up some kerosene tins. The fire was streaking down the cliff face and our weatherboard clubhouse was

threatened. We began racing down to the surf and carting the water back and forth to the fire. It was hot work.

A very well built young man, sunbaking on the beach with a very well built young lady, saw our plight and came along and gave us a hand. He was carting two tins of water to our one.

Luckily we got the fire out and the clubhouse was saved. We introduced ourselves to our Good Samaritan friend and I thanked him on behalf of the club and gave him a well earned mention in my next column.

That young man was none other than 'Gelignite' Jack Murray ...

Kangaroo Jack

In 2003 Warner Bros released an American buddy-action movie called *Kangaroo Jack*. The main story line revolves around a kangaroo that is knocked out by a car and is then dressed in a jacket so that the driver can pose with the animal for photos. To everyone's surprise (including the kangaroo's) the big red revives and runs off with the coat—oh, with a large sum of money in the pocket.

The movie story line suggests that when wearing a pair of sunglasses—yes, you read that right—the kangaroo resembled a fictional American gangster called *Jacky Legs*. The critics' consensus? Quote: 'The humour is gratingly dumb, and *Kangaroo Jack* contains too much violence and sexual innuendo for a family movie.' Apparently the singing, dancing, even rapping, computer generated kangaroo was not a big hit with audiences.

In 1978 Evan Green as the *Sun Herald* Motoring Editor had written an article relating several REDEX stories. It was called *How 'Gelignite' Jack earned his name and a niche in motor history*. Compare the movie storyline to what Evan wrote concerning a fellow REDEX Trial competitor:

> I remember publicity conscious contestants like Frank Kleinig who was always taking photos for his sponsor. He hit a large kangaroo and decided to

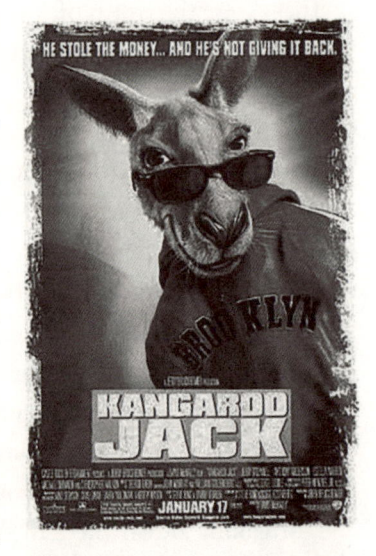

Above: Kangaroo Jack movie poster.

take a special picture. Kleinig draped his sports coat around the immobile roo's shoulders, and busied himself with the camera—which is when the animal regained consciousness and disappeared into the Never Never, wearing the coat—with Kleinig's wallet safely tucked in a pocket.

Coincidence? And why was the kangaroo named Jack?

How an incident/fact/fable from a REDEX Trial in 1950s' Australia became the basis for a multi-million-dollar Hollywood production is a mystery. The movie credits list says 'Story by Steve Bing, Barry O'Brien and Scott Rosenberg'. Perhaps only these Hollywood writers could shed some light on it. As for me, I have absolutely no idea.

Spare Parts

As in a mechanic's workshop, oddities gathered over time are often kept and stored, too 'valuable' to throw away. All our lives are full of these 'spare parts'. People seemed to be naturally drawn to Jack's stories of his adventures. Whether at a motorsport event or simply relaxing on holidays, he would invariably draw a crowd.

Here are a few of Jack's 'spare parts'. The first is from *The Gelignite Bugatti* by Damian Kringas:

Above: 'Gelignite' Jack Murray holding court.

CHAPTER NINE

Brabham would leave Australia and excel at Formula One. Murray would have his car rallies. But Brabham and Murray couldn't have been more different. Brabham, focused and determined, seemed destined to storm the international stage and make his mark. And make it he did. Murray, equally determined, was never going to be knighted by the Queen.

From his mate Evan Green, when asked about Jack's travel kit: 'Jack's necessities? Toothpaste, underwear and gelignite.' Evan, while impressed with Jack's driving ability, certainly saw limitations to his friend's navigational skills: 'Jack couldn't track an elephant with ink on its feet through fresh snow.' He also once declared Jack 'Australia's widest travelled practical joker.'

For reasons best known to himself, Jack had a number of hideous rubber masks which often appeared during rallies or, in one memorable instance from my childhood, greeted me in the dark on my way to the bathroom in the family unit at Vaucluse. The collection included a gorilla face, a haggard witch and a particularly menacing, psychotic looking, bald headed man. When asked about the latter by a newspaper reporter, Jack offered, 'He is a Lithographic man from the Plasticine age.' Paleoanthropologists and geochronologists are still trying to work out Jack's malapropism: Neolithic man from the Pleistocene age.

Jack was a non-smoker and a teetotaller. He once offered the secret of what sometimes seemed his everlasting youth: 'I don't drink grog and never touch cigarettes.' I never saw my father drink beer or any alcoholic drink. But as one mate said, 'If he's like this sober, he would be bloody murder drunk.'

During the 1970 London to Mexico rally, a rather unlikely friendship developed between Prince Michael of Kent, cousin of Her Majesty Queen Elizabeth II, and Jack. The Prince was driving an Austin Maxi along with two of his brother officers (bodyguards?) from the Royal Hussars. The Queen's cousin clearly enjoyed the company of the unaffected, straight-talking Australian who refreshingly treated him as just another competitor and addressed him simply as 'Michael'. Naturally, heads turned. Evan related this confusion of cultures:

> A few days later, one of his crewmates came up to Jack and myself. He was twitching with embarrassment.
> 'You shouldn't really call him Michael,' he said softly.

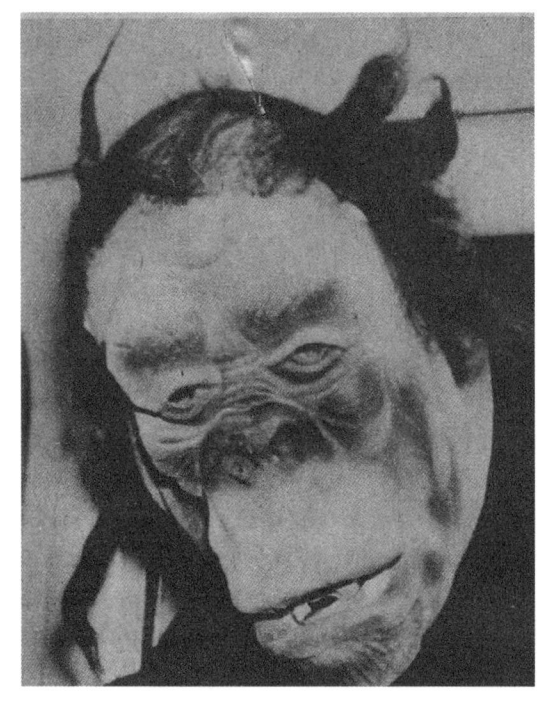

Above: A boyhood memory of my father.

'Shit,' said Jack looking concerned. 'Don't tell me I've been calling him by the wrong name. I'm a bastard with names. What is his name?'

'Oh, it's Michael.'

'That's what I thought. What should we call him? Mike?'

The man looked like someone who's been hit by a low cricket ball, but is still trying to smile. Jack turned to me. 'Well, what do I call him?'

'I think Michael would be better than Mike.'

The other man nodded in agreement, tried not to laugh, and retreated.

Jack watched him go. 'What a queer bastard,' he said.

Heads continued to turn during the course of the rally as Prince Michael began to acquire some of Jack's more colourful expressions, but jaws really dropped one day in Monte Carlo as the Prince and Jack together inspected a less than impressive boat motor. Jack offered, 'Michael, that engine's so weak, it wouldn't pull a sailor off your sister.'

Max Stahl observed, 'Hardly anything [Jack] did was designed to be done alone. He was at his happiest when in the company of other people, having them share in his activities, entertaining them with his wit and repartee and infecting them with his boisterous energy.'

It is difficult in 2016 to convey, particularly to a younger audience, the profile and public affection that Jack enjoyed in 1950s and 60s Australia. As I was collating the hundreds of newspaper and magazine articles about him, I came upon a 1968 *Daily Mirror*. There was a prominent section that dealt with three individuals—the then-

Prime Minister John Gorton, Jackie Kennedy Onassis and 'Gelignite' Jack Murray. When I first saw this, I was struck by the thought, 'Well ... that's fairly impressive company for anyone to share. The fourteen-year-old who left school to play around with bikes and cars certainly did well for himself.'

Number Plate Aficionado

Jack was always a car and boat registration aficionado. All the Murrays have an affinity for a good number plate. Perhaps there is a rego gene?

For many years, on his stable of vehicles, he held JM 123, JM 456 and JM 789. My brother John and his son Jonny now have those plates. For my seventeenth birthday my father gave me white on black number plates PM 115. I have transferred the same number plate to successive cars over the past 45 years and intend to retain them until I hang up my keys for the very last time.

Thirteen

As his close friends were aware, Jack suffered from triskaidekaphobia, and the more crippling and related illness paraskevidekatriaphobia. (Try spelling that after a few dinner drinks.) Jack had a fear or dislike of the number thirteen and of Friday the 13th in particular. It was with great trepidation that I included Chapter 13 in this book. Sorry Jack!

The origins of this irrational concern about the number thirteen are lost in time, but Jack was always loath to make any important decisions on such an inauspicious day and date. It is interesting to note that it was Monday 13 June 1938 when the Mackellar Special lost control and ploughed into spectators at Penrith, killing three people. While Jack did not own the car at this time, this history with 'thirteen' would have caused him some angst.

'Gelignite' Jack and Copyright

In 2007 noted Australian singer and songwriter John Schumann (of Redgum fame: remember the Vietnam veteran anthem song, 'I was only 19'?) released an album entitled *Gelignite Jack*. I wrote to John asking where the inspiration came for his album title.

Here is his reply to my query:

ADVENTURER, HUNTER, DIVER AND FIREMAN

Above: John Schumann and the *Gelignite Jack* album cover.

Hi Phil,

I'm delighted you got in touch. Sadly, I never met your dad but I was aware of him (as were we all). I held him to be an Australian icon. As you will read, I used the 'Gelignite' Jack title with genuine respect—and a wish to remind Australians, yet again, of him and his exploits.

Cheers, John Schumann.

John gives a brief story of the album's origins:

As impecunious young Flinders University students with brand new drivers' licences and really old cars, my mates and I saw REDEX

CHAPTER NINE

rally driver 'Gelignite' Jack Murray as a genuine cultural hero. While we all fancied ourselves behind the wheel, we were in awe of Jack Murray and vastly entertained at the thought of him hurtling along outback dusty roads tossing sticks of gelignite out the window.

As a school student I'd worked as a storeman for my father and done a couple of stints in a factory. I loathed being confined and under constant supervision so I applied for every driving job going. From the end of Year 12 until graduation I drove delivery vans, light trucks, utes and taxis all over metropolitan Adelaide. My mates had always called me Jack anyway, and it wasn't long before some wit in the pub dubbed me 'Gelignite Jack', in recognition of my endless hours at the wheel. The nickname stuck.

After I left Redgum in 1986 I started work on my solo album, *Etched in Blue*. It had always been my intention to call it *Gelignite Jack* but, shortly before its release, some other bloke released an album called *Whispering Jack*. Bugger. 'Never mind,' I thought to

Above: The Grey Ghost outside Gelignite Jack's restaurant, Shoal Bay. Jack did not have any financial interest or involvement in the restaurant.

myself, 'I'll save the name up until 2007 when I'll release a collection of my best songs.'

The name 'Gelignite' Jack is not copyrighted © or registered in any fashion, and its use is unrestricted. Accordingly, it has been used at various times and for various businesses. For instance, a restaurant in the Shoal Bay Country Club used the name for a period and a discounters in Cooroy, near Noosa in Queensland, uses the name Gelignite Jack's.

I welcome the name continuing in public use. Appropriate commercial use of Jack's moniker serves a role in reminding everyone of an Aussie legend and icon.

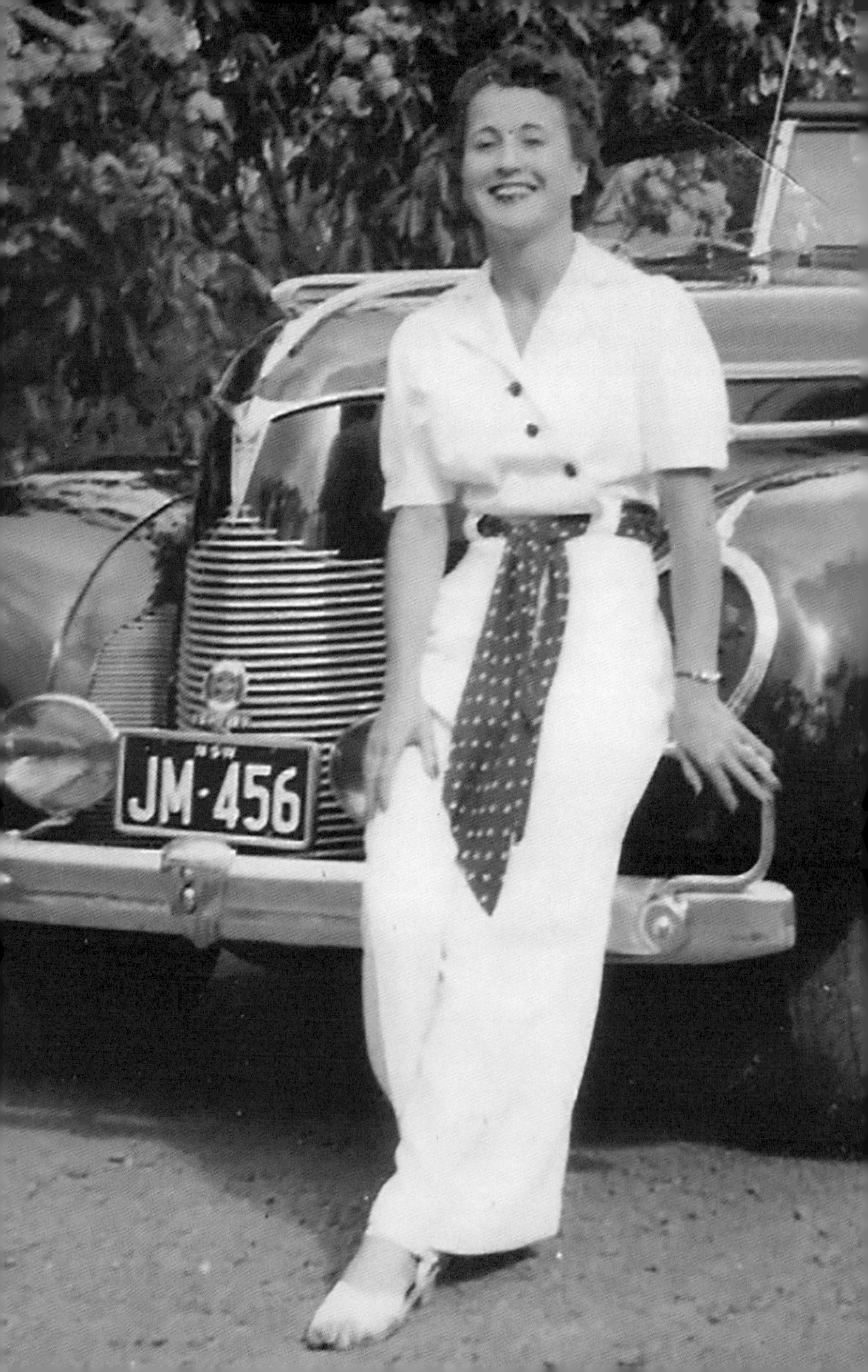
JM·456

CHAPTER TEN

FAMILY

In the late 1950s my father Jack purchased a three-storey block of residential units at 24 Derby Street, Vaucluse. Each floor was occupied by a single unit. The Murray family—Jack, Ena, John and Philip—lived in one, and Jack rented the remaining two. The family home was the top floor, commanding a sweeping view across Sydney Harbour from the Harbour Bridge to North Head. Derby Street was home when I was a boy and Sydney's Eastern Suburbs is where I grew up.

When Jack and Neil Bennetts were recording their 1976 National Library interview, an interesting exchange took place that struck me as an insight into my father's real passions, interests and concerns:

> **BENNETTS**: When did you get married?
>
> **MURRAY**: Oh, I forgot about getting married. Oh, Christ knows—John is 34. About 35 years ago.
>
> **BENNETTS**: 1945?
>
> **MURRAY**: Got married, yeah about 45, I'll just say that. You could say to me, 'When did you have time to get married?' and I'd say, 'Oh yeah, I got married about 1945.' I've got two boys. Got one, Philip—

Left: Ena and Jack honeymooned in Queensland.

CHAPTER TEN

he's 22—and the other guy is 34. And then forget it like more or less, wouldn't you? You can't, don't talk about it (sniffs).

Jack and Ena Byrne were married on 3 July 1942. At the time of this interview, I was actually 21 and John was 32.

The interview continues:

BENNETTS: 1945 was the Australian Grand Prix. [*sic:* but there was no Grand Prix, because of the war. It was 1947 at Bathurst.] Did you go in that?

MURRAY: The car that I was driving was a Brescia Bug [*sic:* Type 39 Grand Prix Bugatti] fitted with a V8 Ford, Edelbrock Ford, parts that you could buy from the States. It had a Winfield camshaft in it—that came from America—and I had a Halibrand rear end. That gave you 14 ratios, just by taking a plate off the back: four nuts, and pull the gear out and just pop it in again; it was on a spline. What else was there? Oh, it was a car—bits of everything. It was a good car: you could go 115-120 miles an hour. I drove that at Bathurst in the Grand Prix.

This interchange shows how Jack could not tell his interviewer the year he was married nor the ages of his two boys, but could in minute detail relay step-by-step instructions on how to change the gearing on a Brescia Bug to deliver 14 ratios—from over 30 years before.

To those who knew him, it comes as no revelation that Jack was not your *Father Knows Best*, patches on the sleeve, 'kick a football around on the weekend' or 'sit by the fireside' style of father. But nor was this unusual for the times. In the 1950s and 60s, the role of raising the children often fell more to the wives, while husbands were pre-occupied with work or play. Clearly, Jack chose play. His real interests lay beyond the family, in the challenges of motor and water sport, adventure travel and his many eclectic interests that led to his becoming an Australian sporting icon.

As a result of the large gap in our ages, just under eleven years, I believe my brother John and I experienced Jack differently. We each grew up in different times with a different family dynamic that changed over the years. In writing

Above: Jean Byrne, Ena's twin sister, at left, with Ena and Jack, enjoying time at the beach.

this biography, it has become apparent to me how relatively little time I had with my father in an adult-to-adult relationship. When I completed my university studies in 1976, I lived for a year in Goulburn, and I spent most of 1980 travelling in Europe. Jack passed away in December 1983, having had three years of intermittent illness. When he died I had just turned 29.

While as a boy I never sensed an absence on Jack's part, as an adult reflecting on those childhood years, there were clearly differences between my life and the experiences of most of my peers. For instance, we never undertook a holiday as a family unit, where my father, mother, brother and I vacationed together. I travelled quite extensively as a schoolboy, to outback Australia, Queensland, New Zealand, Noumea and the Pacific on a cruise aboard the *Oriana*—but always on holiday with my mother. Nor did we ever have anything as banal as a family BBQ, which to people today sounds most unusual.

Early family life in the Murray household, as I experienced it, differed from what was seen as the norm. A young boy who loses his father when aged only five, and then has to finish schooling and make his own way in life at the tender age of fourteen, has not had the benefit of family experience or the role model that prepares him for fatherhood later in life. Jack had to find his own model for parenting.

CHAPTER TEN

Betty Wheeler, family friend and champion waterskier, recounted memories from the early 1950s:

> A usual Sunday afternoon winter outing was to Centennial Park and this is where I first met 'Sparra' [Ena, my mother] and John. Another was to Jervis Bay for a couple of weeks in October and November. Joey [Jack] took his family down and came back to The Garage and maybe went for weekends as well. Bruck and I went there too but maybe just for the day as I can't remember staying anywhere. I know it was a happy group of friends—husbands and wives and children. Another life really.

The expectations and choices available in 1950s Australia, both for men and women, were certainly different from today. My wife Rhonda and I made the conscious decision not to have children. As a couple who have made a lifestyle choice that precluded parenthood, I can certainly appreciate and understand how Jack's interests and activities may well have been focused outside the family.

In the exchange with Neil Bennetts, Jack commented, 'And then forget it like more or less, wouldn't you? You can't, don't talk about it (sniffs).' In my view, this is Jack seeking to maintain his privacy. Given that the conversation is being recorded for posterity by the National Library of Australia, Jack (I interpret) understandably wishes to avoid a discussion about his marriage and the long-term relationship and love outside his marriage which I will describe in a later chapter.

While Jack was a larger-than-life, garrulous and extrovert man, when it came to his relationships, I believe he wished to protect and shield the women in his life, and avoid possible public embarrassment. This explains his comfort and ease with discussions centred on 'the gearing of a Brescia Bug', yet his reluctance to venture into the more fraught subjects of marriage and relationships. On such issues, he was quite coy.

My mother once told me that she had never heard my father swear. Needless to say, as the son of 'Gelignite' Jack Murray, I was f**king flabbergasted. But, in the old school tradition that now seems to have passed, Jack did not swear in front of women. This is another part of the different lives of Jack: he was a man who spoke two languages, English and profane, yet was gentlemanly, almost quaint, in their editing out in the presence of the fairer sex. That was 1950s' Australia.

FAMILY

Where did the family all begin? How did it start? The origins of Jack's story lie in two countries, the United States and Australia, and two states, Victoria and NSW, in Melbourne and in Sydney. The dual identity theme emerged in Jack's life well before he was born.

John Eric Murray

'Gold!' That was the word that in the 1850s caught the attention of the entire world and drew immigrants to Australia, and in particular Victoria, from every country.

The Victorian Gold Discovery Committee wrote in 1854:

> The discovery of the Victorian Goldfields has converted a remote dependency into a country of worldwide fame; it has attracted a population, extraordinary in number, with unprecedented rapidity; it has enhanced the value of property to an enormous extent; it has made this the richest country in the world; and, in less than three years, it has done for this colony the work of an age, and made its impulses felt in the most distant regions of the earth.

Thomas Murray, born in New York and Agnes Main born, in Glasgow, Scotland came separately to this Antipodean Promised Land, looking for a new life and a share in Australia's newfound wealth. Whether it was gold or the wealth that it spawned, they were drawn to the land down under. They married in Carlton, Melbourne in 1875 and had a son, Walter. Walter James Murray (born 9 June 1883 in South Melbourne) met Alice Carse and they married in Fitzroy, Victoria on 28 July 1903.

Alice gave birth to four sons, each roughly two years apart: Hubert James ('Narra'), Raymond Godfrey (Ray), John Eric (Jack) and Leonard Thomas (Lennie, also known affectionately as 'Dopey').

At the time of Jack's birth, his father Walter Murray's occupation was recorded as orchardist. Jack recalled in the National Library interview that when the boys were six, eight, ten and twelve, their father, who was then an engineer at the gas company, died suddenly of a heart attack. Walter's death certificate records he died on the 23 October 1912, aged just 29.

Walter's death certificate shows that Jack had just turned five at the time of his father's death. The boys would have in fact been around three, five, seven

CHAPTER TEN

Above Left: Jack's mother, Alice Maud Murray (née Carse) with her adopted daughter Doreen. (This adoption may not have been legalised.) The portraits show Jack's mother Alice and father Walter.

and nine. Walter Murray died of a mitral valve [heart] problem compounded by over twelve months of pneumonia. His occupation at time of death was still recorded as orchardist.

Jack's memorial plaque at the Northern Suburbs Crematorium incorrectly lists his birth date as 28 August 1907. It was not uncommon for discrepancies to appear in early birth records, particularly for home births. For many years he thought his birthday was in fact 2 September 1907. For reasons forever to remain unexplained, he then switched to celebrating 28 August 1907. I have a copy of the birth certificate, and can verify it as 30 August.

Neither my father's nor my mother's ashes lie beneath this plaque. Jack's were scattered shortly after his death by his wife and two sons on the waters of his beloved Hawkesbury River. Ena's were cast upon the waters of Sydney Harbour

Above: The plaque shows an incorrect birth date for Jack.

near the eastern 'wedding cake' pylon by her two sons and her grandson. Mum loved the view of the Harbour from the window of our Vaucluse unit—and now she is part of that view for all time.

What is certain is that Alice Murray was left as a relatively young widow with four boys under ten to raise.

Jack said that although his schooldays were a lot of fun, he 'could not wait to get out of school'. It is likely that economic pressures alone would have forced him to leave at fourteen and make his own way in life.

In the National Library interview he tells of his itinerant working life as he grew from a boy into a man:

> I was in Melbourne one Christmas there on my own. They'd all gone away and a chap came down. I lived near the garage and he had a tractor. He talked to me in the street. He was a stranger, [but] he said he'd like somebody to drive it back, so I volunteered for the job. I drove the tractor back and I stayed with him for nine months, drove the tractor, ploughed, up in a place called Sea Lake in Victoria where they grow a lot of wheat and all that sort of stuff. Then I lumped wheat at the railway station there for three months. I was about seventeen or something. Lumping wheat—you pick the bag up, put it on your shoulders and walk up the stack with it. At night time you just flop on the bed and don't move, and in the morning you start work again. I stayed there for three months, then I went grape picking at Mildura and I stayed there for about three or four months. A chap staying at the same place as I was, he was a diver's attendant and he was leaving, and he said, 'Why don't you take the job? It's dead easy. You can come down and watch me dress the diver.' And I said 'Right', and I watched. I could do it quite easy, so anyhow I was a diver's attendant for about four or five months till the river flooded ... and then I left Melbourne and came to Sydney.

In the early 1930s Sydney replaced Melbourne as home. By the mid-to-late 1930s, in partnership with brother Ray, Murray Bros Garage was established in Bondi. Jack's lifelong love of cars, boats, speed and adventure had begun.

CHAPTER TEN

Above: A 'happy snap' of early days, the beginning of our family.

Ena May Murray

Are you over 60? If so, you will remember red public phone booths. Now, you may not have realised it, but back in the 1960s if you dialled a number and your call was answered, there was no need to deposit any coins. As the caller, if you shouted into the earpiece—not the mouthpiece—very loudly, the person you had called could faintly hear you.

This is the phone hacking technique I used as a fourteen-year-old, too-young-to-drive surfie, both to defraud the PMG and also summon my mother to pick me up in her car following a day's surfing. She never complained, but simply dropped whatever she was doing and dutifully drove from Vaucluse to Bondi Beach to collect her youngest son. I blush with shame today to think how generous my mother was with her time—and how readily I expected her to be so. But that was my mother. She lived for her sons. Whether she was driving to Queensland with John's VJ sailboat strapped to the roof of her car or taking me on a bus trip to explore Australia, her life was all about ensuring her sons' well being, education and development. Thanks, mum.

My mother was born Ena May Byrne at Luke St, Randwick on 23 April 1915. Fifteen minutes earlier, her twin sister Jean had been born. It was to be the beginning of a sisterly friendship and love that would span nine decades. There were two older brothers, Charlie (15) and Albert (5), and an eight-year-old sister, Marjorie. The Byrne twins grew up in the Coogee and Bondi areas of Sydney's Eastern Suburbs.

To put my mother's life into perspective, she was born just two days before ANZAC Day. Not *an* ANZAC Day, but *the* ANZAC Day—the first, when 1500 troops landed on the shores of Gallipoli. This is often seen as the birthplace of the Australian nation and its spirit. So mum was born at the same time as our nation. In her 90 years she would witness the tumultuous events and extraordinary changes of the twentieth century.

Ena left school at fifteen and started work at the Prince Edward Theatre.

Older sister Marjorie was the head cashier, twin sister Jean was the sound and light monitor and mum worked as an usherette directing patrons either upstairs or downstairs and to their seats. In the days when descriptions were less politically correct, the Byrne sisters would have been described as 'top sorts'. Working in the theatre must have been enjoyable, despite the stories Auntie Jean told me about rats in the chandeliers.

After eight years at the Prince Edward Theatre, aged 23, mum moved on to work as a demonstrator for Colgate Palmolive products.

Around this time Ena Byrne met up with a Bondi character by the name of Jack Murray. Romance blossomed.

The war in Europe was underway and war in the Pacific loomed. The Japanese bombed Pearl Harbour on 7 December 1941, and seven months later, at 12 noon on 3 July 1942, Jack Murray and Ena Byrne were married at St Luke's Church, Randwick. There was no reception and the bride and groom left by car for Cairns and their honeymoon immediately after the wedding service. Friends of Jack chased the car—in fact they chased it as far as

Above: The Byrne sisters: at left, Jean, then older sister Marjorie and Ena at right.

CHAPTER TEN

Newcastle. Mum lost her wedding hat on the Harbour Bridge as Jack's open-top convertible attempted to lose the pursuing wedding guests.

Clearly, those were the days before the police had radar.

The wedding guests and Jack's prankster mates had their moment in Cairns. As Jack opened their beach umbrella, confetti rained down upon the newlyweds. Sixteen months later, my brother John was born. I can only assume he must have been bit of a handful, because it was almost eleven more years before I arrived on the scene. My mother once told me she had been planning a trip to Hawaii, but felt a bit queasy, so went to the doctor. That's when mum heard about me. Given the choice between childbirth or Hawaii, I think I might have chosen Hawaii.

Mum did what women in that era did, devoting herself to her marriage and the raising of her two boys. My mother did not build any structures or sign any major contracts. She did not carve out a career in the business world. What she did do was her very best for her two sons. Whether she was helping out at the Vaucluse Sailing Club, or ferrying carloads of young footballers about in her Volkswagen, she gave nothing but love, encouragement and help to John and me.

My mother had a party trick she used on our holidays together. She was never caught short for a fancy dress costume, whether we were aboard the *Oriana* cruising the Pacific or staying at the Hydro Majestic at Blackheath. At breakfast my mother would purloin a couple of extra slices of toast. That evening she would glide into fancy dress. With me at her side and the toast elegantly pinned into her hair, she drew attention with a sign draped around her neck proclaiming: 'Toast to the [insert appropriate boat or hotel name here].' I was so embarrassed! Then I was

Above: School holidays 1961. Because she had left school early, mum always valued education.

frequently blackened up with boot polish and, wearing my mother's fur coat and carrying an over-sized bone borrowed from the kitchen, I was a cave man—or cave boy. It still makes me laugh to think of these antics.

Today I am still very proud of something I did in 1974. I repaid, in a very small way, the kindness and love my mother and aunt had shown me all my life. As a travelling trio we embarked on a 'Jean and Ena' road trip to Central Australia in my surfie panel van. I must admit, being a university student at the time, my motives were more pecuniary than honourable: Mum and my aunt had agreed to pay all expenses. But I can happily report that Jean, who had travelled the world several times described our holiday as 'the best of my life'.

What an adventure it was! A herd of wild brumbies devoured our breakfast cereal despite the twins' *shoo shoo* and waving hands. A mouse plague at Ayers Rock (Uluru) meant we shared our rather flimsy and very openly constructed hut accommodation with several dozen rodents. Jean stayed awake all night, once more employing the ineffective *shoo shoo* technique. And who can forget the look of apologetic embarrassment on the face of the Tennant Creek camp ground owner? Arriving late at night, I had unwittingly parked on the only green grass lawn within 1000 kilometres. In the middle of the night, midway through a stream of expletives from the owner directing what he thought were surfies to move their 'f**king shitbox car', the twins poked their heads out of the driver's side window. One cried, 'We've paid. We've paid.' What a shock for the owner! What a trip. What great memories.

My boyhood years passed quickly. Mum was a keen tennis player, and some of her happiest times were spent playing or having lunch with 'the tennis girls' (as she called them) or other ladies whose sons went to my high school. They were friends who would remain so for life.

When Jack passed away in December 1983, he and my mother had been married for 41 years.

Ena's Last Years

My mother suffered her first stroke in July 1995. It left her with limited speech and generally weakened. Jean and her son George, through their kindness and compassion, welcomed my mother into their Castle Cove home. Without Jean during that period, my mother would not have had the moments of quality and happiness that they both enjoyed and shared.

Ena lived with Jean for four and a half years. When Jean herself fell ill,

CHAPTER TEN

Ena lived with my wife Rhonda and me at our Sylvania Waters home for six months, before accommodation was found in a nursing home.

Once mum wandered into the kitchen at Sylvania Waters and asked Rhonda, 'What is the date?' Rhonda told her and she walked out. A few minutes later, she came back—with the same question, same answer. She then left the room. Rhonda had noticed that mum was in tears. It was 14 December 1999, sixteen years since Jack's funeral. She had remembered and was still deeply saddened.

I cannot tell my mother's story without thanking Rhonda. She helped me care for my mother, by sharing the worry and burden. Over the years Rhonda has been a support and comfort to both my mother and my aunt. We sat at my mother's bedside with grandson Jonny Murray as mum passed quietly away.

Ena had been blessed with a life full of good health. She neither smoked nor drank alcohol.

Up until her first stroke, at age 80, throughout her life she had only been in hospital to have her two sons. Don't we all hope that we can claim such a record at the end of our lives? Old age did not sit well with her. The stroke, loss of speech and the reduced mobility that comes with age were a source of frustration. 'Oh, blast' she used to say as she struggled with words and became annoyed with her inability to convey a message.

Ena and Jean were inseparable in life—and, as fate would have it, inseparable also in death, passing away within just nine days of one another in 2005. Twins always have a special bond, but Ena and Jean were especially close, given that their marriages and husbands had striking similarities.

Both were married to 'men's men', larger-than-life figures. Jean's husband, Fred Rush, was a very successful property developer and World War II bomber pilot. The partners in both marriages drifted apart and both husbands developed long-term relationships outside their marriages. Given the parallel situations, the sisters were often in one another's company and when Ena had her stroke, it was only natural that Jean should come to her aid.

Thank you, mum. You were everything two sons could ever have hoped for in a mother.

John Vivian Murray

In July 1954 as 'Gelignite' Jack Murray drove the Grey Ghost into the Sydney Showground to win the second REDEX Trial, ten-year-old John watched in awe as the crowd applauded his father's achievement. What an impression that

FAMILY

Above: Big brother John was almost a second father figure to me.

must have made! No doubt the experience kindled in him the love of motorsport that would in later years see 'Cracker Jack' compete against, and with, his famous father.

John attended Vaucluse Primary School and then Vaucluse Boys High School, before completing his secondary education at The Scots College, Bellevue Hill. Schooldays over, he then completed an apprenticeship as a motor mechanic. However, he quickly realised that he preferred to be behind the wheel rather than on the end of a spanner.

When I was still a teenager just learning to drive, my brother allowed me behind the wheel of his beautiful sky blue, two-door Mercury Cougar, an American muscle car. No admonition was required from big brother, as a show-off little brother managed to get the big V8-powered car stuck sideways on Military Road, Bondi. My white knuckles and wide-eyed look told John that I had just learned a valuable lesson.

With his fleet of taxis co-owned with his brother Ray, Jack advised both his boys when they reached 21 years of age to obtain their cab licences as a financial fallback. While we both complied with Jack's instructions, obtained taxi licences and drove cabs casually for a period, we both quickly moved on in our respective careers.

John inherited the motorsport gene. He competed in a number of rallies and motoring events over the years. In 1964, John and his twenty-year-old mate Peter Barnes entered twelve car trials run each weekend by the Sydney Car Club, in preparation for the 1964 Ampol Trial.

On 14 June 1964, John 'Cracker Jack' Murray set off from Bondi Beach in a balloon-filled, lime green Milo sponsored Valiant car, he along with 200

CHAPTER TEN

Above: John 'Cracker Jack' Murray. Photo courtesy Hal Moloney.

others on the 7500 mile journey. As already noted, two weeks later he returned to place thirty-third in the field—while his father could manage only fortieth.

In August 1979, father and son, together with Jeff d'Albora, of d'Albora Marinas, teamed up in the 20,000 km Repco Reliability Round Australia Trial. The trial, like the 1955 REDEX, proved to be controversial, with results disputed and contested. Only thirteen vehicles of 167 entries completed the course. Jack, John, Jeff and their Commodore were placed either twenty-third or twenty-ninth, depending on your source. The boys missed eleven controls.

Jack was certainly less than impressed with how car trials had altered over the preceding 25 years:

That bloody Repco would have to have been the most useless bastard of an event I've ever been in. We went for two bloody weeks and hardly saw anyone; that's not what rallying is all about. Where was the social side of the event, where blokes could sit around a table and tell lies to each other and generally have a good time?

Rest periods and time between sections were not new issues when it came to round Australia trials. In the *Truth* newspaper's *Souvenir REDEX Trial Feature* written in July 1954, we read:

> As contests such as the REDEX are primarily intended to be a test of cars and not of ability to forgo sleep and endure driving fatigue which might jeopardise safety, the determination of the number and duration of rest periods deserves close analysis when conditions for the 1955 trial are formulated.

Clearly lessons had not been learned over the intervening 25 years. The emergence and popularity of fun and charity Variety Bashes in recent years shows the general appeal of what Jack had been urging for many years.

Above: John and Jack rallying together.

CHAPTER TEN

Jack's Grey Ghost entered the 1979 Repco Trial as Car No 72, driven by Maurice Walsh and Don Whitby. It fared no better than Jack, retiring with a broken crankshaft.

While no one realised it at the time, the 1979 Repco Trial was to be Jack's last competitive motorsport event. It was a fitting finale, that father and son—as lovers of motorsport—should get the opportunity to share that one last event together— even if it were 'the most useless bastard'!

Most recently John has competed in the 2008 and 2009 Australian Rally Championships, driving a Commodore in 2008 and a Subaru Impreza WRX in 2009.

As a boy, John was always a keen sailor. He has been a former placegetter in state VJ sailing championships. It was a natural fit when as a young man he entered the private sector, establishing the company Marlin Australia, specialising in the production of life jackets, PFDs and wet-weather clothing.

The company grew and expanded internationally, enjoying great success. It now exports to the American and European markets. Today it is the market leader in marine apparel. John and his wife Wendy live in Vaucluse and have one son, John Charles Murray (aka Jonny), who was born in 1981. A third generation of Murray was about to hit the road.

John Charles Murray

A third generation of Murray has inherited the motorsport gene. With a famous grandfather such as 'Gelignite' Jack and a father who was a keen and successful rally driver in his own right, it is little wonder that young Jonny Murray developed an interest in and displayed a natural ability for motorsport.

In 2007, under the Marlin Australia Team banner, Jonny competed in the World Rally Championships, driving a Subaru Impreza WRX.

He had been raised in Rose Bay and

Above: Like his famous grandfather and his father, Jonny Murray is equally comfortable in a car on four wheels, two wheels or even airborne.

Vaucluse and, following in his father's footsteps, attended The Scots College. After school, he joined his father in the family business, while enjoying motorsport in his leisure time. Jonny's first car was a red Nissan 200 SX, an ex-race car fitted with Recaro seats, body kit and twin turbos, to become a young man's dream car and a father's worst nightmare.

Type in 'John Murray Jnr longest jump' into YouTube and you will be treated to exhilarating footage showing a third generation of Murray rallying, airborne, and obtaining a 'longest jump distance'. In a Subaru WRX, Jonny competed in the 2006 Australian Rally Championship. He retains a strong link to his famous grandfather, living in what had been the family home.

Just as in the 1960s when 'Cracker Jack' was to beat his famous father in the 1964 Ampol Reliability Trial, so over 40 years later, Jonny was to finish twenty-second in the 2007 NEC Australian Rally Championship, narrowly edging out his father who only managed an equal twenty-fourth.

All those years later, as a father was once again passed by his son, no doubt the irony was not lost on John: 'Get cracking dad—this is a tow away zone.' Both Murrays competed in four of the six events staged that year, but Jonny was plagued by mechanical problems and mishaps, particularly in the final events.

In August 2015 a tragic terrorist bomb blast occurred in Bangkok, killing 22 people and injuring over 140. Jonny and his girlfriend Leify Porter were on the overhead bridge at 7pm on a balmy Thai evening when the bomb detonated. Leify was thrown to the ground by the force of the explosion. When interviewed by the BBC, a shaken Jonny commented, 'There was a guy crawling next to us who we tried to help ... the footpath was covered in blood. It's something I've never seen and I never want to witness again.' We all realise how close this event was to becoming a very personal and family tragedy.

Then Jonny and Leify had the misfortune of being in Paris during the November 2015 terrorist attack. Jonny was on his way to attend a boat show in Amsterdam.

The world has become a very different place in just three generations. Throughout this book I have written about 'gelignite' and 'explosions' as I recount Jack's pranks and antics. They were simply good fun, publicity and entertainment, enjoyed by many. But now Jack's grandson has had a brush with death associated with a very different kind of explosion—one born of hatred and callous disregard for fellow human beings.

CHAPTER TEN

Philip Eric Murray

When I was born—less than three months after 'Gelignite' Jack Murray became an Australian household name on winning the 1954 REDEX Trial—I was dubbed 'the REDEX Baby'.

Like my brother, I attended Vaucluse Primary School, followed by Vaucluse Boys High School. For a couple of years in primary school, my fellow classmate was the twenty-ninth Prime Minister of Australia, Malcolm Turnbull.

For my eleventh birthday, Jack gave me a surfboard and a set of weights. Both surfing and body building developed into passions. Like my fitness conscious father before me, I am a non-drinker and non-smoker—save for the odd glass of wine with friends.

I have never ventured into motorsport, but have always enjoyed physical training and keeping fit. In 1982 and 1983, as an amateur, drug free body builder, I managed several third place positions, both as a novice and within my weight category. In 1984, I went one better and won the UBBA NSW Men's Open over 80 kg.

Both John and I were good looking young men (even if I say so myself!) and as boys and youths, we dabbled in part-time careers in modelling, acting

Above: Future Prime Minister Malcolm Turnbull (back row, far left)—unusual for a Liberal, but probably appropriate for Malcolm. I am the blond standing at far left, third row.

and 'extra' roles in commercials, television and films. John appeared in the early 1960s Crawford TV production *Consider Your Verdict*, while I had minor roles in movies such as *The Punisher*, starring Dolph Lundgren and Lou Gossett Jnr, *Facts of Life Down Under* and Australian local productions such as *Luigi's Ladies* and *Come in Spinner*. Because of my body building, I often landed roles as policemen, gangster heavies or (in the very forgettable *Luigi's Ladies*) as the classic muscle-head in a comic pursuit of a dwarf and a well-endowed topless young lady, in a scene shot on Bondi Beach. Shakespeare it ain't—but it was a lot of fun at the time.

I actively pursued surfing, football, athletics and Goju-Kai karate as a boy growing up. My first car was a 1967 Holden HR panel van, complete with surfboard racks and the obligatory mattress and curtains in the back. I was academically inclined rather than mechanical, and when I completed my Higher School Certificate, was school dux in geography. I won a cadetship to join the public sector with the then-MWS&DB [State Government organisation which supplies Sydney's water and sewerage needs, today called Sydney Water]. Continuing my studies, I went on to gain an Honours Degree in Surveying from the University of NSW. I subsequently became a Registered Land Surveyor.

Above: Models and actors: at left, John; in the middle Phil as a wartime US serviceman and at right as a 1940s standover man.

CHAPTER TEN

Above: Our Sylvania Waters home became a film set in 1988 for *The Punisher*. Jack would have been proud of the exploding and burning car in the driveway featured in this action movie.

In a career spanning 30 years, I had a variety of roles within an evolving and changing organisation: land surveyor, sewer and water system designer, system planner, internal consultant, urban development leader, trainer and major projects manager.

I retired in 2005 and today live in Nelson Bay, NSW with Rhonda, a former

Above: On Graduation Day, May 1977, with my mother. My second car, a Datsun 240z sports is on the right.

National Manager for the US-based Honeywell. We were married in 1987.

An Unexpected Daughter, 'Carol'

There are certain moments in one's life that are milestones, forever etched in memory. In early September 2007 I answered our home phone and was met by an unfamiliar middle-aged woman's voice. (For privacy reasons, I will use the pseudonym 'Carol'.) Following the initial introductions Carol, clearly steeling herself, paused and proffered: 'I'm your big sister.' As she later confided, this was a very difficult phone call for her to undertake. She had struggled for three days, building up the courage and preparing to dial our number.

Above: Thanks for the weights, dad. Hours of gym work certainly paid off for me, with 92 kilos of muscle, circa 1983. Those were the days!

This phone call was not totally unexpected. A month or so earlier, I had been contacted by a mechanic friend from Bondi who, via a chain of interconnected people, had met a lady who believed she was 'Gelignite' Jack Murray's biological daughter. Interested to hear her story, I agreed that my friend could pass on my contact details. As I spoke to her, I reassured Carol that there was no need for her fears or apprehension. Curious and wanting to hear what she had to say, I welcomed the opportunity to speak with her.

I learned that she had met my brother the previous year, near Yarra Glen in Victoria. She had approached John, who was competing in a car rally at the time, and informed him that she was Jack Murray's daughter. She asked, and John agreed, to pose for several photos.

I can only imagine that the appearance of an unexpected half-sister must have been quite a shock for my brother. It must have been difficult to hear this news in person and then to instantly change tack, switching gear both literally and figuratively to concentrate on driving a rally car at high speed.

As her story unfolded, Carol revealed her difficult, if not tragic upbringing. At just three months old, she had been abandoned by her mother and handed to her grandparents. Made a ward of the state, Carol had been raised by these

CHAPTER TEN

grandparents. Her mother did not remain in contact, except for a couple of visits each year when she was aged between five and ten.

In 1992, at age 62, having had two heart attacks and two strokes within a 48-hour period, Carol's mother passed away. However, before doing so, Carol told me her mother had a moment of clarity. At her mother's bedside, she seized this last opportunity to seek the truth and uncover a long-held family secret. She set out the following conversation:

> 'I deserve to know who my father was.'
> 'A REDEX rally driver,' her mother replied.
> 'You're not going to tell me my father was 'Gelignite' Jack Murray?'
> 'Yes,' her mother replied. Two hours later, she died.

Carol informed me that in the same year, nine years after Jack's death, she had contacted and later met with Evan Green, related her story and accompanied Evan to Jack's Garage. A signed copy of one of Evan's books is one of Carol's most prized possessions, along with a copy of the TV show *This Is Your Life* featuring 'Gelignite' Jack Murray.

As you would expect, I was rather taken aback by this flood of information.

My initial reaction was to feel uncomfortable with how readily Carol used the term 'dad' when referring to Jack, my father. Carol's easy references to 'dad's garage' and observations such as 'I can't believe I have a big brother and a little brother—and I love my little brother' were all quite overwhelming.

I found our conversations unsettling and disconcerting. As I answered questions about birth and marriage dates and other family details I felt as if a stranger were delving into my personal life.

Carol related how as a little girl she recalled riding in Jack's Cadillac-Allard and the man driving being referred to as 'Joey'—the nickname often used by Jack's friends. This man she said she later 'definitely' recognised on *This Is Your Life* as 'Gelignite' Jack Murray.

Despite the feelings it arouses, I have a great deal of sympathy for Carol's story and empathy for her situation. For 25 years she had been searching for an identity for herself and a family history for her children. She even offered to undertake a DNA test 'to prove I am your big sister'.

So is Carol correct in her belief? I don't know. Did Jack, as a 41-year-old, father a child to an eighteen-year-old girl? Certainly the descriptions 'bit of

FAMILY

a ladies' man' and 'stable of women' have been applied to Jack on more than one occasion. For him there was always that duality, a family life, particularly in the late 1940s and 50s—but another life as well. As a close lady friend of Jack's once remarked, 'It was mostly older blokes with young, attractive women.' Given Carol's childhood memories it seems possible that Jack was—or at least thought he was—her father.

All these years later, I am very conscious that Jack is not here in person and can neither confirm, deny nor offer comment. Sixty years on, there is much speculation and conjecture. I am not questioning Carol's sincerity and honesty, and her firm belief that Jack is her father. However, a multitude of questions remain unanswered in the story she tells.

Carol has no documentation or photos as supportive evidence. Jack Murray

Above: Jack's vehicles and boats certainly attracted the ladies.

CHAPTER TEN

is of course not listed on her birth certificate as her father. Her mother went by three different names in her life—apparently because she 'hated' her given name. Carol is adamant that her mother was lucid when she questioned her. However, she was critically ill, only hours away from death and presumably heavily medicated at the time when she agreed that Jack was Carol's father. Such concerns tend to at least bring into question the veracity, not of Carol's own story, but perhaps of her mother's.

If Jack was part of Carol's mother's life, is it not possible other men were as well? Jack and Carol's mother may have *thought* he was Carol's father. Was a mother racked with guilt on her deathbed trying to placate and appease an abandoned daughter by offering her a famous father as a form of atonement?

What about the DNA test? With today's technology, DNA testing using biological samples from two known siblings and a possible half-sibling could be undertaken to indicate whether or not Jack was Carol's biological father. Unlike, say, a DNA paternity test, a half-sibling test is not conclusive. At best, it can only provide a statistical probability, the *likelihood* of two individuals being related.

Perhaps more importantly the question needs to be asked: DNA testing to what end and for what purpose? Carol is at the end of her quest. She is satisfied in her belief that Jack was her father. Neither my brother John nor I feel any sibling bonds or kinship. We don't feel it's necessary to either prove or disprove Carol's belief.

I think Carol was hoping for something I cannot provide: a half-brother/half-sister relationship. After all, she is at the end of a very long and emotionally draining search that has spanned 25 years.

I, on the other hand, as I talked to her, was on the end of a phone talking to a stranger I had been introduced to only minutes before who referred to my father as 'dad', said she 'loved' me and was looking forward to viewing our family photo albums. This was, you may imagine, quite a surreal experience. I simply felt no emotional connection, nor any desire to establish further contact.

This is what I said to Carol: 'I know this is not what you want to hear. You're going to be upset—and I don't want to hurt you in any way.'

Carol said, 'No—that's OK. I'd like you to have a little more time to take it all in. It took me three or four months to come to grips with it.'

So she agreed that she did not expect me to feel any emotional connection with her, given that all this news was so new and raw. But I felt she hoped that, given time to process what she had told me, I would reach out to her in future. More than ten years later, however, my feelings remain unaltered. No contact has been made during these years. The matter rests there.

In 2007, in a letter, Carol sent me heartfelt details of her life and family. Very poignantly, at the very end she writes:

> I understand your feelings, Phil, because I went through the same for some time. The only thing I now want in my life is just to be accepted or at least acknowledged by my two half-brothers. Please consider my situation.
>
> *Carol*

I hope that in telling her story and including it within Jack's, I have helped her in some way to find the peace, closure and resolution she has sought all her life.

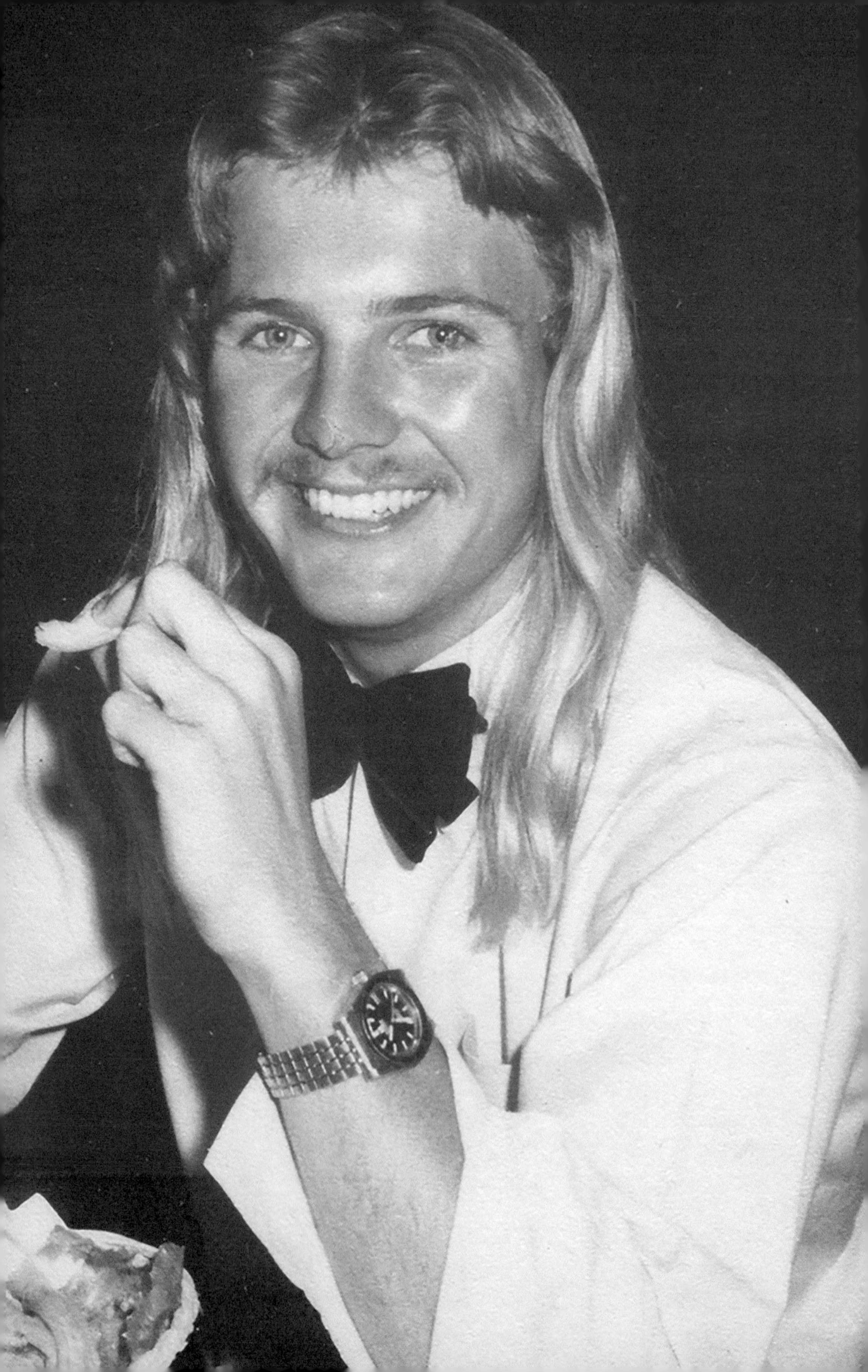

CHAPTER ELEVEN
GROWING UP WITH 'GELIGNITE'

When I was in primary school my dad was famous! Everyone seemed to know him or had heard of him. He always seemed to be in the newspapers. But when I was a headstrong teenager in the revolutionary 1960s, I saw my father as old fashioned. Finally, when the teenager became a man, I came to realise that Jack was also a man, a unique and talented sportsman, whose body may have faded with the years, but whose spirit had not.

When people learn of my heritage, they often ask me, 'What was it like growing up with 'Gelignite' Jack Murray for a father?' And my reply is always the same, 'Well—different.'

Let me give you an insight into exactly *how* different.

Left: The author, University of NSW ball, mid 1970s. Readers be assured, I'm innocently holding a piece of chicken, not a joint!

Above: Twenty-first birthday celebration: Jack, Ena and a cheeky Philip.

CHAPTER ELEVEN

Flying the Red Prince

Jack always kept a stable of vehicles—including a fire engine red 'Prince'. In 1966 and again in 1967 he raced a Prince Skyline at Bathurst. This car was fast. Jack decided to find out exactly how fast one evening, following a family night out.

As Old South Head Road started to steepen and rise up approaching Rose Bay North, Jack put the pedal to the metal—big time. The Prince responded like a greyhound unleashed. Back in 1963, late at night, thankfully there were no other cars on the road. But the narrow, single-lane-each-way road and parked cars left no room for error—and compulsory seat belt wearing was still seven years away.

As the red rocket crested the hill and entered the flat section of the Rose Bay North shopping centre, the vehicle became momentarily airborne.

I vividly recall floating off the seat and hovering in space, shops and parked cars just a blurred smear through a side window. Clearly, Jack was equally comfortable driving on or off the ground.

Ahead lay the sweeping right-hand bend opposite the Diamond Bay Bowling Club. Jack actually accelerated into the right-hander, and I felt the Prince lift. Both right wheels, front and back, were now off the ground. I lay on the back seat, terrified. My mum lay pressed against the passenger door by the G-forces generated. In the calmest of voices she said, without any hope of convincing him, 'Slow down, Jack.'

As the car teetered precariously on two wheels I remember clawing the upholstery, edging my way up towards the right-hand passenger door. Like a motorbike sidecar passenger, I was desperately trying to weigh the vehicle back on to the ground.

When I glanced at the driver, I was mesmerised. Only Jack's fingertips were on the wheel, making lightning-quick micro-adjustments, balancing the centrifugal forces, the weight of the vehicle and the movement in the wheels.

As I watched the instinctive touch adjustments to the steering wheel and his reflex actions, I knew I was watching someone with a special talent.

Exiting the sweeping curve, Jack put the Prince back on all fours. Two minutes later we pulled up outside our home. George Street to Vaucluse: a new land speed record.

At eight years of age the world can seem bigger than it is, and your dad is a hero larger than life. As I retell the story of the night I flew in the red Prince, I remember, laugh and I am eight again.

Above: A fire engine red Prince, as featured in the ABC 500 words contest, which published my story.

Double Bungers

Loud explosions, persistent ringing in the ears, absolute terror and gripping fear: surprisingly, all these and more are associated with one of my fondest boyhood memories.

Guy Fawkes' night—what we kids called Cracker Night—was celebrated with great gusto in the Murray household back in the 1960s. This explosive family festival arose not through any particular love of, or need to, celebrate the saving of the English monarchy. No, our celebration arose more from my father's enjoyment and appreciation of anything that goes 'bang'—preferably very loudly.

No concession was ever made to anything pretty and colourful, anything that whizzed or twirled or swished, encouraging an observer to sigh 'Aaah!' and marvel at the pretty colours.

Cracker Night in the Murray household was strictly and literally observed. It was about 'crackers'; even 'bungers' were unacceptable. The minimum size explosive allowed on the Murray premises was a 'double bunger', a destructive and powerful firework resembling, appropriately enough, a small stick of

CHAPTER ELEVEN

gelignite. Each Cracker Night, Jack brought home several commercial size boxes. As an eleven-year-old, I was barely able to carry a box of double bungers, but I would help unload the car boot jam-packed with a load of munitions. With my cargo marked 'Dangerous—Explosive', I would stagger up the three flights of stairs to our unit, which overlooked the back yard.

It was like preparing for a siege, or perhaps a revolution. Guy Fawkes would have been proud of us. My mother provided the only note of sanity to the night's proceedings. Mum insisted that the cache of explosives be stored upstairs and that I content myself with a Globite school case full of double bungers. Once safely in the backyard, I was to remove a double bunger and close the case to prevent possible detonation from a stray spark. I was then to place the double bunger in the rear of the yard, as far away as possible from the school case, light the fuse and retreat to a safe distance. Should the entire school case have detonated, some of Australia's most expensive Vaucluse real estate would, no doubt, have ceased to exist. I would also have ceased to exist.

I must confess, *listening* to my mother's instructions was the one and only concession to safety made on Cracker Nights.

After several trips up and down the stairs to refill the Globite arsenal, the backyard resembled the Somme during World War 1, a scene of total devastation. A smoky haze hung heavily over the grass. The ground was covered in the paper remains of the double bungers, holes (wherever possible) had been blown in the soft turf, tree branches severed and the Hills Hoist bore several dark scars. I had graduated to placing my double bungers in groups of two or even three on the lower horizontal railing of the small paling boundary fence. I took great delight in watching individual palings being dislodged and blasted into the reserve at the rear of our home with each explosion. Cracker Night was proceeding exceptionally well. By this stage of the evening, I had probably removed three or four fence palings.

It was at this point that I came under heavy and sustained fire.

From the vantage point of the third floor window of our unit, overlooking the backyard, Jack had a commanding view of my operations. Unfortunately, I was also in range of whatever explosive device he chose to lob my way. I didn't suspect a thing. As I prepared to destroy my fifth fence paling, there was an almighty explosion at my feet, directly behind me. Startled, I tumbled forward and crashed into the fence as another explosion burst above me in mid-air. I looked up in utter confusion, as the smoke cleared and paper fluttered to earth. I could see Jack's silhouette and a third match being lit, all framed in the darkness of the third floor window. Cunningly, my father had turned out all the household lights. The unmistakable sight of a lit wick spiralling towards the backyard told me that a third double bunger was heading my way. I grabbed the top of the fence with my left hand and swung myself up and over, landing on the grass of the reserve behind. It was fortunate that I did. The double bunger hit the ground *exactly* where I had been crouched. Jack was not only cunning; he was accurate. It exploded and set fire to the pile of litter that had accumulated at the base of the fence.

Jack, honourable in war, ceased hostilities while I re-jumped the fence, grabbed the garden hose and fought to extinguish the small fire that had now started to consume the remains of the battle-scarred fence and threatened to escape into the lower branches of the liquid amber tree. Laughter and whoops of joy accompanied the closing of the third floor window. Mission accomplished! Jack had successfully scared the living daylights out of me. The fire fighting experience was simply an unexpected bonus.

This marked the end of my 'blitz' and suggested that hostilities had ceased for the evening.

The rest of the night was something of an anti-climax. Nearly blowing up one's son *and* starting a fire are difficult acts to follow—at least in the same evening. I had learned how difficult it is to light double bungers while keeping a wary eye peeled for attacks from above.

Most kids get reprimanded for throwing bungers at one another, blowing up fences and starting fires, however small. My experience was somewhat different. As the son of 'Gelignite' Jack Murray, my only mistakes were to have unwittingly conceded the high ground to Jack and not suspected that he would secrete a stash of his own double bungers with which to rain terror upon his son.

On reflection, it always amazed me that I never got into trouble for my fence demolition program. With hindsight, I now see that it would have been hypocritical for a man renowned for his use of explosives to destroy outback dunnies to chastise a son for demolishing a few fence palings. My defence would have been that my actions could be blamed on genetics.

Condoms, Condy's and Conceptions

Like most teenage boys during the swinging 60s, my sex classroom was definitely *not* the school hall on Father and Son Nights.

CHAPTER ELEVEN

The back of a Holden HR panel van, or prior to that, the thick bush and privacy afforded by the heavily wooded The Glen at Watsons Bay were my preferred venues for learning about love. As a lad, I was always a hands-on, experiential sort of youth rather than a theorist. My father's advice on sex to his younger son was mostly taciturn, but when delivered was certainly unambiguous. Plain speaking could be expected, given that Jack was as well known for his colourful language as his enthusiastic use of explosives. He made for an interesting—even unique—educator when it came to matters carnal.

I recall three distinct occasions when Jack shared his wisdom on the male sex drive, prevention of sexually transmitted diseases and my own untimely procreation.

The Male Sex Drive

Sensing that I had reached the age when a young man's thoughts turn to more than just surfing, his first car and 'What's for dinner, mum?', my father judged it time to assume the role of sex sage and share some worldly advice. Perhaps the fact that the first car I craved was a panel van had given him the heads-up that my youthful interests had broadened.

He endeavoured to convey to me the concept that a hormone-driven youth in the throes of passion might sometimes behave with reckless abandon. Unprotected sex is the likely outcome, he said. Who would have thought? This was the 'use a condom talk' every father has—or should have—with his son. Jack's opening gambit on the subject of catering for the male libido and the need to plan ahead of any horizontal activity was unorthodox, but very Jack: 'Listen, boofhead', he began 'Always remember … a standing prick knows no master.'

With this opening line, my father had my undivided fourteen-year-old attention. My sex education, 'Gelignite' Jack Murray style, had begun.

Prevention of STDs

Several years later, as a twenty-year-old university student with a Hawaiian holiday on the horizon, Jack offered a second gem of sexual advice. He realised that unprotected sex was a distinct possibility. While a condom was the preferred preventative measure, Condy's crystals was Jack's backup contingency plan when it came to sexually transmitted diseases. For those unfamiliar with $KMnO4$, potassium permanganate, it is 'an antiseptic wash or bath for eczema, vulvovaginitis, vaginal thrush and recurrent urine infection'. Suffice to say, it is also said to prevent sexually transmitted diseases.

Jack counselled that immediately following love making (though he did not use this terminology in any of our discussions), it was advisable not only to liberally wash one's private parts with Condy's crystals but pour as much as possible of the pinkish dye down the eye of one's penis.

Leave that striking image at one side for a moment and picture this scene. A Hawaiian hotel room at 5am in the morning. *Aloha*! I had met, entertained and then, gentleman-like, escorted a young lady from Des Moines, Iowa back to her hotel room. Upon returning later to my own room, I thought it prudent to activate the Condy's crystals plan. It was a bit like trying to fill a milk bottle with a fire hose. To say there was 'slight spillage and overflow' with the Condy's crystal mixture is akin to saying the *Titanic* had a problem with a little too much ice. Being a non-drinker, the litre of Mai Tai I had consumed with youthful exuberance earlier in the evening definitely did not assist my dexterity—or aim. Defeated by physics, I thought the best course of action was rest. I passed out cold, slumped over the bed.

'Christ—what have you done?'

It was 6am, and my mate from university and travelling buddy, Peter Dunn, was shaking me awake. Realising I would be entertaining, ever the understanding mate, Peter had made himself scarce for the evening. But with the rising sun, he had returned. Hung over and still sleepy, the look of complete horror on Pete's face was all the wakeup call I needed.

'Shit—there's blood every-bloody-where,' he exclaimed.

It became fuzzily apparent that I had failed in my quest to cleanse my genitals with Condy's crystals. The ubiquitous red-pinkish stain seemed to be splashed all over the room, everywhere but my personal party zone. The bathroom was awash and every towel was pink. The sink looked like an abattoir basin and pink footprints led from the bathroom to my bed. Even the pillow was that certain shade of crimson.

Convincing Peter that I wasn't a serial killer, just a very inaccurate user of a sexual disease preventative, we set about the task of cleaning up and rinsing out towels, sheets and linen. If an afterlife exists, no doubt Jack is there now, relating this story with gusto to St Peter.

CHAPTER ELEVEN

My Untimely Procreation

The third piece of sexual advice offered by my father was to do with my birth. I was conceived on or about New Year's Eve as 1953 fell into 1954. I figured this out when I was about fourteen, maths always being a strong point. But the truly interesting number was eleven. My only other sibling, my brother John, was eleven years older than me. So as a fourteen-year-old, I pondered this, Julius Sumner Miller-like: 'Why is this so?' Maybe my parents had difficulties conceiving a second child? Perhaps they had decided to wait until my brother was older? This question needed answering:

PHIL: Dad, how come there are eleven years between John and me?

JACK: Ah, that's simple. You were a hole in a French letter.

Silence.

We stared into one another's eyes and then, as one, we both roared laughing, throwing our heads back. Another endearing father-son bonding moment, Murray-style.

Confirmation came when my mother recounted to me years later that she had been planning a trip to Hawaii, felt a bit ill in the weeks leading up to it and went to consult her doctor, only to discover that she was pregnant. That Hawaii certainly has its pitfalls for the unwary!

If Jack was not the most orthodox of fathers when it came to dispensing advice on sex, as a fourteen-year-old I appreciated his matter-of-fact style. He talked to, and treated me as he would another man. I've learned over the years that most young blokes respond positively when treated as equals in an adult-to-adult relationship.

Jack passed away over 30 years ago, but my father's sexual advice has left me with a legacy I will carry for the rest of my life. I can never walk down the aisle of a pharmacy or pass a bottle of Condy's crystals without suppressing a boyish grin.

The years passed and as a teenage surfie and later a university student, the battles with my father moved from wars with crackers to a war of wills.

Baking Dish Battles and Other Skirmishes

Hair. To be more precise, the *length* of *my* hair. It drove Jack nuts.

That was the burning issue that lit the fuse in the battles I had with my father during my adolescence. Youthful eyes saw Jack as dictatorial North Korea, while I was the freedom-loving South. Victory eluded both combatants, defeat was unthinkable and an uneasy truce prevailed as I grew ever-more-hirsute throughout my teenage years.

My shining, gleaming, streaming, flaxen, waxen locks irritated my father, cursed with a *Just for Men* tinted and thinning hairline. At fourteen, I realised that I held on my head the tempting power to annoy. Naturally I grew my hair as fast and as long as was humanly possible. In close combat, I once thrust in the line, 'Your hair's so thin—you're just jealous.'

Jack parried with, 'Who wants fat hair'? One to Jack.

Years passed, but the hair war remained unresolved.

Then at seventeen, the subject of my first car arose—or, to be more precise, the subject of who exactly would *pay* for my first car.

Forty years on, as I ease myself into my 60s, I chuckle recalling those inevitable differences of opinion. Struggles and tests of will always occur as boys grow into teenagers and teenagers grow into men. 'Two bulls in a paddock' is the clichéd phrase that best explains the verbal tussles with my father. Older men set boundaries and younger men test them. It has always been like this.

In my case, it was the late 60s: Peace and Love and Rock 'n' Roll, man. I was a surfie, panel van accessorised with mattress in the back, an eight-track stereo system—tie-dyed curtains. For parents with daughters, I was a nightmare on Holden wheels. Of course I was going to have long blond hair and assert my freedom and individuality by copying the dress and fashion of every other teenager. Very cool—and we knew it. The other great advantage I had over my parents when I was a teenager surfing, weight training, shagging and studying my way towards manhood was—well, of course I knew everything worth knowing.

The great hair debate had come to a head, so to speak, the year I turned sixteen. My academic record was impeccable: a straight-A student. As a reward from my high school, several boys were offered the opportunity to participate in a two-week school excursion to Noumea. Jack agreed and offered to pay. The night before payment was due for airfares and accommodation, I asked my father for the cheque. Jack then slowly said, almost as an afterthought, 'Here's the cheque and some spending money—if you get your hair cut.'

Now this took me aback. No previous linkage had ever been made between hair length and overseas travel. Whether Jack had planned this manoeuvre

CHAPTER ELEVEN

all along or it was a spur of the moment gambit in our hairy chess game, I'll never know. Fortunately, as a member of the Year Four debating team I had a better-than-average command of the English language, and had experience in presenting an argument, defending a position and countering opposing propositions.

Accordingly, in what I judged a measured, pithy and well-constructed retort I informed my father:

'You can stick your money up your arse. I'll f**cking pay for myself.'

Jack just smiled. Not the reaction one might expect from a father confronted so rudely by a son. But then again, 'Gelignite' Jack was not adverse to the use of the odd colourful expression himself.

I like to think that his smile reflected his admiration for my youthful exuberance, my teenage pluckiness and being a worthy adversary. But in hindsight, he was probably smiling because he had just saved himself two grand.

Getting my hands on a Holden HR panel van also involved my financial contribution. Jack had made it very clear that, while he was prepared to source and mechanically check my first car, it would be me who would be paying for it. At the time, a number of my mates, who had not enjoyed anywhere near the academic success I had managed, were being rewarded by their fathers. I grew up in one of the most affluent areas in Australia where wealthy fathers were buying their spoilt sons expensive cars.

From the vantage point of a seventeen-year-old, Jack's attitude seemed unfair. Once again I drew on my debating experience and vast vocabulary when attempting to convince my father. I think I used the words 'tight arse' a lot—even excessively perhaps. Clearly, diplomacy was never my strong point as a youth.

Stacking cans at Franklins part-time secured me my own can on wheels. I loved that car, maintained and treasured it.

Thank you, Jack. My father had taught me one of the great lessons in life: we appreciate what we have to work for, not what we are simply given. Jack supported me financially throughout my university years. I lived at home board-free until I was 23. Thanks, dad.

Although I knew everything at the time, I did not know how to say those two simple words to my father.

At age twenty, on impulse, I walked into a barber's shop, sat down and simply said, 'Mate, take all this long stuff off. It's driving me nuts.'

But there were plenty of other issues on which to lock horns. One apocalypse took place in the kitchen of my parents' home, repeated over several nights, with the clash of the titans focusing on a baking dish—the *cleanliness* of a baking dish. Funny? Very—but I don't remember anyone laughing at the time.

Lubricants remove friction within engines. Some people are lubricants who smooth the relationships and interactions within families. Often this role is unseen, unnoticed by those who benefit most. Mum had gone on an extended holiday with her sister; the family lubricant was absent. Jack and I were home alone, left 'batching'. The baking dish blue began to sizzle.

A baking dish in the Murray household is more a piece of heavy industrial equipment than an accompaniment to haute cuisine. No scones or cakes or biscuits ever saw the insides of a Murray baking dish. Picture a massive, metallic tray with upturned sides, a Volkswagen roof cut off and flipped over. Baked lamb or beef dinners surrounded and buried in dozens of baked potatoes and pumpkin were the only contents allowed. Mum learned early that feeding three men is less about *cordon bleu* and more about cordoning off the meat and potato section of the supermarket and loading up a trolley or two.

Unsupervised, the Murray men quickly reverted to their natural state: a primitive hunter and gatherer existence, foraging for ourselves with no structured meals. Each was busy doing his own thing and like ships in the night, occasionally saw one another in passing. During my mother's absence, with the spectre of starvation hovering, I cooked myself a baked dinner. To this day, it remains the one and only item in my list of culinary achievements. I even cleaned up, washing plates, cutlery and the oversized baking dish prior to returning the beast to its lair in the cupboard beneath the sink.

When I arrived home from university the following evening, there sat the baking dish beside the sink. That's odd, I thought. A small note in the middle of the dish solved the mystery of the self-levitating tray: 'Not clean, wash again.' I duly complied. Steel wool in hand, I applied approximately 200 kg of bench press power, removing baked-on oil stains, blackened meat marks and alike. The baking dish, looking five years younger, took pride of place once more in the cupboard beneath the sink.

The following evening the dish materialised once more, accompanied by the now rather repetitive note: 'Not clean, wash again.' No problem. This was a challenge to be met and beaten. I attacked the baking dish with all the vigour and enthusiasm of a gym training session. I scrubbed that sucker within an

CHAPTER ELEVEN

inch of its metallic life, till it was sparkling as brilliantly as a commercial. I respectfully returned the now immaculate dish to its sanctum beneath the sink.

But the following evening: 'Not clean, wash again.' Only on this occasion, Jack was home. Communication and bonding time. The dish provided an opportunity for father and son to sit down, calmly and rationally to discuss the various cleaning techniques available and agree upon an acceptable level of baking dish hygiene.

'Stick the baking dish up your arse,' concluded that discussion. Again, Jack just smiled.

Fast forward almost ten years. Jack is now aged 76, and has had his leg amputated three years earlier. As he lay dying in St Vincent's Hospital, I held his hand. Unbelievably, this was the first time I can recall such an act of intimacy between us. He was drugged, wasted and weakened, only the shell of the man remaining. Sunken eyes stared up at me and seemed to question.

'I'm scared,' he whispered.

I could not believe I was hearing such words from the legend who was my father.

'It'll be all right, mate. Don't worry.'

As we had both grown older, I felt I grew closer to my father. Three years earlier, following the amputation of his leg, I had driven him home to Vaucluse.

'How am I going to get up the steps?' he wondered out loud.

'I'll carry you.'

'You won't be able to carry me up three flights of steps.'

But aged 73, he was a thin man with an amputated leg. I was 26 and had recently returned from seven months touring in Europe—the prodigal son returned. It was a significant moment of transition for both of us. We both felt it, but nothing was said. I scooped him up from the passenger seat and as we talked I floated him up to the sunroom with its magnificent views over Sydney Harbour.

Three years later, almost to the day, I sat at his bedside holding his hand. Jack died on Sunday 11 December 1983.

As a teenager, I thought I knew everything. But I knew nothing. If I had, I would have known to say 'thank you' more often. I would have known that Jack was proud of me, but couldn't say that either. I would have known and understood the lessons my father was trying to teach me.

All those years earlier, when my mother had returned from her holiday and looked around her kitchen, her first words were, 'Jack, what on earth happened to the baking dish? It's never been this clean since I bought it.'

And Jack? Well—he just smiled.

Above: The surfie Holden HR panel van PM 115 that I paid for, my much loved 'shaggin' wagon' that travelled Australia.

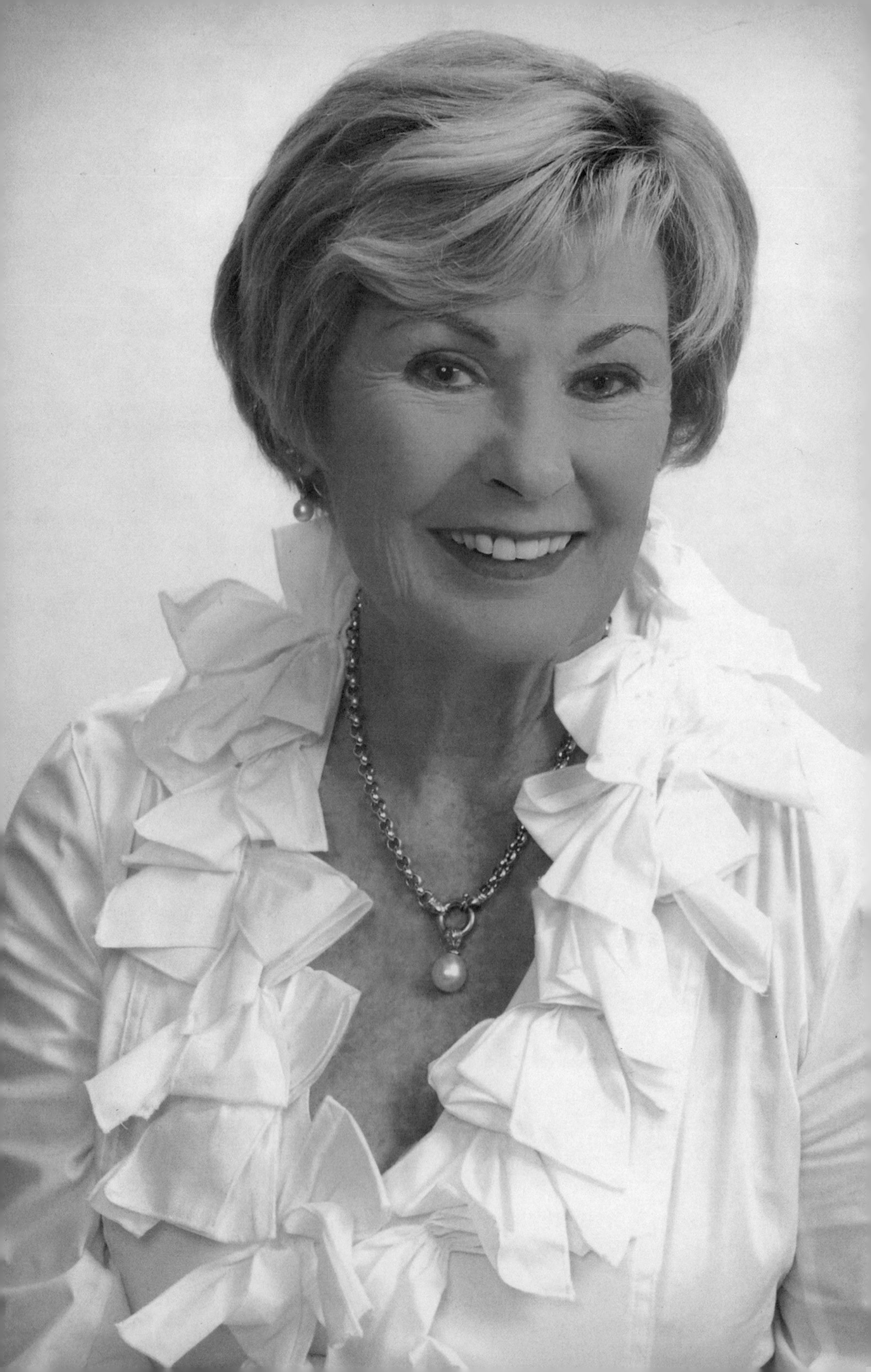

CHAPTER TWELVE
DOROTHY

'A blonde ... brandishing a golden mallet'

In 1973, the world was a very different place. Clearly the concept of inappropriate—even sexist—commentary was unknown to many journalists. On Saturday 20 January 1973, the front page of Sydney's *Daily Telegraph* newspaper bore a smiling photo of Dorothy Rosewell under the banner *She's After Bids*. These lines followed:

> If you see a stunning, long-legged blonde brandishing a golden mallet in Paddington—don't panic. Dorothy Rosewell isn't after heads—just successful bids. Dorothy is Australia's first woman auctioneer. Along with that mallet goes eighteen years' real estate experience, curves not usually associated with auctioneers and a low, well-modulated voice in place of the usual auctioneering rasp.

Good publicity—definitely. Flattering—certainly. Sexist? Well, let's put it this way: no contemporary journalist describing a successful businesswoman would dare include the words 'long-legged' and 'curves'. But hey, the *zeitgeist* of the 1970s was all hot pants and scanty tops and sexist journalism passed unremarked. Forty years on, we have to laugh. As Dorothy herself would no doubt say, 'It was all good fun back then.'

To understand and place in context Dorothy Rosewell's life story, and her relationship with my father, perhaps it is best to begin by summarising: my father

CHAPTER TWELVE

and mother married in 1942 and remained married until Jack's death in 1983. However, in the late 1950s Jack met Dorothy and they fell in love. Their relationship blossomed, grew and endured until Jack's passing. It was a love that spanned 25 years. As Jack lay dying in St Vincent's hospital in Sydney, the two women who shared Jack's life, Ena Murray and Dorothy Rosewell, stood on either side of the bed. The man they both loved lay between them, dividing them but at the same time uniting them in their shared grief and imminent loss.

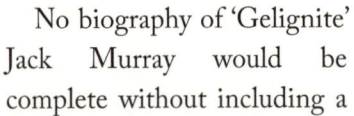

Above: Auction Sales—and Dorothy has a 100 per cent success rate: *Sold! Sold! Sold!*

No biography of 'Gelignite' Jack Murray would be complete without including a chapter dedicated to this remarkable lady. Dorothy's life is one of achievement, a true 'rags to riches' tale championing by example the rights of women in business. It is a fascinating story that stands on its own merits, regardless of her long relationship with Jack.

But her story is also part of Jack's, an integral part of any 'Gelignite' Jack Murray biography.

Fascinated by Old Houses

Dorothy Ellen Rosewell was born on Wednesday 2 December 1931. As she says, 'I was born in Waterloo—a city kid—and I appreciate and love the city of Sydney. I was always fascinated by old houses and their history.'

Dorothy's parents bought their first house in the inner-city suburb of Waterloo in the early 1950s. Their three-bedroom cottage cost £500, on a £50 deposit. In the early 1960s, the house was resold for £1150.

DOROTHY

Throughout the 1970s, D.E. Rosewell Real Estate and its ground breaking owner would often be seen in newspapers and magazines such as *New Idea*, either advertising upcoming Paddington auctions, introducing readers to her Woollahra home office or focusing on Dorothy herself. The concept of the 'successful businesswoman' was an emerging phenomenon of the time and readers were certainly interested. I will quote from several newspapers and magazines, with additional information added and errors of fact corrected. The articles provide a chronology of events and an insight into Dorothy's young life.

The first Women's Liberation Group in Australia was formed in 1970. The 'battle of the sexes' was a hot topic of discussion and a leading question of the day was: 'Can successful businesswomen still be feminine in a man's world?'

Businesswoman Flag Bearer

Weekend Business Review of 10 April 1970 documented Dorothy's life up to that time and the success for which she had worked and was enjoying.

The journalist, Pauline McGrath, approached Dorothy when she was looking for a businesswoman as a flag bearer for what a talented and determined woman can achieve. She certainly found one in Dorothy. The article began:

> After a quick survey in top positions in Sydney I came across one who I believe is an excellent example of how to be a real woman and successful at the same time.
>
> She's not married—by choice not fate.
>
> But married or not, I believe she still would have achieved the fulfilment and success she has. She is that sort of person.
>
> She is Dorothy Rosewell, a charming, extremely feminine and attractive, self-confessed 38-year-old brunette. And she is head of a very successful real estate agency. Dorothy Rosewell wasn't born with a silver spoon in her mouth—far from it, as she freely admits—and she certainly wasn't born with a driving ambition to make a million. She is simply an active woman who has used her talents. Her success goes right back to her teenage years. Dorothy left school at fourteen with a burning desire to be an artist; however her grandmother persuaded her to complete a secretarial course at St Patrick's Commercial College, Church Hill in Sydney. At fifteen Dorothy joined Charles Clarkson, a sign writing company as Secretary to the

CHAPTER TWELVE

Managing Director, and set about to learn as much as she could about the sign writing business. Dorothy additionally enrolled in art classes at East Sydney Technical College in Darlinghurst.

Three years of night school later and with her relatively short experience in the art business she set herself up as a commercial artist and sign writer in a little office in the Queen Victoria Building in Market Street. She built up a substantial list of clients and very quickly was making quite a lot of money for those days. There were many opportunities to be innovative in Sydney retail stores, and when asked to be a demonstrator, she became one of the first demonstrators at David Jones, working a couple of months at a time a few hours a day and still keeping her commercial art business. She also became involved with teaching makeup at night.

After three years of running the studio she decided it was time for a change and when offered a job by Jones Brothers in Campbell Street, Sydney as their house model saw a new opportunity for herself and set off to do what she could. Eighteen months later the Swiss Sewing Machine Company (Helvetia) spread their interests in Australia and Dorothy was asked to join them as a sewing machine demonstrator. The travel involved interested her, so she joined. Again not satisfied simply demonstrating, she became involved with their advertising and public relations activities, almost before any formalised public relations companies were established in Australia. When import restrictions on sewing machines were established in Australia, the Helvetia company decided to concentrate its activities on merchandising, to lay down a formal plan of advertising, and to feed this through an independent advertising agency. This led to the foundation of the Murray Rosewell Advertising Agency. Dorothy Rosewell, with her background in art took over the creative work and Keith Murray, an advertising man, the account service. [Author's note: Keith Murray was no relation to Jack Murray]

Through sheer initiative more than experience, they built up a client list big enough to get accreditation and kept their billings around the medium sized agency bracket.

They moved into merchandising items and approached stores like McDowells. They introduced the first co-ordinated selling operation in the home dressmaking field into McDowells by encouraging the store to stock fabrics, cottons, buttons and the like in the same department as sewing machines. Again for their client Helvetia, they introduced home sewing lessons in retail stores.

For the first time Dorothy Rosewell, after working eighteen hours a day seven days a week for almost two years, began to feel the pressure. She turned over her share of the business to another advertising man, Brian Ogle, and retired for six months. Her next venture into the business world was as a consultant for a firm marketing hair restorers—a far cry from the glamour of the advertising business, but another challenge.

It was around this time her interest turned to real estate. On seeing a small advertisement in a local paper she attended a real estate course for about twelve weeks, applied for a salesman's licence and set about to look for a job.

At the beginning of 1958 there were no positions for women in real estate being advertised, so under 'Men and Boys Wanted' she found an opening and joined the office of Colechin Real Estate in William Street Paddington.

She developed her own style of selling; never keeping a big listing of properties, but setting out to sell those she had before moving onto anything further.

D.E. Rosewell Real Estate

Needless to say she was a success and when her boss Mr Colechin decided to move his business to Manly, a solicitor friend of Dorothy's came to the rescue and offered her a small room in his building in Woollahra, opposite the Paddington Police Station. She got her own real estate licence, and with a fourteen-and-a-half-year-old secretary, in a 9 ft x 8 ft office and without a skerrick of a client, she started D.E. Rosewell Real Estate.

The late Bill Latimer of Woollahra Council gave Dorothy her first two houses to sell. She now says it was sheer luck she moved to Paddington, with the tremendous development in real estate in the area. But it hasn't been through sheer luck that her business has boomed, for it must have taken ability and flair to capitalise on the new trends in the area. The business could be bigger she admits, but then it would lose the personal touch—the touch which is Dorothy Rosewell's motto.

It's her firm belief that a woman can do as she has, but she has her own philosophy on how to do it. Dorothy doesn't believe a woman should be ambitious; this causes women to be hard. They are fighting to achieve something they should try to let come naturally.

Dorothy runs her business with a firm hand, and has very capable and loyal staff. Her clients are important to her and she gives more service than is generally required. Many of her clients have become friends.

The D.E. Rosewell Real Estate Agency is a good, medium-sized agency, with an excellent clientele in a fashionable area where there is an incredible demand for housing.

Property and Strata Management is one of the agency's specialties, and in an average year they would probably manage around 1500 properties.

A Number of Firsts for Women

Keeping her finger on the pulse of what is happening keeps Dorothy fairly busy. She quotes the story of a tiny weatherboard cottage in Paddington she first sold for $4000 and last year re-sold (for the fourth time) for $25,000. So, she says, you can't afford to be out of touch. As well as selling houses she has sold two marinas, Bushes' Boat Shed and Charlie Messengers' in Double Bay—a tremendous opportunity but a feat for the most accomplished of real estate agents.

And not satisfied to keep still, last year she acquired her auctioneer's licence and last November sold two houses by auction, the first woman ever to do this.

She is the first woman delegate ever to be appointed to the Real Estate Institute, Eastern Suburbs Branch and also a committee member for the Wentworth Branch.

But Dorothy Rosewell is still essentially a woman.

She never thinks about being a woman in a man's world. If she did she probably wouldn't have succeeded. But she has achieved what she wants: she is independent and has all the enjoyment of the material wealth that goes with it. Enjoys life, enjoys the freedom her business gives her, and is not about to start campaigning for woman's rights. Why should she? She has them herself through her own efforts.

Woman's Day wrote in 16 September 1985:

> When Dorothy first joined the Real Estate Institute of NSW, its annual dinners were men-only affairs and she did not receive an invitation.
>
> 'I believe in female liberation,' she said 'but I don't believe the way to win it is by jumping up and down on the spot indignantly.' Instead, she sent a tiny doll along to the dinner with her name on it and a message asking whether it was all right for a doll to attend.
>
> Her colleagues got the message and the next year Dorothy was invited to the dinner. Later she became one of the first women to be elected to the Board of Management of the Institute.

'An important man in her life'

In a 1973 *Vogue* article headed *The Activists: Dorothy Rosewell* we read:

> Dorothy Rosewell is tall, slender and deeply tanned, with soft streaky ash-brown hair that gives hint of expensive care. She answers to her 40 years with the serenity of a woman who knows she looks years younger.
>
> A very successful real estate agent, deeply involved in Sydney's picturesque Paddington, where she works from a terrace house on one of the prettier streets, Dorothy was born in Waterloo and lived 'in an old house; I've always been fascinated by them.' She decided to give up the advertising world fifteen years ago, when she was a partner in a small agency:
>
> 'I was working eighteen hours a day all weekend—it just wasn't worth it.' She took a six-month break, then began her new career of selling houses around the Paddington/Woollahra area. 'When I first started I thought I'd have to learn Italian and Maltese, but surprisingly the children acted as interpreters, even clinching the deal in some cases.'

CHAPTER TWELVE

She finds real estate a very personal business; most clients are recommended to her by others she's helped. She starts telephoning at eight in the morning, puts a lot into her job ('I work hard when I'm working') but has learned at last to 'finish the day completely and put work out of my mind'. She's been a member of the Real Estate Institute for nine years, is enormously involved with its various committees and at present is helping plan next year's important International Real Estate Federation Congress, to be held in Sydney. Attending this year's congress in London will stimulate her ideas.

Organisation is a key word with Dorothy Rosewell. She's energetic, active in many areas. 'I've always believed that old thing about if you want something done, give it to a busy person.' There has never been a woman on the Board of the Institute but when it happens she'll be right up there in the running. She belongs to Zonta [Author's note: A worldwide organisation of executives and the professions working together to advance the status of women], plays bridge and chess, waterskis, reads voraciously and is learning how to play the electric organ—a recent purchase.

Although she says, 'Since childhood I never envisioned myself as a housewife, never wanted to marry—children are not me', she's extremely feminine. She speaks about 'we' often, and you guess that there's an important man in her life, someone who helped her become as emotionally secure as she undoubtedly is.

Security is another big thing with her; the tangible form of her own many real estate assets; and in safety, as with the high wall around the new house she's building in Paddington—sandstock brick and iron lace to blend with the terrace environment, huge glass doors to let in the sunshine above a heated swimming pool. When asked about luxury, she laughs, 'My life is one long luxury.' Luxurious indeed is the month's holiday she has taken every year for the past fifteen, relaxing at Shoal Bay where she has an apartment.

She looks forward to 'more time for home days, more time to travel', and says, 'I've tried to create a certain respect for myself. I believe I'm a good real estate agent.' She also believes in luck. 'I'm a lucky Sagittarian!' She describes herself as 'a whole person' and that's how she comes through.

Congress—First Woman Speaker and TV Host

On 12 May 1976, the *Wentworth Courier* told of Dorothy's further success under a banner headline. The article read:

> A Woollahra woman has been invited to speak in San Francisco at the International Real Estate Federation's congress in a special section devoted to women in real estate.
>
> She is Dorothy Rosewell, a member of the Board of the Real Estate Institute of NSW and the first woman to address the congress.
>
> She's been in business as an estate agent since 1959.
>
> Miss Rosewell will be among 300 delegates from all states of Australia who will leave for the conference scheduled from May 22 to 29.
>
> The president of the Real Estate Institute of NSW, Mr Neville Tucker, said that the purpose of the congress was to further education in real estate function and co-ordination of procedures throughout the world.
>
> It is a worldwide organisation which spends most of its time improving the practices in the real estate calling.
>
> 'Much of its time is spent in discussion and addresses the covering of all aspects of real estate, with particular emphasis on the education of people coming in and already in the profession,' he said.

Australian Property News (December 1977—January 1978) featured yet another article on Dorothy in its Real Estate Identities section. Under the headline *Agent with a Difference*, it wrote:

> Dorothy Rosewell is an unusual real estate agent. She lives and works from a comfortable double story terrace in the fashionable Sydney suburb of Woollahra and conducts her business on a very personal level. 'Inspection by appointment', the discreet sign at the gate tells you.
>
> But not all her clients are famous and not all the houses she sells are luxury mansions off the cover of *House and Garden*. 'I have just sold an absolute bomb over at Alexandria for $23,750,' she says.

CHAPTER TWELVE

Far from being a real estate agent for socialites, she sees herself as 'more a person for people'.

Life has been hectic for Dorothy in the last few years. In 1972-73 she sold out her property management business, then built her present terrace home and moved her office 'into residence'.

Then in 1974, she and Joan Crosland became the first women to be elected to the Board of Management of the Real Estate Institute. [*Dorothy retired only that year, 1977, from the Board.*]

And recently, she became involved in hosting a television program dealing with every aspect of buying, selling and owning a home. [*This was called* A Home Affair *and screened on Channel 10 in 1977.*] The thirteen-week series has just finished and has been hailed as a successful contribution to community affairs.

Now she hopes to devote more time to her own business and, in whatever spare time she finds, enjoy such things as waterskiing, kite flying (behind a ski boat!), reading, entertaining and caring for the elderly people in her area.

Dorothy Rosewell is certainly not a run-of-the-mill real estate agent. Apart from her natural rapport with people, it is obvious she loves her job. But perhaps the key to her success can be found in her own description of herself:

Above: Dorothy Rosewell compering her TV show *A Home Affair.*

'I was born in Waterloo—a city kid—and I appreciate and love the city of Sydney.'

But she is no newcomer to the business. Back in 1957, after a short spell in advertising, she took an eighteen week course in real estate and hasn't looked back since.

Her first and only 'job' in real estate was with a small office in Paddington.

'They advertised for a man, but I applied and got the job. In those days there was no salary attached to the job. It was straight commission, so I didn't cost them anything if I didn't work out,' she explains.

But Dorothy Rosewell did 'work out'. Within six months she took out her own licence and opened a small office opposite the police station in Jersey Rd, Paddington.

In those days, Paddington was far from the trendy suburb it is today. Rather, it was a dirty, cramped inner-city area which mainly housed those who could not afford to move further out.

'New Australian families would buy four-bedroom terraces between three families for £3000 to £4000. They would pay them off over three years, then move further out to Kensington, where they would buy a home,' she says.

The scene has changed dramatically since then. Many of Dorothy's Paddo clients now are trendy young solicitors, architects or TV personalities and the houses are mostly—though not all, she adds hastily—in the $70,000 to $120,000 bracket.

Her clients have included advertising personality John Singleton, his wife (before they were married) Maggie Eckhardt, the actor Michael Pate (who is currently renting a mansion in Rose Bay to finish work on the film *The Mango Tree*) and Kym Bonython (Dorothy sold him the premises for the Bonython Gallery).

One Woman among 40 Men

In 1963, Dorothy became the first female member of the Board of Management of the Real Estate Institute of NSW and in 1972 represented Women in Real Estate at the FIABCI World Congresses in London (where she was the public relations officer), Madrid, San Francisco, Sydney and Athens and travelled extensively around Australia.

While most of her work involved selling terrace houses in the Paddington–Woollahra area of Sydney, she also sold properties in Spain, marinas in Sydney Harbour and a million-acre cattle property in the Northern Territory.

In August 1978, she enrolled in a real estate financial management workshop at Armidale University. She was the only woman among 40 men. Her success was clear: the following year she was asked to join the faculty, lecturing on merchandising and advertising in real estate. 'My passion has always been education, education, education,' she said.

CHAPTER TWELVE

The Fateful 1958 Ampol Trial

The year 1958 was significant for Dorothy, for a number of reasons.

Another of her interests was in motorsport. She had been reading about the round Australia car trials of the early 1950s and knew that in 1958 another trial was planned. She entered her VW in the trial only to have it stolen two weeks before the rally started. The car was never recovered, but she was determined to somehow enter the rally. She placed an advertisement in the paper and, being a competent navigator, was quickly selected by Brian and Pamela Parle of Griffith as their navigator.

The race began well for them. The Parles, with Dorothy navigating, were up with the leaders. However, along the Grand Ridge Rd about twelve miles from Welshpool, Victoria, disaster struck. Brian Parle drove off a cliff and plummeted some 300 ft (90 metres) into a ravine; the brakes had locked on a curve. Dorothy said, 'The car rolled over and over. Each time it hit the ground the body came in.' About 200 ft down the ravine the seatbelts holding Mr and Mrs Parle snapped and they were thrown out of the vehicle. The Parles escaped with shock and bruises. Fortunately, Dorothy was wearing a seatbelt and a helmet at the time and escaped completely unharmed. She completed the rally as a guest of the sponsors—in an aeroplane.

Below: Ampol Trial, 1958: From left: Dorothy Rosewell, Pamela and Brian Parle. VW Car No 149 was the first car to be involved in an accident. Photo courtesy Hal Moloney.

BEARDED TRIAL DRIVER HERE

Car's 300ft. horror crash into gully

Survivors of an Ampol Trial crash early yesterday watched a second car rolling end over end down a 300ft. ravine.

The crashes occurred about 35 minutes apart.

Both cars were wrecked, but the occupants escaped serious injury.

The cars were a Volkswagen (No. 149) and a Holden (No. 106).

Brian Parle, 32, of Kooba Street, Griffith, N.S.W., was driving the Volkswagen.

With him were his wife, Pamela, 30, and Miss Dorothy Rosewall, 30, of Glenwood Avenue, Coogee.

Kevin Parker, 37, of Edward Street, Kingaroy, Q., was driving the Holden. His brother, Douglas Parker, 33, of Markwell Street, Kingaroy, was with him.

Parle's car left the road when the brakes locked.

While rescuers were helping the crew Parker's car somersaulted at the same corner, and fell 300 feet down the ravine.

Jim Roberts and Don Garard, of Sydney, took the lead in the Ampol Trial.

They said headlamps of the crashing car flashed "fantastic circles of light."

Pieces flew off the car and equipment fell out.

The car, a Holden containing two men, rolled over 15 times.

It stopped near a Volkswagen which had crashed down the ravine 40 minutes earlier.

The two men in the Holden and two women and a man in the Volkswagen escaped with shock and bruises.

The cars crashed from the Midland Highway, 12 miles from Welshpool, Victoria.

Driver fell out

In the Holden were Kevin Parker, 37, of Kingaroy, Queensland, the driver, and his brother, Douglas, 37, co-driver,

and his feet tangled in the steering wheel."

The Holden ran off the road when Kevin Parker was distracted by rescue of the three people in the Volkswagen crash.

In this crash were Brian Parle, 32, of Griffith, his wife, Pamela, 30, and Miss Dorothy Rosewall, 30, of Coogee.

The Volkswagen's brakes locked on a curve.

About 200 feet down the ravine safety belts holding Mr. and Mrs. Parle in the front snapped and they were thrown out.

Miss Rosewell, who was strapped in the back seat said yesterday: "The car rolled over and over.

"Every time it hit the ground the body squeezed in."

Bearded Ampol Trial driver Doug Parker, signing autographs for young enthusiasts Malcolm Roberts (left) and Dean Donovan at Norwood Oval last night.

Above: A Sydney newspaper report on Car No 149's brush with disaster.

Jack and Dorothy Meet

In preparation for this ill-fated rally, a meeting had been held in Paddington Town Hall, attended by all prospective competitors. While she was diligently taking notes and listening to the presentation by race organisers, Dorothy's concentration was interrupted by a noisy group of fellow competitors behind her. One of these chaps was particularly loud in his laughter—one 'Gelignite' Jack Murray. Confident and self-assured, 27-year-old Dorothy turned to the group and asked them politely, but firmly, to quieten down. The men, suitably admonished, complied.

At the completion of the presentation, one of the group, a friend of Jack's, approached Dorothy and asked her if she would like to meet the garrulous 'Gelignite' Jack. Unimpressed, Dorothy declined and left.

During the rally there were several occasions when Dave Johnson (Jack's navigator) tried to introduce Dorothy to Jack. Dorothy laughed, explaining to me, 'Any move was from your dad, not me.' Following the rally, Jack asked her if she needed a lift anywhere, since she did not have a car. Dorothy accepted and Jack drove her to Coogee where she lived. Jack and Dorothy's paths were

CHAPTER TWELVE

destined to cross again. As she tells the story:

> My life was a very full one, with many friends. A few weeks later Les Holden asked me and several other girl friends if we would like to go waterskiing on the Hawkesbury. Not having skied before, this was another adventure, and of course Jack owned the boat, and we met once again. At the time I was between jobs, and studying real estate. However your father was persistent with phone calls, and invited me to go to a movie, or waterskiing on the weekend. I was unaware that Jack was married, and there was never any mention of family. Guess I may have been a little naïve, and when Jack did tell me he was married, there was still no mention of Philip. I was aware of John from photos of the 1954 REDEX. How your father handled the situation at home with your mother, I guess we will never really know.

Jack had charmed other girlfriends—but Dorothy would prove to be different. Jack was a persistent suitor, and the rest—as they say—is history.

Above: Dorothy trick waterskiing.

A Passion Shared

As well as car rallies, Dorothy shared Jack's passion for waterskiing. She won an Australian Water Ski Championship, a metropolitan tricks title and also competed in the Bridge to Bridge ski classic. She has even flown in a kite behind a ski boat.

Charity Begins at Home

Dorothy has always maintained a strong sense of social justice and community spirit. Throughout her life, she has used her skills to help others. Perhaps it was her humble beginnings in that small house in Waterloo that maintained her empathy for, and

Above: From left to right: 1962 Australian Water Ballet Championships. Dorothy Rosewell, Dale Challinor, Betty Wheeler and Tonia Bevan.

understanding of, those less fortunate than herself.

In 1978, Australian and world hang gliding champion Bill Moyes miscued on a volcano in the Philippines and crashed his hang glider. The following day he returned to the village of Berinayan to retrieve his valuable kite, expecting to find it stripped or stolen. Instead he found a Filipino family of eleven guarding the strange craft that had fallen from the sky. The oldest of the children was a girl named Teresita, then aged 24. In a subsequent letter to Bill, Teresita spoke of her dream to come to Australia to overcome her handicaps of lack of education and poverty. Bill showed the letter to Dorothy and it clearly struck a chord. She could understand a young woman trying to get ahead through overcoming adversity. It sounded familiar.

Despite battling bureaucracy in both countries for over two years, Dorothy and Bill Moyes managed to bring Teresita Ulitin to Australia for six months. During this time, Teresita was sponsored by Dorothy, lived at her Woollahra home and taught herself to type as well as developing language and other skills to take back home to help lift her family out of poverty.

CHAPTER TWELVE

It is one thing to assist with international aid by sending a monthly cheque. It is a far greater commitment to personally become involved, to take responsibility for and invite someone from overseas to come and share your home. In material terms, Dorothy may well have been a long way removed from her humble beginnings in Waterloo, but this act of generosity shows that her heart and empathy for others had stayed with her and made the journey from Waterloo to Woollahra.

For Better or Worse

Jack's last years, during the 1980s, presented major challenges and obstacles.

In December 1980, aged 73, he had his gangrenous right leg removed just above the knee. Barely four months later, in the early hours of 1 May 1981, Jack's beloved Garage was badly damaged in a major fire. With the help and support of the two women in his life, and in typical 'Gelignite' Jack style, he shrugged his shoulders, made a joke or two about needing only to buy one shoe and soldiered on.

It was in the project management of the rebuilding of The Garage that Dorothy's business skills came to the fore. The zoning for the land on which it sat was residential, but it had operated as a mechanical workshop and was recognised as such due to long and continuous usage.

Building applications are long and tedious processes. Finalisation of the project took a number of years and the Council indicated that they would have preferred to see The Garage demolished and a residential development take its place. Dorothy's abilities and persistence ensured that it was rebuilt and once more became operational as a mechanical workshop.

Following Jack's death in 1983, ownership of The Garage passed to my mother, Ena. After her stroke, my mother's long-term stay in her high care nursing home was funded by rental income provided by the Curlewis St property. Upon her passing in 2005, The Garage passed jointly to my brother John and me and remains in family ownership to this day.

Without Dorothy's professional input, and her practical and loving support of Jack at a time of ill-health and need, The Garage would not have been rebuilt and my mother's nursing care requirements would have required funding from a different source. Dorothy's involvement in a number of ways was key to getting through these troubled times. Our family is deeply grateful to her.

City Girl Goes Bush

In 1989 the city girl went bush. Dorothy moved to Jilliby near the Central Coast of NSW, where she established a boutique cashmere goat farm. During this rural period, Dorothy frequently travelled to Inner Mongolia in China, promoting and developing the Australian cashmere goat industry. Around 1999, she also joined local community group Central Coast Living Options, an organisation providing services for the disabled.

In 2007, she had been one of the guest speakers at the inaugural Women in Real Estate Conference. Dorothy inspired delegates with her journey from artist to real estate agent and reiterated the message of an earlier speaker—get involved and keep learning. That year she also studied Mandarin at TAFE while managing to squeeze in two road trips throughout NSW, Victoria, South Australia and Queensland.

In 2009, she moved to a smaller, 2.5-acre property at Brolga Way, Jilliby. Here she contributed to her new local community as a member of the local bush fire brigade.

Thoroughbred horse racing was introduced to Dorothy by long-time friends the Cunninghams, keen horse breeders who owned a property called Branka Lodge not far from Dorothy's property at Jilliby. Mrs Cunningham, when considering retirement, gave two brood mares to Dorothy: Branka Lass and Sonia Girl. The offspring My Joey [Author's note: Joey was also a nickname for Jack], like his namesake, proved to be a very successful racer, winning six races, including a country club race meeting. Sonia Girl was the dam of Prince Dalem, another of Dorothy's horses. Close Balinese friends from Ubud were visiting Australia at the time, and lent their name to the gelding. Winning his first race as a two-year-old, Prince Dalem showed great potential; however he retired early due to an accident.

In 2016, having moved from her rural property to Kooindah Waters residential golf resort, Dorothy's involvement with thoroughbreds is more of a low key interest. She is part owner of Annatime, trained by Kim Waugh and managed by her husband and ex-cricketer Mark Waugh, AM.

The same compassionate Dorothy who had assisted and mentored the young Filipino girl in 1978 also became involved with assisting people with disabilities twenty years later.

Central Coast Living Options Inc. (CCLO), established in 1996, is a community-based, not-for-profit organisation providing services for the

CHAPTER TWELVE

disabled. It is all about improving the lives of people with disabilities. Dorothy has served on the Board of CCLO at various times over the past twelve years and in 2015 was a member of the Building Committee.

On 6 November 2014, she was honoured with the position of Patron of CCLO, in recognition of her invaluable support for the organisation.

'Sweet dreams and love'

Today Dorothy's home is on a magnificent golf course estate, the beautiful Kooindah Waters on the central coast of NSW. Her interests are many, her community involvement continues and her zest for life remains undiminished.

The writing of this biography would not have been possible without her untiring assistance. Her saving of so many newspaper articles, magazines, photos and other memorabilia has made the task of telling Jack's story possible. This material has given me the facts. But beyond that, Dorothy's candour, trust and willingness to share even the most personal and intimate correspondence between herself and my father is greatly appreciated. It has added a new facet to my understanding of him. There have been countless descriptions applied to 'Gelignite' Jack Murray over the years. The last adjective I would ever have thought applicable to my father was 'romantic'. I was wrong—so very wrong.

During 1968 when he was overseas preparing for the London to Sydney Marathon, and again in 1972 when Dorothy was in England, she and my father wrote a series of letters to one another—love letters. One would not expect a boy who left school at fourteen to make his own way in life to

Above: Dorothy at left in November 2007.

be able to express himself well in prose. Once again, I was wrong.

All writers learn that 'good' writing is not about spelling and punctuation, but about conveying feeling and engaging the reader. Jack's letters come from the heart. They tell of a very deep and enduring love and show Jack's tenderness and vulnerability. These are parts of ourselves that can, and rightly should, only be shared with the one we love. That is why I have not requested, and do not wish to reproduce any of these letters in this book. But to give some insight and understanding into the deep and lasting love Jack and Dorothy shared, perhaps allowing just a few of my father's words speak for themselves will be enough. Surely every woman would like to receive a letter from the man who loves her, and whom she loves, that ends with these words:

> I will close, my darling, loving you more than anything on earth. Sweet dreams and love. JM

Above: Dorothy and Jack enjoy a day on Sydney Harbour.

CHAPTER TWELVE

'I would not change a thing'

In June 2015, my wife Rhonda and I sat at The Boathouse restaurant enjoying lunch with Dorothy, as we overlooked the aqua waters of Port Stephens, only a stone's throw from her beloved Shoal Bay. The REDEX baby, then 60, sat beside the Lady with the Golden Mallet, then 83. As you would expect, we laughed when talking of Jack's adventures, reminiscing about the past and speaking of the daunting task I had set myself in writing Jack's biography.

In a moment of reflection, Dorothy paused—and then offered, 'I hope my relationship with your dad did not interfere too much with you as a child.'

I assured her it did not. When I was growing up there were never any arguments between my parents, certainly none that I witnessed. I do not recall how old I was when I found out about Jack's relationship with Dorothy. In the Murray household when I was growing up, Jack arrived home promptly at 6pm for dinner on Monday, Tuesday and Thursday nights. On Wednesday and Friday nights, he arrived home late. Following the usual Saturday baked lunch, he would disappear from the family scene until late Sunday night.

A young Philip was told dad was 'up the river'—which river he had no idea. I grew up with this pattern and thought nothing of it. I never felt a sense of absence nor any tension in the home. My childhood was idyllic and unaffected. Since he was eleven years older than me, my brother John spent time at Shoal Bay and met Dorothy waterskiing on the Hawkesbury, fairly early on in her relationship with Jack.

Dorothy says:

> The Garage was Jack's haven, and waterskiing and his great many other sporting involvements would no doubt have meant he was not always home. And even taking six weeks every February into March for his annual holiday at Shoal Bay—it was just what Jack did.

And what was Ena's attitude to the situation and her husband's extramarital relationship? My mother and I never discussed 'Jack and Dorothy'. I can only recall her occasionally mentioning Dorothy's name in relation to properties I may have been buying at the time [initially a Balmain studio unit, then a Windsor St, Paddington terrace as a home and finally a Surry Hills loft apartment investment]. Only recently, while I have been writing this biography, has Dorothy been frank enough to discuss the situation:

DOROTHY

Never in my association with your father was there a conflict between Ena and myself. I can understand there must have been times between Jack and Ena when questions would have been asked and perhaps some arguments. There were neither conversations nor any arguments between Ena and me personally over the years. I believe Jack played the role of being a good father to his boys, albeit perhaps not the best husband, other than never leaving home. As time went by, Ena knew about Jack and me (as more than friends) but chose not to interfere. Thinking about both John and yourself, only both of you can spell out how you saw me as part of your father's life.

A number of the men in Jack's circle of friends had an extramarital partner, or a 'mistress', as the terminology of the day described it. This seems to have been an accepted part of the culture of the time amongst Jack's contemporaries, as were long absences from home associated with adventures, holidays or motorsport.

Reflecting as an adult, I surmise that an accommodation had been reached between my mother and father by the time I was a teenager. In hindsight, clearly this was a man dividing his time between two worlds and the two women in his life.

Our 2015 lunch over, we gazed out over beautiful Little Beach. I said, 'Dorothy, if I had some omnipotent power to turn back time ... well, I wouldn't change a thing.' And this is the truth.

It was Dorothy's real estate advice, assistance and guidance that in no small part enabled my wife Rhonda and me to accumulate enough savings to retire early, enjoy extensive travel and many of the good things in life that affluence makes possible. Thank you, Dorothy.

To the casual observer, ours may seem an unusual situation, given that 'love triangles' frequently do not end well and children are often the first to suffer when love divides families. But that is certainly not my experience. The stereotypical movie love scenario of the 'other woman' coming between a faithful husband and wife did not apply to us. Dorothy deeply loved my father, and was loved by him in return, for 25 years. She is a remarkable lady and has certainly had a significant influence on my life—for the better.

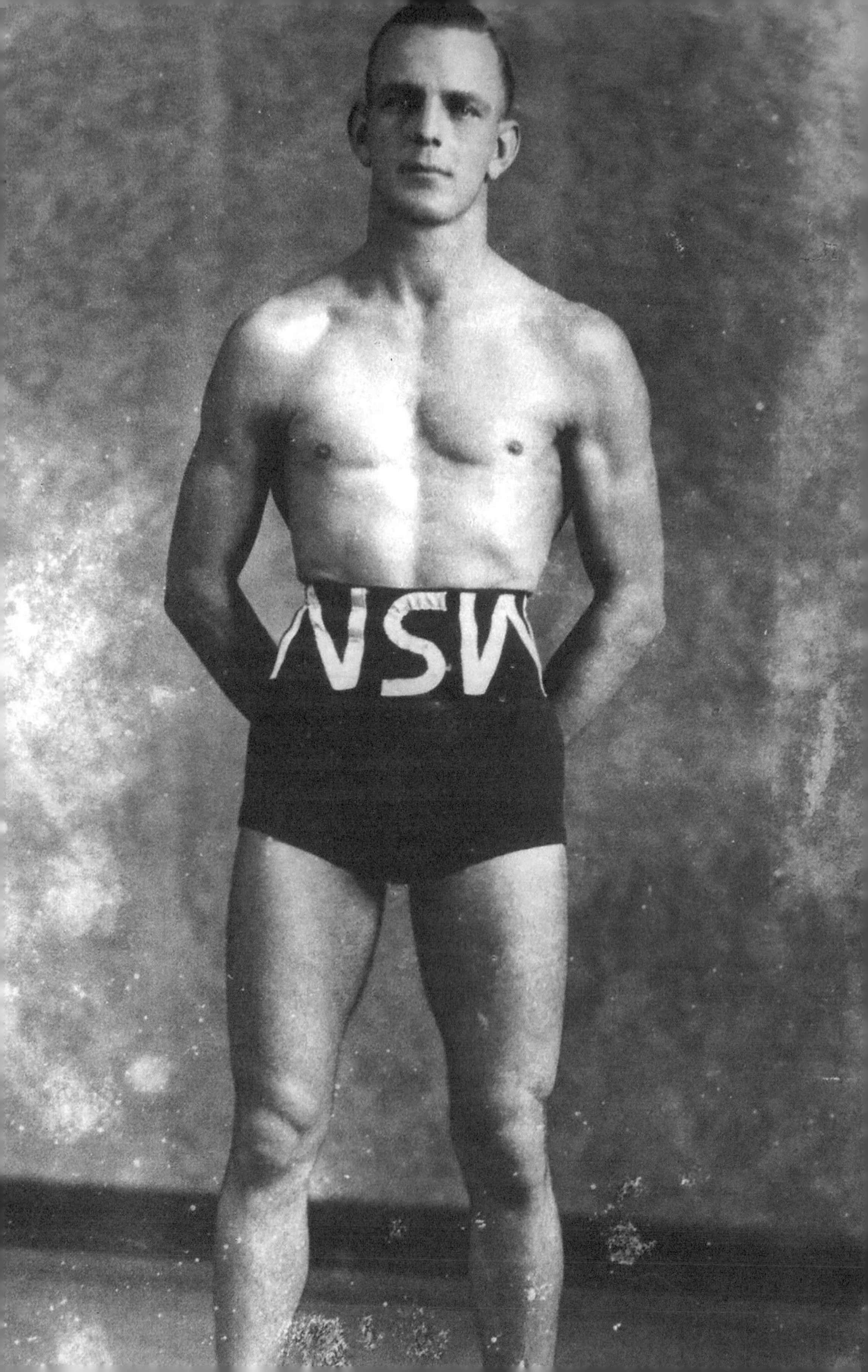
NSW

CHAPTER THIRTEEN
WRESTLING AND WATERSKIING

There was more to 'Gelignite' Jack Murray than motorsports and The Garage. As he told his National Library interviewer:

> During the past 50 years I have been engaged in various sports and various successes: boxing, wrestling—I was State Champion welterweight for about twelve years in New South Wales, and welter and middleweight for about four years. The date I just can't give you offhand. I engaged in waterskiing—actually I formed the first waterski club in Australia with Bill McLachlan. That would be back in about 1943. The skis were brought out by a friend of mine, Bruck Wheeler, on the old *Aorangi* and we tried to ride them with varied successes and a lot of fun. There were some really good athletes among them—Jack O'Hara a Games wrestler, and a lot of other chaps.

The *Australian Dictionary of Biography* says:

> [Jack Murray] was a pioneer of waterskiing in Australia and alleged that he had been the New South Wales welterweight wrestling champion for ten years. Of chunky build, he had an undoubted

Left: A proud and very young Jack as part of the NSW wrestling team.

CHAPTER THIRTEEN

Above: Jack 'commutes' across Sydney Harbour as only 'Gelignite' Jack Murray can.

commitment to physical fitness. In 1964 he won the inaugural BP Ocean Classic for powerboats from Sydney to Newcastle and back. He survived some serious boating accidents: in 1955 he was burned, in 1956 he was knocked unconscious and in 1965 his boat hit an unidentified fish or whale at high speed.

The word 'alleged' certainly suggests the writer's disbelief in Jack's claims. So what is the truth?

Again, 'Truth is stranger than fiction'.

Wrestling

Well before he became known as 'Gelignite', Jack was a very successful amateur wrestler. If he hadn't lost two crucial matches to his close friend, Jack 'Spud' O'Hara, Jack would have represented Australia at both the 1934 London Empire Games and at the 1936 Berlin Olympic Games.

The 'two Jacks' used to flat together in Bondi. Their weekly ritual involved

Above: Jack showing his amateur wrestling technique.

a wrestling match between them. The loser had to pay the rent. Spud's major lament was that while he might have won those two major bouts, Jack kept 'flipping' him for the rent. My concern is with the poor property owner. Surely the weekly tussles must have taken their toll on the property!

To verify Jack's wrestling record, in 2015 I contacted NSW Wrestling. Don Brown, the NSW State President, was kind enough to check NSW Wrestling Association Inc records. He confirmed that during an amateur wrestling career spanning seventeen years (1930-46), Jack won no fewer than thirteen NSW State Championships:

> 74 kg: 1930, 1931, 1932, 1933 and 1934; J.E. Murray was NSW State Champion five times.
> 84 kg: 1930, 1931, 1935, 1938, 1940, 1941, 1945 and 1946; J.E. Murray was NSW State Champion eight times.

In both 1930 and 1931, Jack not only won the lower weight division but also competed in and won the next higher weight division, defeating considerably larger opponents.

CHAPTER THIRTEEN

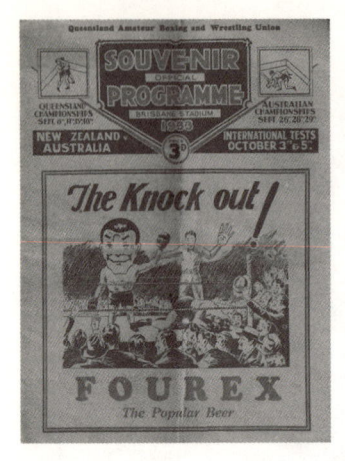

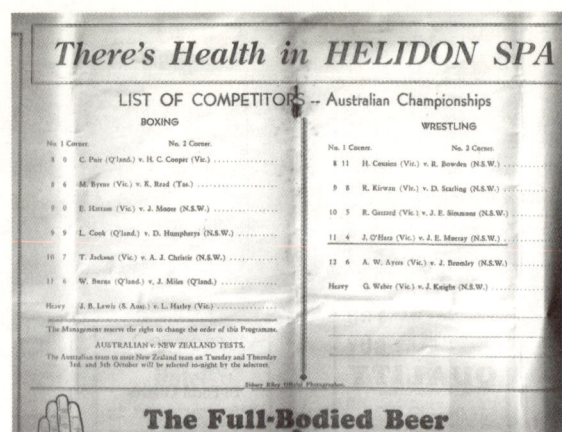

Above: The Program: The 'two Jacks' wrestle for the 11 st 4 lb (72 kg) Australian Championship in 1933.

Jack 'Spud' O'Hara: Great Mate and Champion

John O'Hara was 23 when he represented Australia at the 1936 Berlin Olympic Games, and one of three Australian wrestlers who competed. He and Dick Garrard learned their wrestling at the Victorian Railways Institute gym in Melbourne, and Eddie Scarf was from Sydney. They travelled by ship with the Australian team to the Games and tried to maintain their training while on board.

Scarf, who became Australia's first medallist at the 1932 Los Angeles Games, winning bronze, placed sixth in 1936. O'Hara progressed to the third round and Garrard (who would win silver in London in 1948) was eliminated in the second round.

This was undoubtedly the best Australian wrestling team at any Games, but they came up against some unfamiliar judging rules and were 'unfairly' penalised, according to the post-Games report, which nevertheless refers diplomatically to the judging. World War II stalled their careers, meaning the loss of two Games in their prime years.

O'Hara was Australian wrestling champion in varying weight categories for fourteen years, and in weight lifting, he finished as a heavyweight. In those days natural sportsmen could spread their talent around. He played water polo and rowed in 8s for Victoria, was runner-up in Victorian high-diving contests, surfed on the first big hollow boards at Torquay in the 1930s and 40s and waterskied with Jack. He also drove in the REDEX Round Australia car rallies in the 1950s. Spud would pass away the same year as his great mate Jack.

The many years of training as a young wrestler promoted the physical fitness and sheer strength my father would use for both his motorsport and waterskiing careers.

Waterskiing and Shoal Bay

The names Shoal Bay and 'Gelignite' Jack Murray became synonymous with fun. For decades, Jack's annual summer vacation in the blue water paradise of Port Stephens attracted a number of good friends, mates and locals. Many of them were well-known sporting or entertainment personalities of the time.

Port Stephens is located two to three hours' drive north of Sydney, and the port is actually two-and-a-half times the size of Sydney Harbour. The gently sloping, sandy Shoal Bay beach was an ideal location for all manner of water sports, including fishing, sailing, manned kite flying behind speedboats and waterskiing. Jack and Dorothy Rosewell bought Unit 9, Shoal Towers, directly opposite the beach, with a panoramic view over the Bay. A number of the group of friends who holidayed with them also bought property in the area as holiday homes and for investment, such as World Hang Gliding Champion Bill Moyes and his wife Molly, who purchased a block of units on Shoal Bay Road.

Celebrities and Sportsmen

Television personalities and keen tennis players Bob and Dolly Dyer, best known for the TV show *Pick a Box*, scientist Harry Messel, well-known cricketer and commentator Sid Barnes and Arthur and Joan Fitzgerald were all part of this holiday scene. The Fitzgeralds also purchased a unit in Shoal Towers. The group of friends could swell to 20 or even 80 or more, and a number of boats for skiing or game fishing were often part of the scene. The fishing tournament each February-March was an important annual event. Keen anglers such as Keith Whitehead fished for marlin and shark and visited outer islands with groups of boats.

There was camaraderie between all these people who visited Shoal Bay every summer. February became the time to lay aside a month for the annual visit to Shoal Bay. They were involved in waterskiing, tennis and swimming; hiking over Tomaree and trips to Yaccaba; visits to Soldiers Point, Jimmy's Beach, Hawk's Nest, Moffat's oyster barn and Tamboi at the edge of the Myall lakes; they went to Blossom Point and even waterskied as far as Bungwahl.

It was great fun and Jack was certainly at its centre.

CHAPTER THIRTEEN

Above: Bill McLachlan (left), unknown beauty and Jack (right).

As the years passed, the friends informally tagged themselves The Shoal Bay Club. Members all had numbered, matching fun/souvenir key rings which featured the Dorothy Rosewell rose logo. The Club comprised the Delany family, Maureen, Pat and their four sons, together with Katrina and Harry Potter, the Cheok family, the Moyes family, Jimmy Powers, Hilton Firth, Ron d'Albora—and many more.

Bruck and Betty Wheeler were very much part of the Shoal Bay circle of close friends. Betty, a diminutive and attractive blonde, was a particularly gifted and talented athlete. She started waterskiing in 1953 and in 1961 represented Australia in the world waterski tournament at Long Beach, California. She won several Australian, Sydney and state titles for trick and slalom skiing. Betty was the first woman to ski barefoot in Australia. In 2016 this fact was confirmed by Dorothy Rosewell who spoke with both Betty Wheeler and Betty Leighton, sometimes mistakenly credited with being the first woman barefooter. Betty Wheeler was first and Betty Leighton the following day. Many of Betty Wheeler's skills were honed on the waters of the Hawkesbury River and Jervis Bay south of Sydney as well as at Shoal Bay.

WRESTLING AND WATERSKIING

Above: Bob and Dolly Dyer at rear of boat. Jack is driving.

Above: Jack and Hilton Firth refuelling one of Jack's ski boats.

CHAPTER THIRTEEN

Above: Australian Champion and world-class skier, Betty Wheeler, prepares for a run in Shoal Bay.

Keith Williams, developer of Sea World and Hamilton Island resorts, paid Betty the following tribute:

> Betty played a great role in the growth of Sea World. The *Australian Water Skier* magazine was her personal baby, she managed the administration of the Ninth World Water Ski Championships single-handed and her continued organisation of the Concours d'Elegance over a period of fourteen years is a tribute to her organisational ability. Betty, without your contribution, the history of waterskiing in Australia may well have been very different.

Australian men everywhere owe Betty an eternal debt of gratitude. Like Paula Stafford, the Gold Coast 'Bikini Queen', Betty designed, sewed and promoted the first bikinis both at home and in the USA.

Today Shoal Towers is still a residential block. The plaque that stands opposite reminds visitors of 'Gelignite' Jack Murray and the role he played

Above at top: Fun and games as Bob Dyer and Jack lie, clearly defeated by the girls at tennis. Beach fun included manned kite flying behind boats as another highlight.

in the local community. The invitation to its unveiling in Easter 1984 read as follows:

> For over two decades 'Gelignite' Jack Murray, who died on 11 December 1983, and a group of colleagues celebrated Christmas and Easter at Shoal Bay where a number of his friends have waterfront units. On Easter Sunday this year to mark the contribution Jack made in teaching children and visitors to Shoal Bay the hazards of the water and the need for safety measures at all times, combined

CHAPTER THIRTEEN

Above: From left, Marie McLachlan, Betty Wheeler, Lorraine Sargent and Dorothy Rosewell. Shoal Bay, February 1961. Photo courtesy of University of Newcastle Cultural Collections.

with his diligent teaching of waterskiing to all and sundry, it has been decided by a group of local residents to mount a plaque in a small reserve on the beach. It was formerly a windswept sand patch.

With the planting of trees and the growing of grass, which Jack supervised, it has been made into a very nice picnic area. Jack Murray and his friends tended the area with great care and it is used by all beach enthusiasts as somewhere to sit in ideal surroundings.

The Port Stephens Shire Council has given permission for the plaque to be mounted in the area, which will be done on Easter Sunday. A great number of Jack's friends are making the trip to Shoal Bay in memory of the Murray spirit of adventure.

'Gelignite' Jack Murray Memorial Plaque

In July 2015, the plaque and its granite mount were moved a few metres east in order to accommodate the construction of a wider and much improved path along the Shoal Bay foreshore. But it is still positioned in front of Shoal Towers, in a concrete area with a seat for visitors to enjoy the same view he once described as 'the best in the world'.

In the Shoal Bay Country Club Hotel, adjoining the refurbished and updated Ramada Resort Shoal Bay, a wall display of 'Gelignite' Jack Murray memorabilia is also to be found.

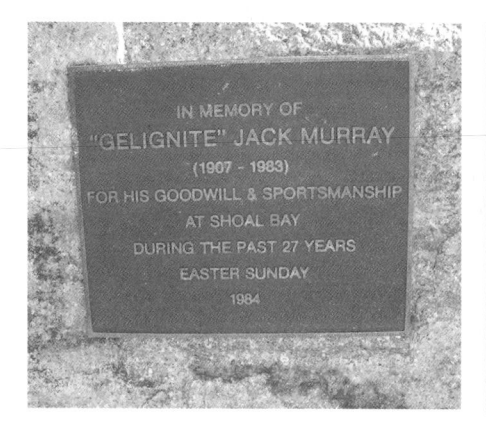

Above: 'Gelignite' Jack Murray Memorial Plaque.

Above: Jack's grandson, Jonny Murray and the author viewing Jack's memorabilia in 2011.

Above: Floral tribute to Jack featuring the waterskiing Gold Oscar.

Jack's Gold Oscar

The coveted Gold Oscar is awarded to a skier who wins all three events; a slalom title, trick event and jump event at the Australian Water Ski Championships. Betty Leighton, long-time friend of Jack, was the first person to receive this magnificent trophy. A bronze replica of the Oscar is also produced which is awarded to winners of individual events. The trophy was modelled on a photograph of Jack.

CHAPTER THIRTEEN

The Father of Waterskiing in Australia

So why do people remember Jack so fondly? He probably loved waterskiing as much as he did motorsport. He was not the first person to waterski in this country. However, due to his pioneering involvement, including securing sponsorship for the initial Bridge to Bridge ski race, and his extensive participation in the sport, he is often described as the Father of Waterskiing in Australia. Jack was a Life Member of the NSW Water Ski Association and holds the distinction of being one of the group of seven who first barefooted in this country.

In November 1979, Bob Wing wrote to Jack requesting his help:

> Dear Jack,
>
> I am at present compiling a book on the history of waterskiing in Australia, along with the basis of how to learn to ski. Because of your involvement in the history of the sport, a chapter relating to you would be an integral part of the book …

He concludes his letter by adding …

> PS A book without your story would be quite incomplete and if you could spare an hour sometime, I could come out and put your information on tape.

Jack did assist Bob and also wrote a letter to Alan Gibbons in Darwin, introducing Bob to Alan, thus ensuring that Carl Atkinson's story, as another pioneer of the sport, was told to Bob.

Bob went on to publish his book, *Water Skiing in Australia*:

> In 1934, during the month of either July or August, Edward Arthur (Ted) Parker of 18 Schofield Avenue, Earlwood, became the first person in Australia to waterski. The epic event occurred on Hen and Chicken Bay, Sydney Harbour, behind a three pointed boat powered by a 22 horsepower Johnson outboard motor. The boat was driven by Carlisle Arlington Rochester of Burwood. The skis were made by Ted Parker's neighbour, Doug Facoral of Undercliffe, who was

a patternmaker by trade, and the skis were made from photographs seen in American magazine *Popular Mechanics*. The design was copied and a pair of shoes securely fastened onto the skis for foot grips. Ted Parker was aged twenty at the time and was born in Sydney on the 11 February 1914.

... It was a popular belief that the first Australian to ski was Carl Atkin [*sic:* Carl Atkinson] from Darwin in the NT who in 1936, while visiting Sydney, skied on Sydney Harbour. Then World War II curtailed any further skiing activity until the 1940s when the era of Bill McLachlan, Jack Murray and Reg Johnson took over to set the sport on fire as we know it today. Reg Johnson, a photographer at the RPA hospital, was the first person to waterski after the war and he started on the Hawkesbury River. Reg used to work shifts and have plenty of days off. It was through this that he used to invite people up to the Hawkesbury and amongst the first he invited were Bill McLachlan, Jack Murray and Ray Leighton. Their first experience of waterskiing was when the Hawkesbury River was in flood and was a muddy and not very impressive sight—but once up on skis they were hooked.

The Hawkesbury

It was not until after World War II that waterskiing began in earnest at two places on the Hawkesbury River near Sydney: Sackville and Wisemans Ferry. These parts of the river have long, straight stretches of water; they are tidal and bordered by lush green banks. They are, in short, ideal for waterskiing. At these locations, the sport began to blossom into a pastime not exclusively for the well-to-do. You could hire or share a boat, skis and equipment at the towns of Sackville and Wisemans Ferry.

Waterskiing encouraged the powerboat and trailer making industries and an entirely new holiday and recreational scene began to grow. A party of skiers might go up for the day, or camp over the weekend, so enjoying picnicking as well as waterskiing. It was this democratic and easy way of conducting skiing which turned it into a nationwide sport in a comparatively short time.

CHAPTER THIRTEEN

Sea World

One of the more spectacular developments of waterskiing in Australia took place at Surfers Paradise on the Southern Queensland coast. There, on the Nerang River Surfers Paradise Gardens, an imitation Cyprus Gardens, the original of which was in Florida, USA, was developed. Aquatic attractions included marvellous displays by individuals and groups of waterskiers—and, of course, a waterski ballet. Relocation to Sea World on the sand spit north of Surfers CBD occurred in 1972. Sea World offered full-time waterskiing opportunities to skiers and those who wished to gain experience of a wide range of waterskiing events.

Another of Bob Wing's articles shed light on the history, characters and origins of waterskiing in Australia and Jack's foundation involvement. To paraphrase Bob:

The Dawn of Waterski Racing

It was in the 1950s that waterski racing became very popular in Australia. One of the earliest venues was Sackville. Unfortunately, an accident in the early days impacted the sport. Kemble Barclay fell while leading one of the races and was struck by a following boat and fatally injured. Kemble's death changed the whole attitude of waterskiers to racing and saw the introduction of safer time trials and marathon skiing.

Among the early races were the 100-mile Ampol Trials. Another Australian innovation was introduced as skiers competed in pairs, better known now as 'two up'. Whatever the reason, whether it was a shortage of boats or Australian mateship creating the teaming up, the popularity of two up racing became the accepted format for Australian ski racing.

As in all sports, there was always the team to beat and in the early days it was Jack Murray and Ginger McEwen who were picking up the trophies.

Jack and Les Holden as skiers, with driver Hilton Firth, won the 1957 and 1959 Ampol 100 Mile Water Ski Trials.

Founder of the Bridge to Bridge Ski Race

In 1961, Jack, noting that there had been for a number of years a Bridge to Bridge boat race, rang Jeff Lovatt, then sales manager for Mercury. He said,

Above: Jack skiing and being towed behind a seaplane.

Above: Bill McLachlan attempting a speed record behind a seaplane.

CHAPTER THIRTEEN

Above: Jack enjoying the sport he loved, spray flying.

Above: Perfect balance: foam and spray fly as Jack Murray and Noreen Borg speed along at 40 miles an hour. Jack and Noreen were two of Australia's top-line waterskiers.

'What about we have a ski race as well?' Mercury sponsored the first Bridge to Bridge Ski Race for £100: £50 went to the winner, £30 to second and £20 to third placing.

In the first race, conducted by the Aqua Ski Club, there were twenty entries. Jack entered his boat with a side-valve Dodge engine, and came second last! From those small beginnings developed the world's biggest ski race.

The Bridge to Bridge Race, from the Hawkesbury River Bridge at Dangar Island to the Windsor Bridge, a distance of 70 miles (112 kilometres) is now a world classic in waterskiing. It attracts the fastest machinery afloat and the keenest skiers from both Australia and overseas.

Winners of the first race were Chica Courtney and Fred Crofts, skiing behind an outboard, *Yogi Bear*. In those days the race had a different character. Competition was keen, but not professional. For many competitors and spectators the race was simply a social ski outing. Average speeds were in the 40 mph (64 km/h) range and an honest 50 mph (80 km/h) gave a good chance of a win. Until the late 1960s and the early 70s, the competing boats were largely centremount inboards.

There were fun and games. Not many boats had the luxury of a rear-facing seat! It was always comical when a boat went by with an observer busily talking to the driver and missing a skier. Much time often went by before discovering they only had one up and had to double back to find and pick up the missing racer.

Wing's work highlights the importance of the Hawkesbury River, and in particular Sackville, in the development of waterskiing in Australia. The town stretches along the road beside Sackville Reach on the Upper Hawkesbury River, about 80 km northwest of Sydney. It was here, in 1946, that Jack, Bill McLachlan and Alf Nagar established the country's first waterski club. Jack was the first one to ski the entire length of the Hawkesbury River and in March 1951, he and Bill McLachlan skimmed over the water at 130 km/h on a towline from a light seaplane. This was the first time in Australia that waterskiers had been towed by an aeroplane and made the front page of the Sydney Morning Herald.

'Two pieces of beech and a pair of sandshoes'

Fred Williams is another famous pioneering name in water sports in Australia. Fred Williams' Water Skis is today a large and highly successful supplier of water sports equipment. Jack and Fred were mates, and Fred was interviewed at the time he was being inducted into the Australian Water Sports Hall of Fame. He was asked:

> *How did you make your first set of skis?*
> 'Gelignite' Jack Murray was a friend of mine. He and his mates were messing around with old planks on the water, and he encouraged me to give it a try. We thought we'd make something similar to an

CHAPTER THIRTEEN

aquaplane—we made it out of an old garage door! I also read about a bloke by the name of Waller in an American magazine who'd made a set of long skis.

I got two pieces of beech and hung them over the veranda with two house bricks tied to the end. I poured boiling water over them to make them bend and left them overnight. I attached two sandshoes and painted a bulls-eye in the middle—and that was my first set of skis!

Ocean Boat Racing

Neil Bennetts asked Jack in his National Library interview:

BENNETTS: Have you been in much of the ocean racing?

MURRAY: Oh yes—I'd forgotten all about that, more or less. It would be about ten years ago. They suggested a race from Sydney to Newcastle and back. I think there were about 26 starters for the first

Above: 'Gelignite' Jack Murray and Keith Whitehead win the inaugural Sydney-Newcastle-Sydney Ocean Race in 1964, in *Tact*.

one, using Bertram boats, Savage, all the well-known makes of boats. We had a Bertram. It was an 18-footer with two outboards on the back of it, Keith Whitehead and myself. Keith had the boat and had the motors, and I think they were loaned to us by Mercury. We were lucky; there's a lot of luck in that. It was really rough this day. We got to Newcastle and stopped there for half an hour, pulled up at the Maritime Police up there, and they looked after us, gave us a meal. Then you turn round and you go back again. I think we averaged 50 miles an hour for that. It was a good average. We didn't have that much trouble. Belted hell out of us. Won two of those—Bob Dyer was in one of them, he had a cruiser with a couple of V-8 Chevs in it. Anyway, he broke all the engine mounts and I think he got towed to the finish or something like that.

Then we went down to Victoria and they put on one down there round Port Phillip Bay and we were lucky enough to win the first one of that, Keith and myself. And I think we got a first or a second

Above: Keith Whitehead (at left) and 'Gelignite' Jack Murray (at right) won first place in the BP Ocean Classic 1964.

in the third one they held. That's right—it rained all the time and the chap said, 'How do you go, do you use a compass?' I said, 'No, you just go out and turn left.' He said, 'One of these days you won't do that.' A few years after, Keith Whitehead—I wasn't with him—was going to Newcastle and it did rain, and he got outside and he didn't know where he was. He pulled a trawler up to ask them where he was. They said, 'You're going in the wrong direction; follow us'—and they took him back in round Dee Why there. When we used to race to Newcastle, we used to just go out and turn left. It was fine weather and that was it: we'd just go straight up the coast. Mug's luck. (Laughs) Ah, a lot of fun, though.

BENNETTS: What sort of speeds would you get out of the boat?

MURRAY: The boat could do about 60; you could average 50. It's nearly always rough out there, of course. I've never been to Newcastle ever when it's really smooth. By ten o'clock the nor'easter's blowing, and away you go. It does a lot of damage to the boats. Half of them don't finish. When you get up to 45 [on] some of those waves, it loosens the fillings in your teeth a bit—you know, it's really rough.

London to Sydney Marathon 1968

No matter what adventure he tried, Jack would always find time for some fun and games along the way. With a few days to spare before the start of the London to Sydney Marathon, he thought he would try his hand at a bit of waterskiing on the Thames—right in front of the Houses of Parliament.

The London to Sydney Marathon provided the opportunity for a waterskiing first—behind a liner in the middle of the Indian Ocean. Jack had planned to ski behind the *Chusan* during the nine-day trip from Bombay to Perth, and the ship's radio room had been fitted with a 'picturegram' transmitter so that photographs could be radioed to Sydney.

MURRAY: In India we had a bit of fun. We didn't have bombs; we just had a bit of jelly and we dropped it in the harbour at Bombay. The Indians like a bit of a cracker; I think everybody all round the world likes crackers. Anyhow we came down to Sydney [*sic:* Perth]

Above: Jack's adventure was interrupted by the local constabulary. And his punishment? Transportation by rally car to the colony, leaving Battersea Park on 24 November 1968.

and we were going to have a ski on the boat. The first three days it was dead calm, and the skipper—we had the head of the *Daily Mail* from London here; he escorted the cars all through the rally; we'd run into him and he said, 'Is there anything you want?' I said I'd like to have a ski and he said, 'Alright, we'll have a pair of skis made.' So the ship's chippy, I think they call him, the carpenter, he knocked up the funniest pair of skis you ever saw. He got two boards and then he put a bend in them and he nailed a bit of board on each side to keep the bend in. Then he got an old pair of sandals and he screwed these on, and we had it all ready to go. They were going to let a lifeboat over the side, slow the ship down. I believe it would [have] cost $1200 to turn the boat off from 20 knots an hour back to five. That was the cost, just to turn it off and then bring it back up to that speed; that's what it would have cost to do.

So they agreed on this, it was all done and I signed an indemnity form to exonerate them. So the skis were made, and the next morning it started to get a bit rough, and one of the guys said, 'It will be rough from here to Perth. I've done twelve trips and I bet

CHAPTER THIRTEEN

you it's not calm again.' And it never was. They let the water out of the swimming pool and they lashed everything down. It was rough from there all the way to Perth. Before that—oh, I'd have loved to ski behind the liner. I don't know anybody who has ever skied behind a liner, anywhere in the Indian Ocean. What a gimmick!

And I could have done it. Their boats had six-cylinder motors in them, beautiful dories, they'd do 20 knots. They would just let it down off the davits, I'd get in that, and it would follow the ship and I'd come up and pick the rope up off the ship. They'd let it off the second deck at the back and I'd just pick it up, skiing backwards and forwards behind the ship, you know. It would have been something, that. And like a fool, when I got off the ship in Perth I forgot to get the skis. I just left them on the ship. What a souvenir to hang up in The Garage—but that's another story.

'Gelignite' Jack's Last Ski Boat

Jack owned a number of ski boats throughout his life. His last boat went on to provide spills and thrills for many years after his passing—and continues to do so today. Since that's what ski boats are all about, I'm sure Jack would have approved and enjoyed every run.

A number of Jack's previous boats and his last boat were named, appropriately enough, *Ski*. The last boat is an 18ft Fred Williams Hustler Mark One, an American design with a deep V, fibreglass over marine ply. Fred built the Hustlers here in Australia under licence. *Ski* is what is termed an 'inboard/outboard'—basically a 'marinised' car engine. Jack bought the boat new in 1968 and at the time of his passing, it was driven by a 307 Chev engine, with the power being transmitted through a Sea Tiger sterndrive. It provides a comfortable, yet powerful, smooth ride and its chrome dash screams 1960s. *Ski* was, and is, a great recreational ski boat.

When Jack passed away in December 1983, his assets, which included *Ski*, passed to my mother, Ena. For a year or two *Ski* sat under covers in The Garage, occupying scarce Bondi parking space that could have been better used for the repair and servicing of motor vehicles. At the time The Garage was a mechanical workshop and had already been leased for a number of years to mechanic and family friend, Jeff Stevens (aka 'Fishcake').

Rhonda and I were living in Sylvania Waters, only metres from the perfect

Above: Burrill Lake, near Ulladulla on the NSW south coast, with the author 'on one'.

skiing waters of the sheltered Georges River, so for a few years *Ski* enjoyed a new life and did what it did best. It woke up the Kangaroo Point and Kogarah Bay residents at first light on Sunday mornings as the big V8 kicked in and keen skiers took to the water.

Ski boats in general can be temperamental beasts and they love to be used regularly. With the passage of time *Ski* began to show her age. Rhonda and I, together with good mate, work colleague and former mechanic Laurie Miante spent a weekend with a hired engine hoist and a set of tools in hand. No doubt Jack would have enjoyed the sight of his non-mechanical younger son, head down in the engine bay, legs straight up in the air, applying about 300 pounds of breaking strain to uncooperative engine mounting bolts. The nuts had not moved since 1968, and clearly, after nearly twenty years, saw no reason to do so. Laurie and his inexperienced crew managed to swap the tired 307 Chev, upgrading to a big 350 Chev power plant.

Blind Skier Saves *Ski*

A neighbour with whom I skied regularly, Wayne Lee, once brought a blind friend along for a Sunday ski. Wayne yelled instructions as his talented mate skied on one ski. Later in the morning, as he sat in *Ski*, the friend commented

CHAPTER THIRTEEN

that he could smell petrol. No one else had noticed. Sure enough, on closer inspection, I realised the ageing fuel tank located in the bow section had rusted out along the seam. Under load and acceleration, as the bow lifted fuel was soaking back through the carpet under the seats.

Jack had three ski boats blow up under him. If not for the highly attuned senses of the blind skier that day, my mates and I may well have joined Jack's 'blown up' club. A new fuel tank, especially designed and built to fit the non-standard space near the bow, was installed.

With both a mechanic and an aviation electrical expert as part of the regular ski crew, I managed to keep *Ski* afloat and running for many a weekend. A broken shaft high in the stern drive meant the boat spent several months in Ulladulla awaiting parts. Carburettor, electrical and engine cooling hose problems became all too common. On one occasion, due to a rusted wheel bearing on the ageing trailer, a disaster was narrowly averted when a wheel almost came adrift on Taren Point Road.

Ski and d'Albora Marinas

The name d'Albora is synonymous in Australia with marinas, boating and the marine industry. Ron d'Albora and Jack were great mates for many years and Ron's son Jeff competed alongside Jack and John Murray in a Commodore in the 1979 Repco Reliability Trial.

Ski was eventually sold to d'Albora Marinas.

Having acquired the Grey Ghost, my brother John set about returning *Ski* to the Murray stable. He was prepared to fund and undertake a full restoration program. As described in *Powerboat* magazine, August-September 1997, Bruce Carroll from Pro Paint near Windsor restored *Ski* to her former glory. Apart from some colour changes across the running surface and upholstery updates, the 1997 restoration meant the boat looked much the same as when Jack first laid eyes on her way back in 1968.

Following this first restoration, *Ski* still bore the chrome number '1' and letter 'N' on either side near the bow. They contributed to a true representation of the boat when Jack owned her and had held that prized 1N boat registration for New South Wales.

But we found that the actual New South Wales 1N registration had been transferred to another boat when *Ski* was owned by d'Albora Marinas. The article in *Powerboat* suggested that the chrome number 1 had 'been souvenired at some stage'. It is more than likely that the chrome 1s were removed due to the transfer. In 2017, a pontoon party boat temporarily bears New South Wales registration 1N and is located at Soldiers Point Marina, Soldiers Point, Port Stephens, only a few kilometres from Jack's much loved Shoal Bay.

Prior to boats requiring registration, an accident on Sydney Harbour had occurred which resulted in a death. It was clear that due to their growing popularity and proliferation, boats would need to be identified and registered. All registrations for boats in NSW end in the letter 'N', and the prized number '1' was originally secured by George Benyon, president of the Water Ski Association at the time, while '2' went to Ray Leighton, '3' was unknown, '4' was acquired by Noel Miles, and Jack was issued with '5'. All these people were good mates. Jack skied with registration '5N' for many years. When George Benyon passed away, his wife Judy was kind enough to offer Jack the coveted New South Wales '1N' registration.

So it's a pity that the NSW '1' registration was lost to the Murray family. In the 1980s there was not a market for low boat registrations as there was for car numbers. *Ski*, unlike the Grey Ghost, had not been used to set records or win races. Restoration or transformation into a tribute boat were not on the agenda. And so *Ski*, together with her coveted registration, was sold to d'Albora Marinas for around $5000. Given the tribute boat condition of *Ski* today, the sale is something I regret. Of interest is that Jack had another 19ft boat which was originally purchased in Hong Kong and used at Shoal Bay for several years. The registration of that boat was SK1N ... written as SK1 N on the side of the boat; it also read as *Ski*.

From Restoration to Tribute Boat

Ski's story continues. Following the 1997 restoration, Jack's grandson, Jonny, became enamoured with both waterskiing and the boat, now re-registered:

> I used to use the Hustler all the time. My friends and I waterskied behind it endlessly. After school we would go to the marina and ski all afternoon on Rose Bay sandbar. We took it down to the back of the Spit on weekends, as the water is very flat.
>
> However, by 1999 the original OMC leg kept playing up and it was becoming too expensive to maintain. Shortly after, the 302

CHAPTER THIRTEEN

Above: All chrome and all 60's dash.

engine seized near the sandbar. The boat was then parked in our garage and never touched until 2012 when I finally convinced dad to do a full restoration.

Jonny recalls the previous engine as a 302, but when sold to d'Albora Marinas, *Ski* was definitely powered by a 350 Chev. Perhaps the engine had been changed yet again in the interim?

In 2012, heading towards middle age at 44 years old, *Ski* required some more TLC. Over a period of about a year, a boat builder and Jonny dedicated many hours of hard yakka to the task of rejuvenating the ageing beauty.

Jonny comments, 'I really loved it. It was a proud experience for me.'

The Hustler was completely stripped down to her stringers and rebuilt from the ground up. The boat was fitted with the latest engine from Mercruiser, a top of the range Merc Magnum V8 350, and the cable steering was brought into the 21st century and replaced with hydraulics.

Jonny enthusiastically describes the process:

> I added my touch to the boat as I felt it would be nice to give her some luxury features. I added teak timber flooring instead of carpet and timber side edges to sit on when getting in and out of the boat.

I added a removable teak marlin board so you could get in and out easily after swimming. I also added Silent Choice, an exhaust system that allows you to hear the engine scream along through the pipes at the back—or you switch it to silent mode and the exhaust goes through the leg. The 'JM' initials in the back of the seat were originally in box letters, I changed this to something more related to racing and had Grandpa's initials covered in a racing wreath. It was a strange coincidence to find out later that Dorothy had done a similar thing for his funeral. In December 2014 we had a custom show trailer built for her, for the purposes of exhibiting the boat at shows.

In 2015, Jonny commented:

I have used the Hustler four times over the last three years. My plan was not to use it. However, I have a real love for the boat and am starting to want to use it. Leify [Jonny's girlfriend] and I have really taken to waterskiing and have talked a lot about using her this summer. I think the boat should be enjoyed *and* admired. The times I have taken her out I have been harassed; people just think she's beautiful.

In one instance, an older couple saw us anchored at Camp Cove. When we left they drove to Rose Bay Wharf and waited for us—just to see the boat up close. When the man found out it had belonged to Jack, he almost passed out.

Today the Hustler is stored in a warehouse away from the elements. The transformation of *Ski* from simply a 'restored' boat, looking as close to the original as possible, to a 'tribute' boat means that she retains her usability and relevance. Rather than becoming just an historical, dry-land showpiece, *Ski* continues to serve as a reliable boat that can be used to tow skiers as well as safely cruise the waters of Sydney Harbour.

Jonny has further plans for improvements and transformation:

In October 2015 she is going to the painter. He is putting a thin white boot line strip around the bottom, to give her a more classic

CHAPTER THIRTEEN

look. From the photos, you might notice that the bottom of the hull is black. I did this for a few reasons.

One, paint chips easily when you hit the side of the trailer so the black antifouling is an easy touch-up. Second, when you beach a boat the sand scrapes the bottom, which doesn't look nice. Again an easy touch-up with antifouling.

Dorothy sent me a photo of the boat which I had never seen before. At the front under the nose cone there used to be a chrome hull protector that ran down the 'V'. I soon will have a guy measuring that for installation. He is also doing the registration numbers in chrome. I originally didn't put chrome numbers back on as I was hoping to get better numbers, possibly including a '1'. But I haven't had much luck, so it might just be lucky number 8, as the Chinese say.

I think the boat should be enjoyed *and* admired.

Well said, Jonny.

Hit It

Jack would have been both pleased and proud to see *Ski* continue to provide fun and enjoyment for many people. No doubt the shout of 'Hit it' or 'Go' will be heard from skiers behind the Hustler for countless summers to come.

Above: Leify Porter at the helm of a transformed and updated *Ski*.

Above: 'JM' initials and racing wreaths decorate *Ski*'s seats.

Above: Some of Jack's previous *Ski* boats. This boat was originally bought by Jack in Hong Kong and shipped to Australia. The registration is quite clever: *SKI 1* at left became in the photo on the right taken in The Garage *SKI 1N*, which reads as 'Skiing' or 'Skiin'.

Shoal Bay Today

To escape the ever-increasing congestion of Sydney, Rhonda and I moved in 2007 to the Port Stephens area. Today we live a few kilometres from Jack's monument at Shoal Bay.

Long-time locals, upon learning that Jack was my father often comment, 'Well, you must have come up here a lot as a kid? Is that why you chose to move here?'

Well—'no' and 'no'. I smile and go on to explain that when one's father is holidaying with a lady friend who happens not to be his wife, it is unlikely his youngest son is going to tag along.

While my older brother John, who was a grown man at the time, did visit Shoal Bay with Jack and Dorothy, I had to wait for retirement before discovering the blue water wonderland. Perhaps there is an as yet undiscovered 'geography gene' which has led me to love and enjoy an area that obviously had a similar pull and appeal for my father.

Relax—Go Boating

As noted, there are few surviving examples of Jack's writing. But we do have the presentation he prepared for the Queensland Boating Industry Association seminar on 23 June 1978. He called it: *Relax—Go Boating:*

CHAPTER THIRTEEN

My talk today no doubt will be most unconventional. Standing here to make a speech is not my way of feeling relaxed ... but the theme is one of interest and certainly dear to my heart. There are many ways to relax and I guess boating has given more relaxation and pleasure to more people than I can count.

Going back over 40 years, it was in the late 30s that I first became interested in boating. In later years, having seen a short film with Preston Peterson standing on a board behind a boat, it looked a great idea for a lot of laughs. Bruck Wheeler, who lives here at Surfers, was working on the *Aorangi* and I asked him to bring back a pair of waterskis from the States. That was in 1943.

Standing on those pieces of board was not an easy task, but after a lot of hard work and not much relaxation, we mastered the art of standing up on two skis. I called my first boat *Flash*: One flash and you're ash.

Going back over the years safety precautions have improved and in NSW I was responsible for boats being registered. You might say waterskiing, kite flying, barefoot skiing and the like is not relaxation—more like hard work. Well, going back over 30 years, there were only one or two boats skiing on the Hawkesbury River.

I normally ski from a tin hut right on the banks of the river at Sackville—and even if I don't ski it's one of the most beautiful places in the whole world. Having competed in both the London to Sydney and London to Mexico Marathons I've seen most of the world—and Shoal Bay in NSW and the Hawkesbury I consider the best.

I have been around Australia by air and car. When you consider the miles we all travel on the roads, boating is a complete joy at any time, to get away from the crowd.

Australian Waterski and Wakeboard Hall of Fame

In recent years the Australian Waterski and Wakeboard Federation has been developing a Hall of Fame. There is work yet to be done and further nominations to be considered.

Paraphrasing the AWWF website:

> The Board has approved the commissioning of an AWWF Hall of Fame. The concept is aimed at recognising those people who have

contributed to the sport of waterskiing as an official and/or as a competitor. Several other Halls of Fame have been examined and it has been recommended that the new Hall of Fame be placed on the AWWF website. The categories will be Official, Athlete and Legend.

Our existing Life Membership will continue to be recognised and incorporated into the new site. The process is that States or Divisions e.g. Tournament Waterski Australia, make the nominations for consideration to our selection panel.

In 2015 I sent a draft copy of part of this book—a chapter then entitled *Shoal Bay and Waterskiing*—to Gary Humphrey, Executive Officer of Waterski and Wakeboard Australia. Gary advised me: 'Yes, I have heard of your father's career over the years and have lodged that document and accompanying emails with the selection panel.'

The selectors will not meet until late 2016 and the next induction is due 2018. Should Jack be considered eligible for a nomination, Gary Humphrey will contact me requesting more information.

As Jack's son I must concede a degree of bias. I think 'Gelignite' Jack Murray's inclusion in the Legend section of the AWWF Hall of Fame is more than justified considering his pioneering contribution and competition results in the sport of waterskiing. Jack's role in initiating sponsorship for, and his personal participation in the Bridge to Bridge Ski Race alone would warrant his inclusion in a Hall of Fame.

If successfully inducted in 2018, Jack would be the only Australian to be inducted into the Waterski and Wakeboard Hall of Fame, the Rally Hall of Fame and the Confederation of Australian Motorsport Hall of Fame. What an achievement!

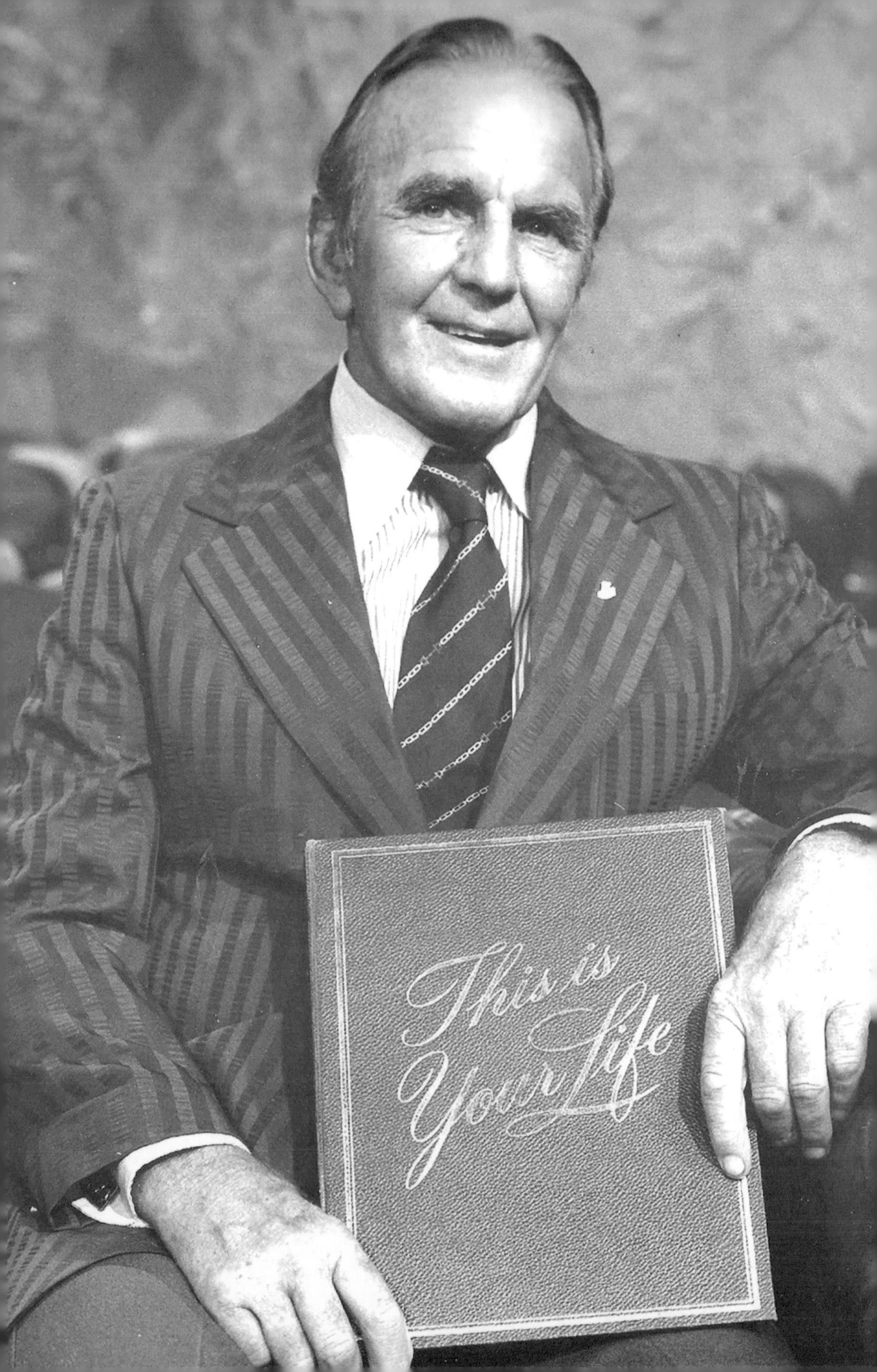
This is
Your Life

CHAPTER FOURTEEN
THIS IS YOUR LIFE

On 3 March 1978, the Guest of Honour on the popular TV show *This Is Your Life* was 'Gelignite' Jack Murray. The show was hosted by Roger Climpson and shown on the Channel 7 network. In preparation, background notes were compiled and a draft script written, a large part of which was indebted to Evan Green's writings. The producers also needed a capable and knowledgeable contact/liaison person to assist with compiling a guest list, organising and providing background information. Naturally, given her special knowledge and skills, this role fell to Dorothy Rosewell.

The actual show at times varied quite markedly from what was initially prepared—but you would expect this to occur in a program filmed live. I recall having a discussion with the host when Roger commented that there had only been a couple of occasions—and he did not elaborate—where the Guest of Honour had prior knowledge that they were to be the subject of an episode. Since it's difficult to fake surprise, he thought both fell flat as a result of the guest being pre-warned.

No such concerns with Jack. His shock—and horror—are palpable. As I look at the footage and read his body language, I can see that Jack is gripped with angst. This is particularly true at the start of the show. As it progressed and his old mates started to appear in rapid succession, he quickly relaxed and became his normal jovial self.

I surmise that his fears centred on the manner in which the show was going to present to the public the issue of his being married, yet at the same time being involved in another long-term relationship. As can be seen in the show's

CHAPTER FOURTEEN

transcript, I had a role to play—and a script to deliver—which would answer any questions that might have arisen and at the same time allay Jack's fears.

Below is a transcript of the show that went to air—with added descriptive comments and explanations. So, sit back, relax, put your feet up and let AMP present *This Is Your Life*:

The show opens with Roger Climpson seated in the back of a vehicle. The Grey Ghost is on its way to meet up with tonight's Guest of Honour. Roger is holding book No 112 of the series.

Roger Climpson: Hello, Roger Climpson. Welcome to *This Is Your Life*. The car that I am travelling in is called the Grey Ghost and it is very much a part of our Guest of Honour because together in the 1950s they made national headlines. 'Give It a Go'—that's the only way to describe our Guest of Honour. He's been a cyclist and a footballer; he's been a champion boxer and a champion wrestler; he's been called the father of Australian waterskiing. He's been a rally driver, trial driver, speedway driver and stock car driver. He hunted crocodile and buffalo and he's a speedboat champion. He's quite a character and he's going to get quite a surprise when he sees me in this car.

The Grey Ghost enters The Garage at Curlewis St. It stops and Roger alights. Jack is seen in the foreground instructing a lady on how to use a new 'anti flat tyre' product called Tireseal. There is quite a crowd of onlookers. Jack has his back to the Grey Ghost and is totally unaware of the arrival of Roger Climpson. Jack was set up by telling him that a TV commercial for Tireseal was being made—hence the cameras, lights and crowd.

It was a genuine surprise for him.

Jack: Shut the valve, and then push the front down ...

Jack continues to give instructions to the lady until he is tapped on the shoulder, turns around and sees Roger Climpson:

Roger: Hello Jack. Isn't that the car you won the REDEX car trial with in 1954? That right?

Jack is stunned, confused and trying to make sense of it all. Such genuine surprise is TV gold.

Jack: This isn't *This Is Your Life*, is it?
Roger: Would you believe, Jack, we are on national television—you and the car and me. And this is indeed 'Gelignite' Jack Murray: *This Is Your Life*.

Laughter and applause from all those gathered. Roger shakes Jack's hand, with the book resting between them, while Jack looks around at the crowd in utter shock. The music swells and the final scene in The Garage shows Jack on one of those rare occasions he had nothing to say. As the scene fades he can be seen looking at Roger, saying simply 'Shit'. After an ad break, the show resumes with Jack and Roger walking into a studio full of rows of seats containing the night's audience.

Roger: Would you like to sit down, Jack? (*gesturing to the couch. What choice does he have? Jack sits*)
Roger: (*opening the book for the program*) Jack Murray, you are one of Australia's best known, most versatile and longest lasting sportsmen. You bring derring-do and pizzazz to the sports arena. Now, for example, during the first REDEX Round Australia Reliability Trial in 1953, you grabbed the headlines and the whole nation's attention.

Throughout the introduction, Jack looks very uncomfortable with this praise. But soon he relaxes and his demeanour changes. Video footage is shown of Jack's 1953 Plymouth rollover and his famous string of expletives when asked what he thought about the crash.

Roger: Well I guess, Jack, we can see how you earned your reputation for using colourful speech. As you yourself say, Jack, 'I speak two languages—English and—
Jack: Profane.
Roger: Profane. Exactly.
Roger: You enter the REDEX Trial two years running and in 1954 of course you win it.

CHAPTER FOURTEEN

Footage of Jack entering Sydney Showground in 1954. Enormous applause from the audience. The camera returns to a still-stunned Jack and he raises his eyebrows in acknowledgement of someone he recognises in the audience.

Mystery Voice 1: He blew up the roadside.
Roger: Your good friend and co-driver Bill Murray.

The doors open and Bill Murray appears, resplendent in a white suit.

Bill Murray: G'day Joey (*smiles and shakes hands heartily*). They got you this time, haven't they?
Roger: Bill, OK—now what did you mean when you said that 'he blew up the roadside'?
Bill: Well, that's how he got his name: 'Gelignite' Jack Murray.
Jack: 'Cause of you.
Bill: We used to carry the gelignite to clear a track for the car. But we found after going around a couple of times that we didn't need it. There were no obstacles, so Jack used to amuse himself by throwing sticks out the window and stirring up the cars behind. And you are still stirring, you ol' bastard. (*Bill slaps Jack on the shoulder before moving off set.*)
Jack: Ohhh—not me.

314

THIS IS YOUR LIFE

Jack's reaction to the use of the word 'bastard' on television, now so routine as to pass unnoticed, is rather quaint.

Roger: On that note, Bill Murray, thank you for being with us.
Roger: Sit down, Jack.
Jack: Fall down.
Roger: Jack, you are a devil on dry land and something of a demon on water. I'm sure that not many of our younger waterskiers know that you are hailed as the 'father of waterskiing' in Australia.
Jack: Grandfather.

Video footage of Jack skiing in front of the Houses of Parliament in London.

Mystery Voice 2, a woman's: They modelled the Australian (Water Ski) Championship trophy on Jack's beautiful body.
Roger: Your very good friends on water and land: Betty and Bruck Wheeler.

The doors open and Betty and Bruck appear. Jack embraces Betty warmly and shakes Bruck's hand.

CHAPTER FOURTEEN

Bruck: You look surprised.

Jack and Bruck (*in unison*): You rotten thing!

Roger: Now Betty, let's keep the party clean. Betty, you were the Australian Water Ski Champion. What can you tell us about Jack?

Betty: Oh …

Jack: Don't. Don't tell them nothing.

Betty: That he has done great things for waterskiing in Australia. And for me. And he's still teaching people to ski.

Roger: Thank you, Betty. Now Bruck, I know that you've had some pretty hair-raising experiences with Jack.

Jack: (*interjecting*) More lies.

Roger: Can you tell us about a few of them?

Bruck: Well actually, we taught each other to ski. In those good ol' days no one else was doing it. And each weekend we'd get up around the Hawkesbury and we'd ski up and down. Must have done thousands of miles actually—behind a boat. But one day a fellow came up in a float plane and Jack hooked up on to that. Well, I won't tell you that story but I'll tell ya we've had gutsers all over the Hawkesbury River: limbs in the willow trees, and barks everywhere, shins missing and all that. But I've also seen, been there at the time when three boats have blown up under Jack. And he's probably had every inch of his body burnt—

Jack: Singed … singed.

Bruck: To his millions of friends, old mate, Jack, you really are indestructible.

Bruck and Jack shake hands.

Roger: Thank you very much.

Betty and Bruck leave the set.

Roger: Now Jack, you have a secret that even our sleuths at *This Is Your Life* could not uncover—and that happens to be your age. So Jack, just for tonight: what age would you like to say?

Jack: Nineteen-o-seven. (*He meant he was born in 1907.*)

Roger: Ninety-o-seven? (*Jack looks at the audience wide-eyed.*)

Jack: Work that out.

Roger: Well, shall we say it this way? You say it and we'll believe it.

Jack: That's it—70.

Roger: 70?

Jack: Yeah.

THIS IS YOUR LIFE

Roger: Congratulations Jack.
Jack: OK pal—good.
Roger: He told us the truth.
Roger shakes Jack's hand.
Jack: So help me God (*throws his hands up in the air*).
Roger: Anyway Jack—Jack, you were born John Eric Murray in Melbourne. In your early teens you display your great talent for sports. You captain the Aussie Rules team at Albert Park School and you win the Victorian Junior 5 Mile Cycling Championship.

> *[Correction: On 8 November 1924, aged just seventeen, Jack won the Port Melbourne Junior Club Championship over a distance of five miles— not the Victorian State Championship. A newspaper report described Jack as having 'won easily' but his time of 17.45 (if correct) is slow. Port Melbourne was not one of the stronger clubs for juniors at the time. My source is Denis Setka, Cycling Australia 2015.]*

Mystery Voice 3: Jack was very particular about his looks.
Roger: Your brother Bert, better known as 'Narra' Murray.

The doors open and Narra enters, no doubt without socks, which he never wore—but like all the others in a suit. Jack shakes hands and promptly grabs Narra by the neck and shakes him about.

Roger: Narra ... now Narra, we know that Jack left home when he was only eleven *[sic: actually fourteen]*. He sold newspapers and he worked on a river dredge—just about turned his hand to everything. But look, Narra will you tell us about his—his little vanities.
Narra: When we were kids, our weekly pocket money was three cents ... threepence ...
Roger: Three pennies.
Jack: Six half-pennies.
Narra: You were always very particular about your appearance, lard head.
Jack: Yeah.
Narra: And he saved his threepenny pieces—until—no, he had a tooth that needed a bit of straightening. That's right, wasn't it?

CHAPTER FOURTEEN

Jack: Yeah, I straightened it myself with a pair of pliers (*audience laughs*).
Narra: Yeah, he saved his threepenny bits until he had enough money to have the tooth straightened.
Jack: Oh get out.
Narra: And at school you were a bloody villain.
Narra: He wasn't too bad a scholar if he concentrated, but he never concentrated. Ah ...
Jack: Did you come down with Bruck?
Narra: I did.
Jack: Well go back with him.

With that, Jack resumes the hand grip on Narra's neck and spins him about once more, sending him away in the direction of the other former guests.

Roger: Good luck, Narra. Goodbye Narra and thanks for being here (*laughter all round*).
Roger: (*amidst further laughter*) Anyway Jack, you leave school and join the Navy and for a number of years you hold the title of Royal Australian Navy Lightweight Boxing Champion.
Jack: Er (*shakes his head in a negative way and covers his mouth with his hand. The body language says it all: No!*)
Roger: ... but by 1928 you are a landlubber once again and take on various jobs around Melbourne. Then it's a move to Sydney, where you become involved in motor car racing, swimming and wrestling.

[A television show host is not an historian, and the researchers behind shows rely heavily on information from sources such as newspapers and magazines and the memories of friends and family. Inaccuracies are to be expected and omissions will occur. Myths, once created, tend to have a life of their own. I once read that Jack was a proof-reader for a French language newspaper! Perhaps said as a joke—some journalist took it all in. My investigations confirm that Jack was never in the Royal Australian Navy and consequently did not hold the title of Royal Australian Lightweight Boxing Champion. Ian Pfennigwerth, former Captain of HMAS Perth 2 and a naval historian, has been unable to find any record of John Eric

Murray in the 1920s in the Royal Australian Navy. Jack did not mention being in the Navy during his 1976 interview with Neil Bennetts. He was already in Sydney in 1930, aged just 23, winning state wrestling championships. Jack did, however, serve with the US Small Ships during the war.

But imagine Jack's predicament: still stunned at having been whisked away from The Garage and flung into a television studio, with Roger Climpson in full flight. He was the single focus of cameras, lights and audience. It is understandable how he would have let these two lines of Naval inaccuracy remain unchallenged, allowing them to 'go through to the keeper'.]

Mystery Voice 4: I had to beat him to go to the Berlin Olympics.
Roger: It's your good friend—wrestling friend—Jack 'Spud' O'Hara.

The doors open and Spud O'Hara enters with a heavy limp. The old friends shake hands and embrace. Jack applies a semi-wrestling hold to Spud's neck—no doubt a sign of affection!

Jack: You were in The Garage the other day.
Spud: No.
Jack: They said you was.
Spud: Yes, I was.
Jack: How I fell for this I don't know.
Roger: But we've got you now, Jack. Spud, by the time he gave up wrestling in 1946 Jack had won twelve amateur NSW titles *[sic: actually thirteen]*, but he lost two major bouts to you. Will you tell us about that?
Spud: Yeah. Remember, Jack it was 1934 for the trip to the Empire Games and there was

CHAPTER FOURTEEN

only you and I left. And I won that one.

Jack: That's right. We both stayed together at North Bondi where we went home for a sleep in the afternoon. Went down to the stadium and I think we wrestled under the floor most of the bout. And er—

Spud: You kept pushing me out under the ropes.

Jack: Yeah—and Potatoes left me for dead. He went to Germany.

Spud: And in 1936, remember going to Brisbane?

Jack: That's right.

Spud: And that was for the trip to Germany. The first one was to England.

Jack: That's right.

Spud: Jack, it was a real tough bout but it's good to be with you. But you got even when you kept tossing me for the rent each week when we lived together.

Much laughter, hand shaking and shoulder slapping. Spud leaves the set.

Roger: Jack, in our audience tonight is one of your very good friends—in fact a friend for the past 48 years: Viv Hamilton.

Jack: There he is.

After pointing into the audience, Jack goes over and shakes hands with a very old man in a wheelchair; he kisses Viv's wife.

Roger: Viv, give us a wave.

[After the filming I went across to introduce myself to Jack's close mate, whom I had never met. As I extended my arm to shake hands with the old man he extended what seemed like a paw from a grizzly bear. 'Viv' had been a shearer in the days when hand clippers were used. I have never seen a man with a larger hand. Viv's fingers were like sausages. As I shook hands with him his fingers enveloped most of my forearm—something I have never forgotten.]

Roger: I believe you've known Viv since you first established The Garage workshop in Bondi in partnership with your late brother Ray. Now Viv tells us you are only afraid of one thing, Jack—Ssss—

Jack and Roger (*in unison*): Ssssnakes!

Roger: But we've also heard you're too fast for them. Anyway Jack, you've been

Above: Jack and close friend, Viv Hamilton.

Above: Jack croc hunting in the Northern Territory.

Above: Ray is second from left and Jack on the far right, at The Garage, circa mid 1930s.

a champion all your life, a man who cannot resist challenges. And we'll learn more of the challenges of Jack Murray in just a moment.

As the camera fades to the ad break, Jack can be seen saying something to Roger Climpson. While it's not audible, I'm guessing the comment 'more bullshit' or something very similar was uttered under his breath.

CHAPTER FOURTEEN

Roger: Jack, speed is the challenge—on land and water. First, cars. From 1931 till 1948 you accumulate trophies and stock car speed records. You marry and you have two sons, and as they grow up you cannot help throwing challenges to them.
Mystery Voice 5: Dad, do you remember how I got that boat?
Roger: Your sons, John and Philip.

[The doors open and John and I enter the set. Just moments before I remember turning to him and asking, 'Are you nervous?' 'A little,' he replied. I said, 'Don't be—there's only a few million people watching.' And with that the doors parted. As we shook hands and were greeted, Jack, off camera, looked at me and mouthed, 'You bastard' I smiled—the normal Murray response to such a greeting.]

Roger: Now John, what was the challenge that he threw out to you?
John: Well Roger, I was a very keen sailor and wanted a boat. Jack had it in mind that I should play the piano, so he said to me one day, 'If you want that boat, you play the piano for half an hour a day for the next twelve

months and I'll buy you a boat.' So I played it for eleven months and he said—er, I came home very late one night and he said, 'Listen, about that boat: forget it.' I said, 'What have I got to do?' He said, 'Well, play it, play the piano for another half hour for another seven months—and you might get it.' Eventually I got it, didn't I?

Jack: You did.

Jack: (*to me and as an aside*): You were at The Garage today and you never said a word. (*'Not a word', I replied.*)

Roger: Now there are thousands of stories about your father, Philip. Do you have a favourite one as well?

Philip: Yes, Roger. My favourite story, or escapade if you want to call it that, is the time you set the speed record for Curlewis St, Bondi in the Cadillac-Allard. You were preparing it for a forthcoming race and apparently you did over 100 mph up Curlewis St and then put the car back in The Garage and covered it with a dust cover. Well, all would have gone well when the police finally arrived except one of them happened to lean against the car and almost burnt his hand off. (*Jack mouths 'Oh shit', amidst much laughter.*)

By the way Roger, we bring a message from mum, who as dad knows is away on holidays at the moment up at Surfers Paradise, and she wishes you all the best for tonight.

Jack: Good.

> *We all shake hands and move off set.*
>
> *[This was one of the most difficult and sensitive issues of the process: how to explain to the public my mother's absence from the evening. Although I was not involved, this question was extensively discussed during preparation of the show. The director agreed that 'it was not necessary nor desirable to have the wife on the program, since they have lived their own lives for many years.' This is essentially true. As I have written this book the reality has become even clearer to me. But Jack still lived at the family home in Vaucluse.*
>
> *My mother, like Jack, was totally unaware that the program was being planned. My comment before John and I left the set was designed to avert any embarrassment due to mum's absence. She was on the Gold Coast— but obviously could have returned for such an important event in Jack's life. In later years, she shared her disappointment with me in not being*

CHAPTER FOURTEEN

included that night. Reflecting back nearly 40 years, while acknowledging my mother's disappointment, I think what I said was as empathetic a solution as possible on the night.]

Roger: Jack, in Adelaide you discover a new love. Now will you listen to this: (*music plays*). A friend from the Adelaide speedway days introduces you to music and *Ruby* becomes your favourite tune of course—and still is. And here is the man responsible, former *This Is Your Life* Guest of Honour, Kym Bonython.

The doors open and Bonython appears.

Roger: Kym, I know that you and Jack became very good mates when you ran the Adelaide speedway. So will you tell us about Jack?

Kym Bonython: Well, after Jack made his sensational appearance at Rowley Park, he tried to teach me rather unsuccessfully to waterski up on the Hawkesbury. After a while I felt the call of nature and disappeared into the bushes, followed about 30 seconds later by a stick of gelignite. It upset my … er … my life cycle for about a year thereafter.

Roger: Kym Bonython, thank you for coming from Adelaide to tell us (*much laughter as Kym leaves the set*).

Roger: All right Jack: cars, waterskiing and then speedboats. In 1964 you tackle ocean racing.

Mystery Voice 6: Hey Jack, will you ever forget the first Sydney to Newcastle and return speedboat race?

Roger: Your co-driver and good friend to tell us about that event, Olympic water polo player Keith Whitehead.

Keith Whitehead appears.

Roger: Keith, will you tell us about Jack and about that race?

Keith Whitehead: Yeah, he'll deny this, but on the return leg from Newcastle to Sydney we were neck and neck with Bob Dyer. We were in a small boat and I was driving at the time and Jack said, 'If I sit down the back, do you think this thing will go any faster?' And I said 'It may do'. Jack said, 'I'll get down the back. But it's pretty rough.' So he climbed down the back and had his head resting on a battery and the boat definitely went up 2 mph in speed. I looked back as we headed off in front of Bob Dyer at that stage and I looked back and he's grimacing, the pain, and the actions. I thought, 'He can't stand this for too much longer.' I kept looking back. 'Are you all right?' 'Yeah arrghh, I can stand it.' So this went on for about ten minutes and we hit the front and then Bob had a mechanical breakdown. So then Jack climbed back into the front and in due course we did win the race. And I said to him when we got back to Rose Bay and the celebrations were on, I said, 'How do you feel?' He said, 'Good as gold.' 'But you were in agony and pain back there!' He said, 'If you'd known how good it was back there—I nearly drifted off to sleep. You would have made me bloody well drive and you would have gotten back there.'

Laughter and handshakes as Keith Whitehead leaves the set.

Roger: Thank you Keith Whitehead. Well, after that, Jack, we have a new challenge. A 13,000-mile figure eight circuit through the heart of Australia. Castrol Oil devises this tough test for a new oil product.
Video is shown.
Mystery Voice 7: Jack, where did you leave the leopard spotted underpants?
Roger: Your partner on the gruelling test, *Sun Herald* editor—yes, Evan Green.

The doors open and Evan, wearing a red-haired witch mask, enters.

Evan: (*referring to the mask*) I'm sorry, Roger, but we used to make Jack wear this mask so that he wouldn't frighten the children.
Roger: Evan, tell us about the test—and more particularly about that pair of underpants.
Evan: Well, Jack and I have been involved in nine trips around Australia and we have driven from London to Sydney and from London to Mexico, but I think the journey that remains in my mind was the one in which the underpants were involved. That was the first—he always wore underpants, but not this way—that was the first ever crossing of Australia through the middle, from east to west.
And we were in the northern region of the Simpson Desert. There was Scott Polkinghorne, Alan Kemp, Jack and myself and the track disappeared beneath

CHAPTER FOURTEEN

drift sand. And we couldn't find the way, so Jack and Scotty and myself, leaving Alan in charge of the cars, went walking through the sand dunes trying to find a firm path back to the track. And the only way to mark it, 'cause Jack was driving, was with articles of clothing. Well Scott sacrificed all he was prepared. He took off his hat, his shirt, and a handkerchief. All Jack had to offer were his leopard skin underpants. He was trying to set the record for being the first person to cross Australia wearing only underpants, you see.

So by the last marker, Jack had left his underpants and walked back in naked embarrassment to the car. We push-started him so he wouldn't cut through the sand. And once he got going, in a blinding fit of enthusiasm, Jack forgot the hat, the handkerchief, the shirt and his own underpants, took a different track and disappeared. And for two hours we walked through the desert trying to find him till finally in the dark we found the car over an embankment, nose first on the ground, tail up, and a naked Jack saying, 'I found the track.' (*much laughter*) But he didn't find his underpants.

Roger: Well, I believe there is bit of a postscript to that story, isn't there, Evan?

Evan: Four years later, a drover was going through the bush chasing some wild cattle and he came upon the underpants and I believe they are about to be made a national monument in the Northern Territory.

Roger: What a lovely story. Anyway, you two of course join forces again in 1968 for a stunt race around Australia between a car and a plane. And later on you

Above and Left: Jack in Afghanistan and getting a haircut from local barbers in Kabul: London to Sydney Marathon.

even race a train, I believe. But in fact every year brings fresh challenges to Jack Murray as we will find out in just a moment.

Ad break.

Roger: Jack, you love testing yourself against anything that moves.
Mystery Voice 8: He always travelled deluxe.
Roger: 2GB radio personality, John Pearce.
Jack: Ohhhh ...

The door reveals a white-suit-clad John Pearce, hand outstretched in friendship. Jack and John shake and embrace and exchange a few words.

Roger: John, what is the most interesting part about driving with Jack?
John: Roger, halfway across Australia he providored a car like you have never seen. We stopped and he produced turkey, two lots of chicken, bread from Bondi ...
Jack: Leg ham.
John: Leg ham. I haven't forgotten the leg ham. Then we had four savouries, strawberries in cointreau. It was a quiet afternoon. The ... the ... the kangaroos hated it *(hands upturned to signal 'that's it'.)*

CHAPTER FOURTEEN

Roger: Well, thank you John very much for telling us about the situation.
John: Yes, I'm totally confused ... I'm glad he is.

And with that John Pearce slaps Jack's shoulder and walks off to join other guests.
   [This segment went totally off the tracks. Before the show each of the guests was given the opportunity to practise. Each had a run-through of the story they were going to deliver. I believe that John Pearce, as a radio professional, saw himself above this; there was no need for him to do it. As a result, he was unprepared and lost his way during the segment. As he himself summed it up, 'I'm totally confused.']

Roger: Now Jack, we know that you are quite prepared to take a risk of any kind—and very often your friends are involved as well.
Mystery Voice 9: Jack, remember the rocks at Forster?
Roger: Former world kite flying champion, Bill Moyes.

Bill Moyes enters in a green Australia blazer.

Roger: Bill, I know that you and Jack were involved in a kite flying endurance record. Would you tell us about it?
Bill: Well, that was a funny one. Jack towed me out of Sydney Harbour in '69

328

bound for Brisbane. And we were to attempt a dual world record attempt. He was tackling the Sydney to Brisbane speed run and me the kite endurance record. It was a pretty tough and gruelling run and up off Taree, Jack hit a log and he split the hull of the boat and she began to flounder and sink. So I had to glide down and land in the water, where we got the boat dragged up on the rocks and we started to wander through the countryside to find some form of habitation. We found a kid ploughing a field on a tractor. And the kid took us on the tractor to his father's farm and at first the father thought we were Russian.

Jack: Communists!
Bill: Ah, but when he realised that Jack Murray had been shipwrecked on his property he grabbed hold of Jack's hand (*which he does*) and he said, 'Jack, you have made my place famous.'
Roger: I guess he did, too. Thank you. Thank you very much for taking time off from the kite flying championships in Melbourne to be here especially with us tonight. Thank you very much, Bill.

[I recall Jack telling me that as they approached the young boy in the field, both wet and bedraggled, Jack's first words to the young fellow were, 'What country is this, son?' Apparently the boy's eyes became as big as saucers.]

Roger: Now Jack, I want you to listen to this voice.
Mystery Voice 10: It's a damn nuisance—but I'll do it for Jack.
Roger: He's interrupted his holiday to be with you tonight, Jack. The Managing Director of Castrol Oil. From London, your very good friend, Max Roberts.

The doors open to reveal the final guest dressed in a smart, dark tailored suit. This is Max Roberts.

Jack: God!
Roger: Max, I think that of all the people here tonight, you are probably the only person who can really tell us about Jack Murray.
Max: Roger, I've known him for too long. It wasn't a damn nuisance; I owe him one or two.
Jack: You coot.
Max: He ought to be roasted.

CHAPTER FOURTEEN

Jack: Coot.

Max: He's too old to boil in oil.

Jack: In oil? Oh Gee!

Max: But Jack, we've enjoyed one another's company for a long, long time—

Jack: We've had many laughs, haven't we?

Max: Yes.

Jack: London. You've just come from London.

Max: The Brylcreem specialist. (*Jack laughs*) You've been a great character, but Jack—you have made a lot of friends (*Jack tries to interrupt for once unsuccessfully*) and I'll say this for you: you must be able to cash a lot of cheques round this place.

Jack: He said to me once, he said, 'When Castrol or when I finish with you, your name will be on jam tins.' (*laughter*). Nearly right too.

Jack: When do you go back?

Roger: Thanks, Max. Can I just say, Jack, in an age when so many of our people have lost the will to 'give it a go', you are a unique example of the special qualities that make up the Australian spirit (*Jack sneaks a look, a wink and a smile at Max during Roger's summation. This is a wonderful moment and one of the most endearing in the show: so typically Jack.*) and may your remarkable story go on and on because 'Gelignite' Jack Murray: *This Is Your Life*. (*Roger hands the book of the show to Jack.*)

Jack: Thank you.

THIS IS YOUR LIFE

Roger and Max both shake hands with Jack as the other guests stand and begin to gather around Jack, talking, catching up and shaking hands. I manage to position myself right next to the man of the hour and accordingly get a lot of airtime as the credits roll. As the camera pans the audience, in the front row our girlfriends including Wendy, who would become John's wife, and Tamara Navin clap enthusiastically.

Above: The Murray men: John, Jack and me.

Above: From left to right: Roger Climpson, Viv Hamilton (in the wheelchair), Viv's wife, Kym Bonython, John Murray, Evan Green, Phil Murray, Jack and Max Roberts (seated), Betty and Bruck Wheeler, Keith Whitehead, Bill Moyes, Hubert 'Narra' Murray, Bill Murray, John Pearce and Jack 'Spud' O'Hara.

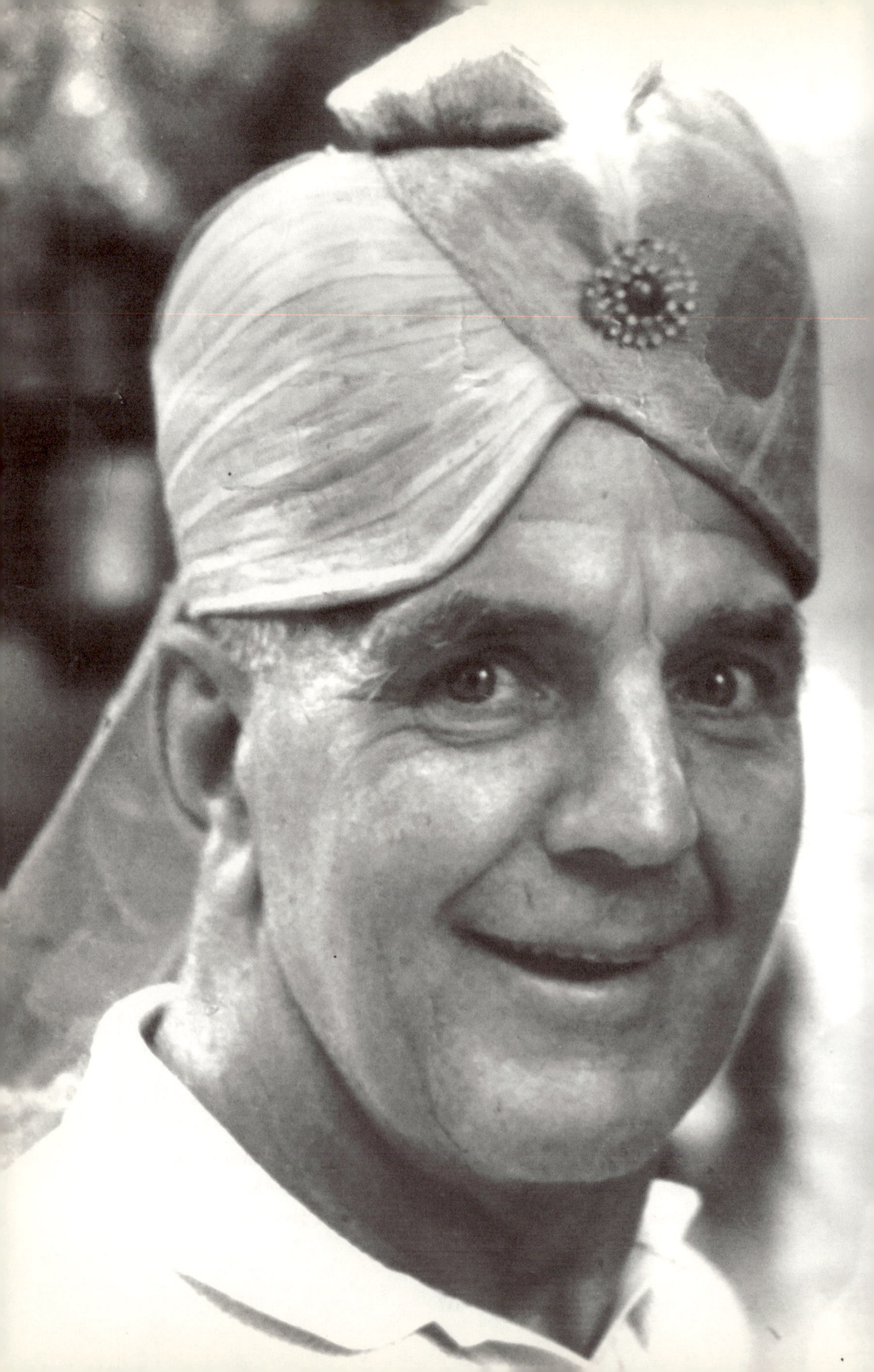

EPILOGUE

Writing my father's biography has proven to be an unexpectedly personal journey.

As I travelled through Jack's life, a new perception of my relationship with my father has developed. I have come to realise how that relationship changed over the years, from a young man butting heads about hair length to a son carrying a proud man who had lost a leg up a flight of stairs and today, the retrospective view of a middle-aged son. The biographical task that I naïvely thought was simply to research, verify and document became so much more—a journey of understanding and discovery.

The adventures, stories and exploits in Jack's life are legendary. I was unaware of the sheer number and variety of motor racing and sporting events in which he had participated. Little wonder that many of his friends and even members of the public who had never met him, but read about his achievements, viewed Jack with an almost cultlike adulation. His good friend Brian McEwen told me of those early days of waterskiing, rallying and working as an apprentice mechanic for Bill McLachlan. Since Brian was born in 1937, Jack and Bill were father figures to the much younger Ginger:

> Your father—I idolised the bloke. As a poor kid growing up in Campsie, I wanted to live my life the way Jack and Bill did: cars and boats. Bill was a fantastic bloke too. They took me up the river and there was Betty Wheeler in a bikini, on one ski cutting back and forth across the wake. Gee, as a young bloke, I'd never seen a girl in

EPILOGUE

a bikini before. They taught me to waterski. For five or six years we skied on the Harbour and did exhibition skiing on different dams to make the sport more popular. Your dad loved his milkshakes. Ski all day and then back to the Wilberforce Milk Bar for a chat and a milkshake. Jack and I must have skied a half-dozen Bridge to Bridge races together, but we never won it, though.

Once, Jack took me rallying in Canberra and gave me a drive, a six-cylinder car Jack had wrangled out of Nissan. The car went into a slide at a T-intersection and I almost lost it. *Whack.* Jack hit me across the back of the head and said, 'You bastard, don't do that again.' It hurt, so I made sure I didn't. Another time, Jack was driving. We came over the crest of the hill and there was this tubular gate right in front of us. I'll never forget this. No brake. Jack ploughed into it, straight on. The gate flew back and hit the backstop, then bounced back and re-shut itself. Jack didn't even slow down, just kept on going.

As a young bloke, I used to love just going to The Garage in Bondi and hearing all the stories.

The stories are literally endless. Everyone who knew Jack has a story or two or more to tell. The memories, the practical jokes and good times recounted by old friends are warming to hear. Among the memorabilia on display at the Shoal Bay Resort, there is a sentence that struck a chord with me when I first read it:

> You quickly realise that even though his life was full of some of sports' greatest achievements, it isn't that which made Jack great, but the way he lived his life.

How true. In describing the various competitors and characters that competed in the REDEX trials 60 years ago, Evan Green once commented, 'There were the amateurs, the eccentrics, the professionals ... and then there was the professional eccentric—'Gelignite' Jack Murray.'

'Professional eccentric' still seems to be the most apt description of Jack.

We will not see the likes of 'Gelignite' Jack Murray again. Australia will undoubtedly continue to produce outstanding athletes and sportsman who

EPILOGUE

set new records and achieve great deeds. But the world of the 1950s and 60s that allowed, even encouraged, the professional eccentric, the amateur who participated purely for the joy of it, is now gone.

Picture Jack in his prime in contemporary Australia. Can you imagine, for instance, a Mark Winterbottom winning at Bathurst and then the following week competing and winning a Sydney-Newcastle-Sydney speedboat race? Would a Cameron McEvoy hop out of the pool, dry himself off, then charge off to the Sydney Stadium and win thirteen NSW wrestling titles? Would a Steve Smith walk off the SCG, lay down his bat for a couple of weeks and compete in and win a round Australia car trial? I wonder if Cadel Evans can barefoot waterski, ski behind a float plane or ski 'on one' on the Thames in front of the British Houses of Parliament? Of course Jack was also a fellow cyclist and won a Port Melbourne Junior Club Championship.

While displaying these multiple talents, picture our modern day Mark, Cameron, Steve or Cadel all wearing rubber gorilla masks and occasionally letting off sticks of gelignite in various public places to amuse the locals.

The other major distinction between Jack and most contemporary sportsmen is that he never set out to make money from any of his sporting endeavours or achievements. While professional in approach and application, Jack participated in all these sports, trips and adventures just for pure fun. As Roger Climpson so succinctly put it, 'He just wanted to give it a go'.

In the years since his passing, the legend that is 'Gelignite' Jack Murray has been immortalised in many ways. He has been remembered on radio, in eulogies and quotes appearing in the press and by inductions into Halls of Fame—as recently as March 2016. Poems have even been written about my father.

'What a load of bullshit,' I can hear Jack saying, with a laugh and a dismissive wave of the hand. I smile just picturing it.

Australia All Over

One of the most popular programs on Australian radio, *Australia All Over* hosted by Ian McNamara (Macca), devoted considerable time to Jack on 18 December 1983. A week after his passing, the show re-broadcast a 1979 interview with Jack by Mike Jeffries. Below are just a few extracts:

EPILOGUE

MCNAMARA: Give me a good car and point me in the direction of the Australian outback and I'm happy. That was the philosophy of rally driver and all round sportsman 'Gelignite' Jack Murray who died last week in Sydney. Murray as a young man was a champion cyclist, boxer and wrestler but he achieved fame for his daredevil exploits tearing round Australia in the REDEX Reliability Trials of the 1950s. His nickname 'Gelignite' came from his habit of taking a case of gelignite on the trials to clear the road of obstacles. In 1979 Jack Murray made a comeback in a Repco Trial.

In this interview from our ABC archives, Mike Jeffries talks to 'Gelignite' about his explosive exploits:

JEFFRIES: Some of those trials are pretty rugged. What kept you at it? Why do you keep doing it?

MURRAY: Why do I keep doing it? Well, you might say why does a guy play tennis—he tries to better his score or as a golfer he tries to get better at it. In rallies, well, you go in a few and you don't get anywhere then all of a sudden you'll start to learn to drive. You get wrapped up in it—and I used to like the outback. The people you meet, say, out Birdsville and around those places—they're fantastic people. They live out there. There was nothing in the old days. You got TV nowadays and all this sort of stuff. In the old days they were real—oh—real people. They'd do anything for you.

MCNAMARA: Real people out at Birdsville. 'Gelignite' Jack used to spend a lot of time out there, blowing things up around Birdsville. He was talking there back then in 1979 to Mike Jeffries. And we've got someone who has rung us who knows, or knew, 'Gelignite' Jack—Russ Hammond from Coffs Harbour. Good morning Russ.

HAMMOND: Good morning to you, Ian, I enjoy your program very much—it's great.

MCNAMARA: Thanks very much. Where did you meet 'Gelignite' Jack?

EPILOGUE

HAMMOND: I was in the '64 Ampol Trial driving a Valiant station wagon and Jack helped me prepare it out at his Garage and he was about the only fella I ever met in me life that was larger than life. You know, you see publicity about people and so on but Jack was really a bigger guy than what he appeared to be in any publicity or anything.

MCNAMARA: What sort of car was he driving in the '64 trial?

HAMMOND: He was driving a Peugeot.

HAMMOND: Yeah, he was quite a character. We were leaving Bourke at two minutes to three in the middle of winter in '64 and I'd only had about a total of about—I'd say—eight hours sleep in the last four or five days. I did all the driving in that trial—something I set out to do and I'd never attempt it again. It was the hardest work I ever tried. But I got home, and I'm really dog tired you know. Jack just drove away and the cars are going away every two minutes and then next thing—*whoompa*—the old dunny went up down alongside the river. He set a charge. Well look, I was awake from there to South Australia (laughs). No worry at all.

MCNAMARA: Thanks Russ for telling us about 'Gelignite' Jack.

HAMMOND: Yeah, well he was a terrific bloke. I'd say that anyone who ever knew him would agree with me. He really was larger than life.

[In the 1964 Ampol trial Russ Hammond driving a Valiant station wagon finished thirty-eighth. Jack, driving a Peugeot 404, finished fortieth and Jack 'Crackerjack' Murray, driving a lime green 'Milo' Valiant sedan finished thirty-third]

Remembered in Verse

Jack was not averse to a bit of poetry. His favourite work was the 1934 *The Man in the Glass*, by Peter Dale Wimbrow Snr. It no doubt would have both amused and surprised Jack, to learn that he was the inspiration for the following:

EPILOGUE

That Cunning Old Bastard
© Gregory North, April 2009

A cyclist, wrestler, waterskier and gliding pioneer,
an all-round sportsman, garage-owning motor engineer,
Police Boys Club instructor, speedboat racing larrikin
who didn't drink or smoke, but wore a cheeky grin;
Quite fluent in two languages, both English and profane,
he always drew an audience that he would entertain.
But driving brought him household fame that few had known before
when he won the REDEX Trial, back in 1954.

He was always in a hurry
He was 'Gelignite' Jack Murray.
How he did it had them tossed
Jack checked in with no points lost.

Cloncurry through to Mt Isa was a tree-choked, narrow track
when Jack surveyed the route before his '53 attack.
A breakdown here could block the road and trap your car in tight,
unless you made escape routes ... blasting through with gelignite!
This problem never did arise when on the REDEX run,
so Jack then used his gelignite to have a little fun.
A long fuse to a dunny put an old bloke on the hop
in Townsville, while Jack was chatting calmly to a cop.

He didn't have a worry.
He was 'Gelignite' Jack Murray.
Over problems, he had glossed.
Jack checked in with no points lost.

'You got a spanner?' Jack would ask of passing REDEX teams,
while perched atop his upturned wreck, the killer of his dreams.
They reckoned it a symptom of when madness overtakes.
Said Jack, 'I thought while upside down, I'd just adjust her brakes!'
But that was back in '53 and with the lessons learnt,
the next year, in a V8 Ford, the record books were burnt.

EPILOGUE

He dominated start to finish, outback to the coast,
and finished in an ape mask in that trusty old Grey Ghost.

He would finish in a flurry
He was 'Gelignite' Jack Murray.
With his fingers firmly crossed,
Jack checked in with no points lost.

The REDEX route was gruelling—more than 15,000 Ks
of shocking roads, no time for sleep, and all in eighteen days.
Competitors were heroes cause the public never knew
you could drive around our continent—and do it quickly too!
They were reeling from Depression and those awful years of war
and Jack reminded ev'ryone that fun is what life's for.
A master when it came to pranks and talking his way clear
from water pistols, gelignite or bending someone's ear.

He always gave them curry.
He was 'Gelignite' Jack Murray,
And without a thought of cost,
Jack checked in with no points lost.

Pulled over by police while on a speedy jaunt through town,
'So who do you think you are?' asked the copper with a frown.
'Jack Murray, Eastern Sydney Branch Police Boys Club,' Jack said.
'Ah, well, you follow me, old mate! I'll get you well ahead.'
But most cops were suspicious of this geli-tossing lout
At the South Australian border they were set to sort him out
Inspectors were kept busy as police stood resolute,
while Jack unpacked the car he'd filled with vegetables and fruit!

Through the pack he'd always scurry.
He was 'Gelignite' Jack Murray.
Cause he never would be bossed,
Jack checked in with no points lost.

While on a rest stop out in Broome Jack used his gelignite
to break the boredom through the streets and liven up the night.
When rival teams awoke in fright, Jack's witticisms flew,
'Hey, you blokes here got any flies? My flywheel needs a few.'
When dashing through the Snowy Mountains, Murray took a spell
to stop and make a snowman, and to throw some snow as well!
The passing targets shook their heads and quipped about his age,
but Jack still averaged 80 miles an hour through that stage.

He would hammer through the slurry.
He was 'Gelignite' Jack Murray.
Whether rain or hail or frost,
Jack checked in with no points lost.

A winner in the REDEX Trial, hero to the crowd,
who never lost a single point and made a country proud
that someone saw a lighter side. A charismatic bloke,
dependable and lovable, who revelled in a joke.
In later life he lost a leg, but still was full of glee,
until finally he parked for good in 1983.
An even if St Peter locked those Pearly Gates up tight,
I reckon Jack just talked him 'round—or used his gelignite!

He was always in a hurry.
He was Gelignite Jack Murray.
And his score card was embossed:
'Jack checked in with no points lost.'

Remembered in Prose

Evan Green wrote an article in December 1980, shortly after Jack had his right leg amputated:

'Gelignite' Jack Murray, one of Australia's most outstanding all-round sportsmen, is thinking of driving in a car rally from Peking to Paris in 1982. This wouldn't be remarkable, except for two facts. One:

EPILOGUE

Jack was alive and well when the first Peking to Paris rally was held 73 years ago, and two: two weeks ago, he lost a leg.

Doctors at St Vincent's hospital amputated his right leg above the knee after blood circulation problems in the limb threatened his life. He is now in the rehabilitation unit at Royal South Sydney Hospital, working out in the gymnasium and making such remarkable progress that doctors believe he will start walking again in two weeks.

'The man's a miracle,' a nurse told me. But then, 'Gelignite' Jack always was.

I saw him during the week, on the day he moved to the rehabilitation centre. I thought he might be feeling low, and would want us to talk about the past, the old adventures we had shared—six trips around Australia, the 1968 London to Sydney Marathon (which we might have won) and the 1970 World Cup Rally from London to Mexico.

Not a bit of it. He was talking about future adventures. To start with there was the challenge of learning to walk on a new leg.

'This place has got a fantastic gym,' he said, eyes shining like a small boy who has glimpsed a toy store. 'I start tomorrow. The doctor says it's dead easy walking these days. Then when I've got the leg I think I might go to Botswanaland,' he said. 'Harry Turner [an American friend] came back from there raving about the animals. I think I might have a look. Harry reckons he can get me an American leg if I want one. He says they're the best in the world.' He paused for a moment. 'No, maybe not. That'd be left hand drive and the bloody thing would want to walk on the wrong side of the road.'

An old mate, Ron d'Albora, came to see him.

'You cunning old bastard,' Ron said. 'Now I can't call you bandy legs anymore.' They exchanged insults for a few minutes. Jack's friends are like that. No roses or chocolates from his mates. Instead, he's had low-priced offers for his right shoes and accusations that losing the leg was just a plot to give new meaning to the phrase 'skiing on one'.

He's serious about driving in the Peking to Paris run—and why not. He proved his amazing resilience last year when he and his son John drove a Commodore in the Repco trial and finished in the top third of the field. 'I might choose an automatic, though,' he said, in the only concession I heard him make to his disability.

'Gelignite' Jack Murray, one leg or two, is still a step ahead of most of us.

Following the amputation in 1980 and his passing three years later, several notable eulogies were published. After the operation, Jack had his own contribution:

> I am in good spirits. 1981 is the Year of the Disabled. I am not disabled; I still have my left foot. Just as well I can ski on one foot.

Following the amputation, Prime Minister Malcolm Fraser wrote to my father:

> I greatly admire your spirit in tackling the latest challenge life has presented you, and Tamie joins me in wishing you a speedy return to everyday life.

The eulogies from those that knew him were both heartfelt and poignant. In the *Daily Mirror*, Wayne Greer wrote:

> Although it was his heart that failed him in late September, those who knew him still say his heart was his greatest asset.

Journalist Ken Anderson commented in the *Daily Telegraph*:

> He blasted his epitaph into history. It was the ability to smile at adversity that will be regarded as the most endearing trait of the veteran motor rally and racing champion.

Phillip Christensen in *Chequered Flag Magazine: The Last Hero*, January 1984, said:

> The death of Jack Murray on December 11 sealed the life of one who could well have been our last true hero. Jack Murray passed

through a lifespan when our country needed to react to the deeds of the common man—and for most of his life there was no such thing as television to make easy the glorification. 'Gelignite' Jack Murray was a man of the 1950s, of the Menzies era. He was probably as well known throughout Australia as Sir Don Bradman had become in the 1930s and 40s.

John Pearce, radio broadcaster said simply:

Jack Murray—they came no greater.

Max Stahl, journalist and editor wrote in *Racing Car News*, February 1984:

That one man could pack so much into one life, make so many friends, entertain such a vast public and achieve notoriety on a grand scale is hard to comprehend—unless you met the man. Jack Murray did it, and we'll never forget it.

'Gelignite' Jack Murray, one of Australia's most colourful, outspoken, witty, mysterious and outrageous heroes. But on December 11, 'Gelignite' Jack Murray finally found the obstacle he would not blast through.

Post magazine perhaps summed it up best of all:

Jack Murray, to give him his correct name, was one of the more memorable Australian characters, a laconic larrikin who managed to turn his entire life into one great adventure.

Hall of Fame

Over 30 years since he passed away, Jack's life was celebrated once more.

On 18 March 2016, the Confederation of Australian Motor Sport held a Hall of Fame Gala Dinner. This inaugural induction was held at the Melbourne Convention Centre, the night before the Australian Grand Prix and in front of a capacity audience of approximately 500 guests. Jack was one of 30 inaugural inductees.

EPILOGUE

Above: From left to right: The family and Dorothy gathered for the special occasion. Phil Murray, Rhonda Murray, John V. Murray, Dorothy Rosewell and Jonny Murray. Photo by George Hitchens.

Above: Jonny Murray and Phil Murray accepting the award on behalf of grandfather and father 'Gelignite' Jack Murray. Photo by George Hitchens.

EPILOGUE

Above: Jack in a collage of the video presentation which preceded the award.

Inductees or their representatives were allowed 45 seconds to respond. Below is my acceptance speech on behalf of my father:

> If Jack could be with us tonight, this would be a very different induction.
>
> There would be firecrackers off stage, no doubt a smoke bomb would be rolling about somewhere on the floor and Jack's idea of black tie always seemed to involve a gorilla mask.
>
> But behind the fun and games there was always a very serious and a very successful competitor.
>
> Jack would have been truly honoured tonight, for there is no greater recognition than that of your peers, the men and women of Australian motorsport.
>
> So, on behalf of my father, my mother Ena who has passed, my brother John who had a successful rally career, Jack's grandson Jonny, who rallied with Subaru, myself, our wives and last, but certainly not least—Jack's partner for 25 years, Dorothy Rosewell, who is with us

this evening—on behalf of all of us who loved him, thank you for this great honour.

The Last Word

Jack passed away on 11 December 1983 in St Vincent's Hospital, Darlinghurst. A combination of factors was listed as the cause of death:

> I (a) Cerebral infarction 2 minutes (b) Cerebrovascular disease 10 years, II Septic arthritis left shoulder 2 months, Congestive cardiac failure 10 years and peripheral vascular disease 15 years.

In layman's terms, Jack died from blood circulation problems—blockages and/or restricted blood vessels. These were the same issues that had led to his right leg being amputated above the knee three years earlier. As a non-drinker and non-smoker, neither diabetic nor obese and a regular exerciser, Jack was an unlikely candidate for such health issues. But Jack's father had died at a very early age due to heart problems, so perhaps genetics played a role. And my father enjoyed dairy products, his favourite being milkshakes, all his life. I never heard him use the word 'cholesterol'. It is only speculation, but perhaps diet was a contributing factor. Jack always reckoned, 'If milk is good enough for babies, it can't hurt you.'

Jack finished his 1976 interview with Neil Bennetts by sharing with us his philosophical view on the weighty subjects of life and death. It's only fitting that the last words in this biography should belong to the man himself. This is what 'Gelignite' Jack Murray had to say:

> I'll go off in a flash one day.
> But I think if you can get a laugh out of life, you're not here that long, and you've got to go sometime, don't you? There's nobody dodged it yet. I say it's something that you're used to because you die every 24 hours. You'll go to bed tonight and you'll fall asleep. You only go to sleep because you think you're going to wake up—so you die every 24 hours. Everybody does.
> Half your life is spent sleeping, and when you get up to 70, you've done 30 year's sleep, so dying doesn't worry me much. You do it every

EPILOGUE

night. I'm going to do it tonight, I'll be asleep at nine o'clock, out like a light till six o'clock tomorrow morning.

So what? That's it, that's life. Live every day, that's my motto. I think I'll go for a ride on my bike. Where is it?

'Live every day, that's my motto'—and 'Gelignite' Jack Murray—my dad—certainly did.

"UH-HUH! THERE GOES THE PEARLY GATES... 'GELIGNITE' JACK MURRAY HAS ARRIVED..!"

Above: *The Herald,* Melbourne, 17 December 1983.

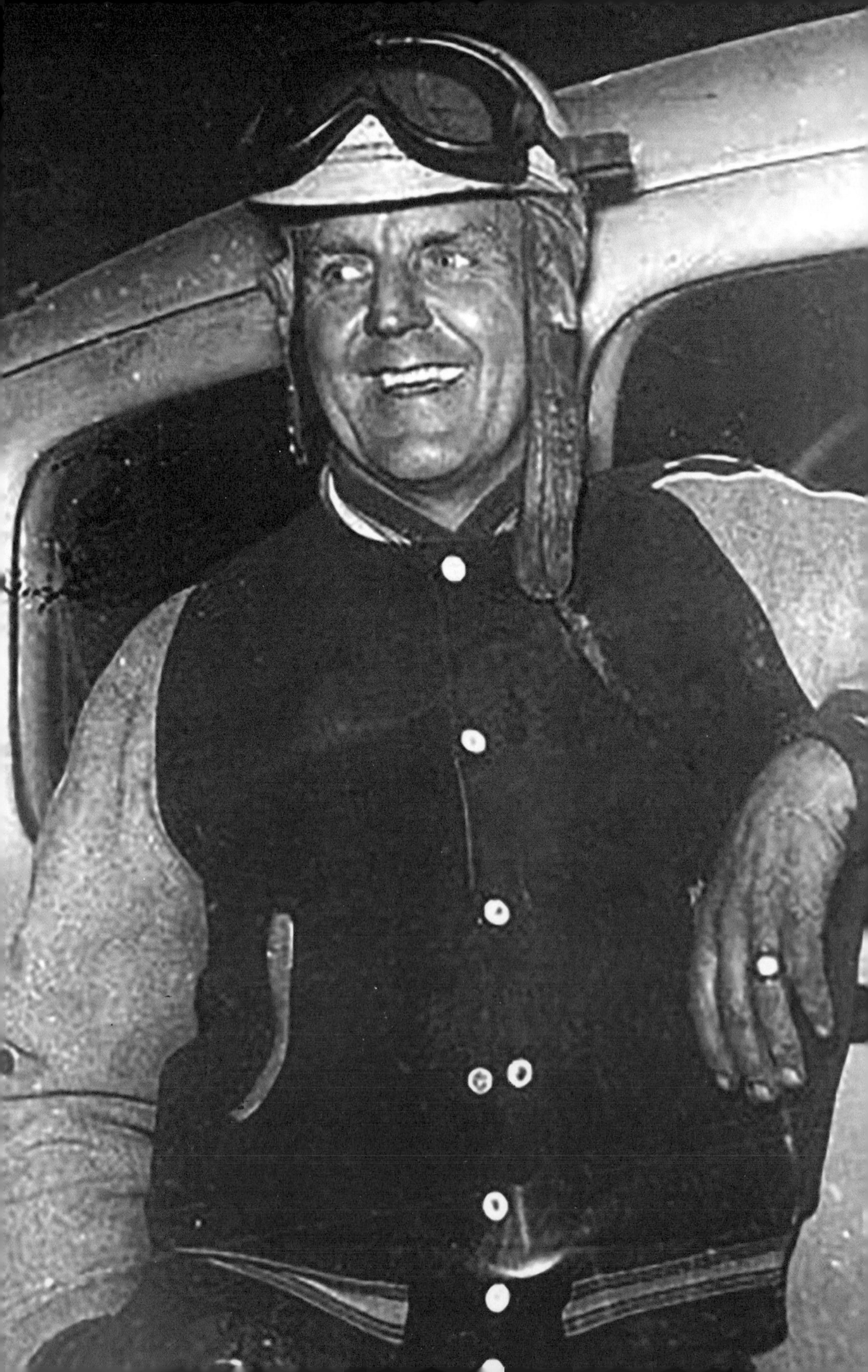

ACKNOWLEDGEMENTS

Trainers are taught never to begin any presentation with an apology—always start with a positive. Having said that, let me begin my acknowledgements with an apology.

I have made every effort to ensure that Jack's biography is comprehensive and accurate. As shown, newspaper articles, magazines and even television shows are often peppered with inaccuracies and errors of fact. To be fair, journalists are not historians—but nor am I. While endeavouring to verify and confirm all the various race results, competitions, dates, people, places, vehicles, trips and adventures, let me apologise now for any omissions or errors. There are many 'Jack stories', races, wins and events I have not covered, such as Jack's race record at Rowley Park in South Australia. To include every race, one book would become a library.

All of the events of this book occurred 30 or more years ago—some over 100 years ago, when talking of Jack's boyhood. Records are often sketchy or non-existent and even first-hand accounts and memory vary, fade and change over time.

I am a keen short story writer who has enjoyed some success, but I am certainly not a professional writer. Short story writing prepared me for writing a biography much the same way as a once-a-week jog prepares one for a marathon. It helped, but the task was much more complex and demanding, larger than I had ever imagined. But I thoroughly enjoyed the challenge and the experience. Just creating a chronology of the events in Jack's life gave me a greater appreciation of my father's many and diverse achievements.

ACKNOWLEDGEMENTS

The biographical process necessitates that an author research, evaluate and reflect upon his subject's life. While any writer learns about his subject, as the son of that subject, I also learned and reflected on my own life and family dynamics. I feel as if my understanding and appreciation of my father have grown as a direct result of writing his biography.

I am indebted to a number of people for their invaluable assistance, information provided, patience and generosity. Without them, this biography would not exist. My sincere thanks go to the following:

Dorothy Rosewell: Dorothy is a natural record keeper. Literally hundreds of newspaper articles, magazines, photos and personal recollections provided the initial information base upon which this book was built. 'File Murray' meant that years of clippings and documents, from an age decades before the Internet, were fastidiously kept and preserved. I could not have written this biography without her information. Let me especially thank Dorothy for her candour and her willingness to share and trust.

Evan Green: Evan passed away in 1996, but his writings live on forever. I have always appreciated his talent as a writer and have quoted extensively from his works in this book. His friendship meant a great deal to Jack, and his writings show the respect, depth of friendship and bond that existed between two great mates.

Dick Smith: I am grateful to adventurer, entrepreneur and former Australian of the Year Dick Smith for giving some of his very limited and crowded time to write a Foreword for my father's biography. Thanks Dick, much appreciated.

Hal Moloney: I call Hal *Mr REDEX*—and with good reason. I would suggest there is no greater authority or enthusiast more knowledgeable when it comes to the REDEX trials, subsequent rallies and historic off-road motorsport in Australia than Hal Moloney. Generous with his time, information, photos and records, Hal frequently corrected, added to and enhanced this book.

Diana Giese and Karen Whitelaw: Writer and editor Diana Giese's mentorship, expertise and insight enabled me to bring my dream of writing my father's biography to reality. This book would not exist without Diana's professional editing, advice and guidance. Karen Whitelaw was my first creative writing teacher and encouraged me to—Jack-like—give it a go.

Max Stahl: Max was at the helm of *Racing Car News* from the 1960s to the 80s. He competed with distinction in touring cars and loved rallying. In the New Caledonian Rally in 1967, in a Volvo with John Keran, the pair won, becoming

ACKNOWLEDGEMENTS

the first Australian crew to win an international rally. Max generously sorted and lent me over 70 copies of Australian Motor Sports magazines featuring articles on Jack and proofread this manuscript.

Bob Selby-Wood Jnr: I must thank Bob for the *Piddler on the Roof* anecdote.

Ian Pfennigwerth, PhD: Naval historian, author and former Commander of HMAS *Perth 2,* Ian's research, suggestions and advice in confirming Jack's wartime service with the US Small Ships were most helpful.

'Bill' and Chris McLachlan: Another of Jack's great mates, Dougald Andrew ('Wild Bill') McLachlan was only 54 when he died on Boxing Day 1971. Bill's *The Manuscript*, parts of which are included in this book, is a great read. I would like to also thank Bill's son, Chris, for information, photos and assistance.

Neil Bennetts: Neil sat down with Jack in 1976 and for an hour recorded Jack as he related the story of his life. For the National Library, Neil recorded 86 such interviews, mostly with leading sportsmen and sportswomen who had retired in the previous 10-20 years. A successful sportsman and yachtsman in his own right, Bennetts had his oral histories purchased by the National Library of Australia between 1975 and 1995. I became aware of the online access available a few years ago, thanks to my nephew Jonny Murray. After all these years, hearing Jack's voice, his nuances and expressions brought memories flooding back. As a result of the work of Neil and the Library, today we can still hear Jack telling his own story in his own words.

Damian Kringas: Author of *The Gelignite Bugatti,* provided historical information.

Rob Rowe: Owner of the Day Special, who generously provided information and connected me with the network of race historians. And Rob enabled me to hear the Day roar!

Brian Lear: Motor racing historian, generously supplied copies of various magazines.

John Medley: Author of *Bathurst: Cradle of Australian Motor Racing*, added some good stories, photos and comprehensive Bathurst race results.

Betty Wheeler: Mogo provided photos and kindly sent letters with background information.

The late Professor Harry Messel: Confirmed the Wernher von Braun story and had fond memories of Jack.

John Schumann: Singer and songwriter, aka 'Gelignite' Jack, sent good wishes and background on his album title.

ACKNOWLEDGEMENTS

Kathryn McLeod: She provided a copy of *This Is Your Life* from the National Film and Sound Archive.

Lisa Savage: Seven Network Ltd. For kindly granting permission to use transcript from *'This Is Your Life'*.

Don Brown: As NSW Wrestling State President, Don confirmed Jack's state wrestling titles.

Bob Wing: Bob contacted Jack in 1979 asking for information to incorporate in his book *Water Skiing in Australia 1934.* Jack assisted with that project and I have quoted extensively from Bob's work on the history of waterskiing in Australia.

The late Bill Lunney and Ruth Lunney: Authors of *Forgotten Fleet* and *Forgotten Fleet 2*, the story of Australians who joined the US Small Ships during World War II.

Denis Setka: I was directed to Denis as a cycling historian by Cycling Australia, in 2015.

Meryl Lee: Waterski historian. She checked waterski records for me and provided a copy of a rare 1964 racing program.

Dave Johnson (inductee Rally Hall of Fame), Barwon Stagg, Phil Arnold, Trevor Poulsen, and *Tom Ryan* supplied photos and/or information.

Bob McEwen: 'Ginger' shared fond memories.

Paul Graham and Terry Andrews: They provided the yarn about Bill Moyes' speedboat meeting the Hume Highway before it met the rocks at Forster. So many stories guys, so little space!

Bruce Wilkinson: Bruce was a young competitor in the 1954 REDEX. Inviting me to his Melbourne home, Bruce was generous with his time and recollections.

Fiona Shultz, Alan Whiticker and all the team from New Holland Publishing for taking a chance on a first-time author and in so doing helping to preserve our Australian history and the memory of the characters that shaped us as a nation.

Rhonda Murray: Last, but certainly not least, I wish to thank my wife Rhonda who has supported and encouraged my writing efforts and patiently listened to the repetition of countless stories. Writing is a selfish and at times all-consuming task. Thank you my darling for your boundless patience as a 'writing widow' for the last few years. And it is very handy to have a well-read wife, who can readily double as an insightful sub-editor and competent literary critic.

ABOUT THE AUTHOR

Son of the legendary Australian larrikin 'Gelignite' Jack Murray, famous REDEX Reliability Trial driver and sportsman of the 1950s, Phil has inherited his father's genes when it comes to adventure, seeking personal challenges and embracing all life has to offer. Just as his father did, Phil believes life is best lived following some pretty simple instructions: 'Don't take yourself too seriously' and 'Always sprinkle in a good helping of humour.'

Phil's adventures and achievements have included: white-water rafting the Grand Canyon; trekking on three continents (Himalayas, Africa and Australia); as well as travelling extensively throughout Europe, Africa, South America and Asia. Whether spending time as a patient in a Soviet hospital during the Cold War period, sailing a yacht to Morocco or experiencing the midnight sun over Hammerfest in Norway, Phil's journeys and experiences have enriched him, both as a man and a writer.

One of his adventures which provided inspiration for his writing involved following in 'the footsteps of heroes'— walking the iconic Kokoda Track in Papua New Guinea and experiencing Anzac Day 2009 at the Isurava Memorial.

That same year Phil received a Highly Commended award in the prestigious Port Stephens Literature Awards for a story based on his Kokoda trek. In subsequent years he has received several Most Highly Commended awards— top-ten placings in a short story competition that annually attracts hundreds of entrants from around the country. Phil's prize winning stories have also been published in *Australian Traveller* magazine and several Newcastle-based Catchfire Press short story anthologies. In 2014 he won the NSW Neighbour

ABOUT THE AUTHOR

Day writing competition with his poignant story, *My Neighbour Alex*.

While he was growing up in Vaucluse, in Sydney's Eastern Suburbs, Phil attended the local public schools. As a young man he moved to trendy Paddington before meeting his future wife, Rhonda. The couple then lived for twenty years in the 'first reality show' suburb of Sylvania Waters in the Sutherland Shire, before both retired early and headed north to the Bluewater Paradise of Nelson Bay on the NSW mid-north coast.

After obtaining a Bachelor of Surveying Honours Degree from the University of New South Wales, Phil's professional career has been varied. He worked for many years as a registered land surveyor, consultant, trainer and major projects manager for Australia's largest water infrastructure company.

Writing has always been a passion and the move to Nelson Bay introduced him to a creative circle of local writers and artists. Now in his early 60s, he has been happily married to Rhonda for 30 years. His interests, like his writing, are eclectic, and include golf, sailing, surfboard riding, mountain bike riding, scuba diving, volunteering as a Native Wildlife Rescuer and, having been a competitive bodybuilder in the 1980s, Phil remains a gym junkie maintaining a high level of fitness for his active and varied lifestyle.

Phil has also been dubbed by the local media 'Kangaroo Phil'. After more than four years with the University of Sydney undertaking kangaroo research on Nelson Bay Golf Course, he founded Kangaroo Encounters Tours. Tourists are guided on to the course and introduced to unique Australian wildlife. All funds raised go towards kangaroo research.

Free from work, short story writing has grown in his life both as a pleasure and a pastime. Phil enjoys writing and trying his hand at all types of short story and other genres: describing actual events, historical fiction, humorous anecdotes, travel, science fiction and even children's short stories.

Phil gained a great sense of achievement and satisfaction by writing his father's long-overdue biography.

SOURCES

Chapter 1 Sources
This Is Your Life, National Film and Sound Archive, Title 32220, *This Is Your Life*, EP 4/10, Rack No AVC005358.

'Gelignite' Jack Murray, interviewed by Neil Bennetts, 18 May 1976, ORAL TRC 391/24-25, National Library of Australia, Canberra.

Creswell, T. and Trenoweth, S., *1001 Australians you should know*, Pluto Press Australia, 2006.

Scott, P., *Modern Motor* 28 (3), August 1981, page 46.

'Souvenir REDEX Trial Feature', *Truth*, 25 July 1954, page 23.

'Gelignite Jack's Outdoor Family', *Courier Mail*, Brisbane, 24 July 1954, page 9.

Daily Telegraph, 13, 15 July 1954.

ABC Radio interview with Mike Jeffries, 1979.

Green, E., *Journeys with Gelignite Jack*, Rigby, 1966.

Moore, A., *Australian Dictionary of Biography*, Volume 18, Melbourne University Press, 2012.

Tuckey, B. and Floyd, T.B., *From REDEX to Repco*, Gregory's, 1979.

REDEX Round Australia Car Trials, 1953, 54 and 55, Video, ScreenSound Australia, produced 1999, narrated by Mike Whitney.

The Last Great REDEX Trial 1955, Video, produced and directed by Allan Keen, commentator Peter Whitchurch.

Australian Motor Sports, August 1954, page 80.

Chapter 2 Sources
Tuckey, B. and Floyd, T. B., *From REDEX to Repco*, Gregory's, 1979.

National Museum of Australia, Canberra website, Birtles' Sundowner Bean Car exhibit.

'Gelignite' Jack Murray, interviewed by Neil Bennetts, 18 May 1976, ORAL TRC 391/24-25, National Library of Australia, Canberra.

Sydney Morning Herald, 26 and 28 November 1932.

The Motor in Australia and Flying, 1 October 1934.

The Referee, 20 September 1934, 22 November 1934.

Daily Telegraph, 22 November 1934.

YouTube: *Tragic Speedway Car Crash In Australia (1938) British Pathé (The Mackellar Special)*.

Damian Kringas, *The Gelignite Bugatti*, Independence Jones, 2012.

John Barraclough, *Australian Motor Sports, Spotlight*, 15 September 1947, page 4.

Australian Motor Sports, 15 October 1948, pages 29-30.

John Medley, *Bathurst: Cradle of Australian Motor Racing*, Turton and Armstrong, 1977.

Chapter 3 Sources
Bill Lunney and Ruth Lunney, *Forgotten Fleet 2*, Forfleet, 2004, pages 195, 253, 314-15.

National Archives of Australia, research by Ian Pfennigwerth, author, naval historian, veteran of 35 years service in the Royal Australian Navy (RAN) and former Commander of the guided missile destroyer HMAS *Perth 2*.

'Gelignite' Jack Murray, interviewed by Neil Bennetts, 18 May 1976, ORAL TRC 391/24-25, National Library of Australia, Canberra.

Chapter 4 Sources
Medley, J., *Bathurst: Cradle of Australian Motor Racing*, Turton and Armstrong, 1977, page 51.

YouTube: *1946 NSW Grand Prix*

Bathurst. Video of the race.
Australian Motor Sports, 15 February 1947, pages 28-29, 15 August 1947, page 35, 15 October 1947, page 4, 15 April 1948, page 4, 15 June 1948, page 41, 15 February 1949, page 22, 16 May 1949, page 3.
Sydney Morning Herald, 4 October 1947.
The Sun, Sun Motor News, 19 April 1949, page 21.
Baird, P., *Australian Motor Sports,* October 1949, page 45.

Chapter 5 Sources
Australian Motor Sports, February 1950, page 41, October 1950, page 7, October 1951, page 30, February 1952, page 38, May 1952, pages 26 and 35, June 1952, pages 45-46, July 1952, pages 21-23, September 1952, pages 21-25, November 1952, pages 34-37, 52-57, December 1952, pages 51-55, January 1953, pages 40-43, February 1953, pages 19-27, April 1953, pages 39-43, May 1953, pages 55-57, June 1953, pages 23-27, August 1953, pages 47-50, October 1953, pages 45-47, November 1953, pages 28-30, February 1954, pages 42-45, May 1954, pages 25-33, October 1954, pages 191-92, November 1954, page 233, January 1956, page 23, September 1956, page 342, September 1957, pages 354-58, July 1958, pages 316-17, 334.
Modern Motor, May 1950, April 1950, December 1954, page 37.
'Spotlight', *Australian Motor Sports,* April 1950, 3, July 1950, page 3.
Wheels, October 1953, page 420.
'The Gelignite Bugatti', *Sydney Morning Herald,* 1950, page 99.
Kringas, D., *The Gelignite Bugatti,* Independence Jones, 2012.
Medley, J., *Bathurst: Cradle of Australian Motor Racing,* Turton and Armstrong, 1977.
YouTube: *1952 Australian Grand Prix Bathurst.*
Just Cars, advertisement, January 2012, page 24.
Sydney Morning Herald, 30 June 1952.
Cumberland Argus, 15 October 1952, page 7, 19 November 1952.
Wheels, May 1953.
The Sun, 15 October 1953.
Australian Motor Manual, 15 September 1954, 1 November 1954, 15 February 1955, page 49, circa July 1955.
The Sun, It's a Grudge Match, advertisement, 1 October 1954.
Cars, April 1955, page 22.
'Gelignite' Jack Murray, interviewed by Neil Bennetts, 18 May 1976, ORAL TRC 391/24-25, National Library of Australia, Canberra.
Modern Motor, Sportlight, March 1955, page 29.
Wheels, the Sport, April 1956, page 50.
Internet re D-Type Jaguar: *XKD532* Coventry Races.

Chapter 6 Sources
Green, E., *Journeys with Gelignite Jack,* Rigby, 1966, page 15-16.
This Is Your Life, National Film and Sound Archive, Title 32220, *This Is Your Life,* EP 4/10, Rack No AVC005358.
Rosewell, D., *Letter to Mrs Whitby and family of Don,* 14 May 1983.

Chapter 7 Sources
Medley, J., *Bathurst: Cradle of Australian Motor Racing,* Turton and Armstrong, 1977.
Blanden, J., *Historic Racing Cars in Australia* (first edition), Museum Publications, 1979.
Jaguar Registry online: Coventry Racers.

SOURCES

Wikipedia, 1960 Armstrong 500.
Racing Car News, July 1961, pages 7, 12, September 1963, page 17, May 1964, pages 19-20, September 1964, page 33, November 1964, pages 21, 24-25, May 1965, page 43, June 1965, pages 44-45, July 1965, pages 34-35, September 1965, pages 41-42, March 1966, page 40, April 1966, page 3, June 1966, pages 41-43, October 1969, page 61.
Modern Motor, November 1963, pages 43, 95, 96.
Green, E., *Journeys with Gelignite Jack*, Rigby, 1966.
'Gelignite' Jack Murray, interviewed by Neil Bennetts, 18 May 1976, ORAL TRC 391/24-25, National Library of Australia, Canberra.
Tuckey, B. and Floyd, T. B., *From REDEX to Repco*, Gregory's, 1979.
Selby-Wood, B., *We Build Utzon's Dream, Piddler on the Roof*, unpublished.
Pix magazine, 4, 11 and 18 February 1967, Vol. 84 Nos 10, 11 and 12.
Sunday Telegraph, 12 May 1968, pages 110-11.
Racing Car News, Bits and Pieces, by Max Stahl, March 1969, page 5.
YouTube: *Jack Murray road safety video*, 1970.
This Is Your Life, National Film and Sound Archive, Title 32220, *This Is Your Life,* EP 4/10, Rack No AVC005358.
Autopics, an online source for over 40,000 motor racing photos: *http://autopics.com.au/*.

Chapter 8 Sources

Courier-Mail, 27 April 1970, page 4.
Stahl, M., *Racing Car News, Bits and Pieces,* June 1970, page 5.
Browning, M., *Wheels Magazine, The track winding back*, March 1975, pages 46-49, 80-81.
Stathatos, J., *The Long Drive*, Pelham Books, 1978.

Chapter 9 Sources

'Gelignite' Jack Murray, interviewed by Neil Bennetts, 18 May 1976, ORAL TRC 391/24-25, National Library of Australia, Canberra.
Wikipedia, Sir Malcolm Campbell and Donald Campbell.
McLachlan, B., *The Manuscript*: *The Other Side of the Story. The Sequel to Journeys with 'Gelignite' Jack*, written 1971 (unpublished).
This Is Your Life, National Film and Sound Archive, Title 32220, *This Is Your Life,* EP 4/10, Rack No AVC005358.
Gordon, A. L., *In Utrumque Paratus* (meaning 'prepared for both' [events]).
'Sharkbait Sam', *Nambucca Heads Surf Lifesaving Club magazine,* Golden Anniversary 1980-81, page 45.
Bing, S., O'Brien, B. and Rosenberg, S., *Kangaroo Jack*, Warner Bros, 2003.
Kringas, D., *The Gelignite Bugatti*, Independence Jones, 2012, 88-89.
Wheels, August 1978, pages 89, 74-78.
Stahl, M., *'The Long Fuse' Racing Car News*, February 1984, pages 59-61.

Chapter 10 Sources

Wikipedia: The Victorian gold rush.
Birth Certificate copies: Walter James Murray (Jack's father) and John Eric Murray (Jack).
Death Certificate copies: Walter James Murray (Jack's father) and John Eric Murray (Jack).
Marriage Certificate copy: John Eric Murray and Ena May Byrne.
Carnage in Bangkok, ABC and BBC News Websites, 18 August 2015.

SOURCES

Chapter 11 Sources
Memories from my youth.

Chapter 12 Sources
'She's After Bids', *Daily Telegraph*, 20 January 1973, front page.
McGrath, P., 'Weekend Business Review' *Sydney Morning Herald*, 10 April 1970.
Murray, J. [no relation], 'Dorothy Rosewell's no blow-in despite the wind surfer', *Woman's Day*, 16 September 1985, page 115.
The Activists: Dorothy Rosewell', *Vogue Australia* June/July, 1973, pages 62-63.
'Congress—first woman speaker', *Wentworth Courier*, 12 May 1976.
'Real Estate Identities', *Australian Property News*, December 1977 January 1978, page 24.
'Women of Substance', *Real Estate Journal* 58 (10), November 2007, page 79.

Chapter 13 Sources
Daily Telegraph, 13 November 1974, page 8.
'Gelignite' Jack Murray, interviewed by Neil Bennetts, 18 May 1976, ORAL TRC 391/24-25, National Library of Australia, Canberra.
Moore, A., *Australian Dictionary of Biography*, Volume 18, Melbourne University Press, 2012.
Jack O'Hara: Australian Olympic Committee website: *corporate.olympics.com.au/athlete/jack-o-hara*
Bob Wing, *Water Skiing in Australia: how it all began*, 1982.
'Waterskiing Behind a Seaplane', *Sydney Morning Herald*, 19 March 1951, front page.
'Perfect Balance'(photo), *Australian Women's Weekly*, 5 November 1952, page 15.
Ampol 100 Mile Water Ski Trial, Program of Events, 2 February 1964.
Powerboat magazine, August-September 1997, page 36.

First published in 2017 by New Holland Publishers Pty Ltd
London • Sydney • Auckland

The Chandlery 50 Westminster Bridge Road London SE1 7QY United Kingdom
1/66 Gibbes Street Chatswood NSW 2067 Australia
5/39 Woodside Ave Northcote, Auckland 0627 New Zealand

www.newhollandpublishers.com

Copyright © 2017 New Holland Publishers Pty Ltd
Copyright © 2017 in text:Phil Murray
Copyright © 2017 in images: Phil Murray, Chapter Opener illustrations: New Holland Publishers

All rights reserved. No part of this publication may be reproduced, stored in a retrieval system or transmitted, in any form or by any means, electronic, mechanical, photocopying, recording or otherwise, without the prior written permission of the publishers and copyright holders.

A record of this book is held at the British Library and the National Library of Australia.

ISBN: 9781742579788

Group Managing Director: Fiona Schultz
Publisher: Alan Whiticker
Project Editor: Laura Fulton
Designer: Andrew Quinlan
Production Director: James Mills-Hicks
Printer: Hang Tai Printing Company Limited

10 9 8 7 6 5 4 3 2 1

Keep up with New Holland Publishers on Facebook
www.facebook.com/NewHollandPublishers